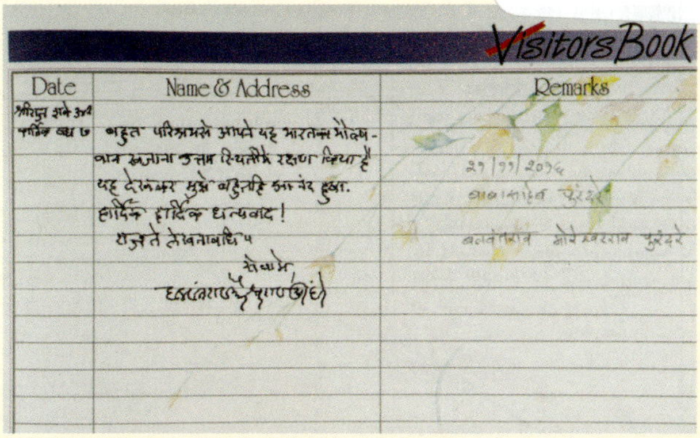
Visitors Book
Date
Name & Address
Remarks
बहुत परिश्रमसे आपने यह भारतका मौल्य-
वान खजाना उत्तम स्थितीमें रक्षण किया है
यह देखकर मुझे बहुतहि आनंद हुआ.
हार्दिक हार्दिक धन्यवाद!

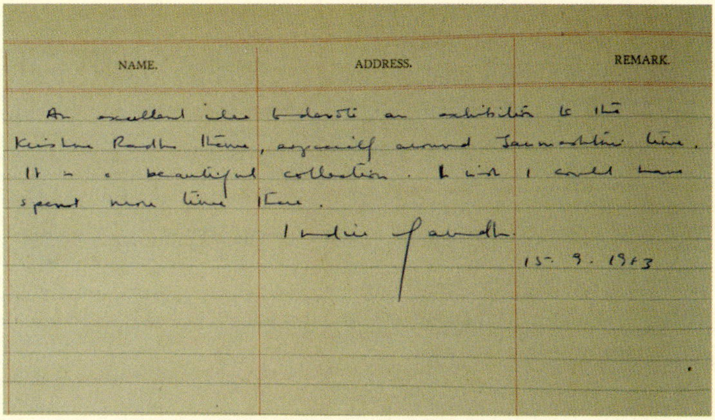
NAME.
ADDRESS.
REMARK.
An excellent idea to devote an exhibition to the
Krishna Radha theme, especially around Janmashtami time.
It is a beautiful collection. I wish I could have
spent more time there.
Indira Gandhi
15. 9. 1973

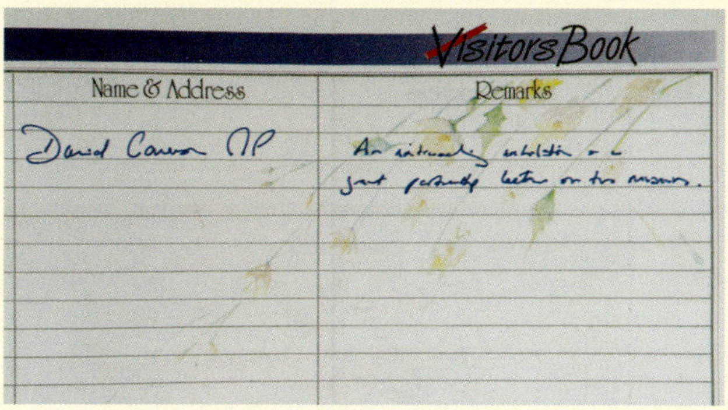
Visitors Book
Name & Address
Remarks
David Cameron MP

Musings in the Museum

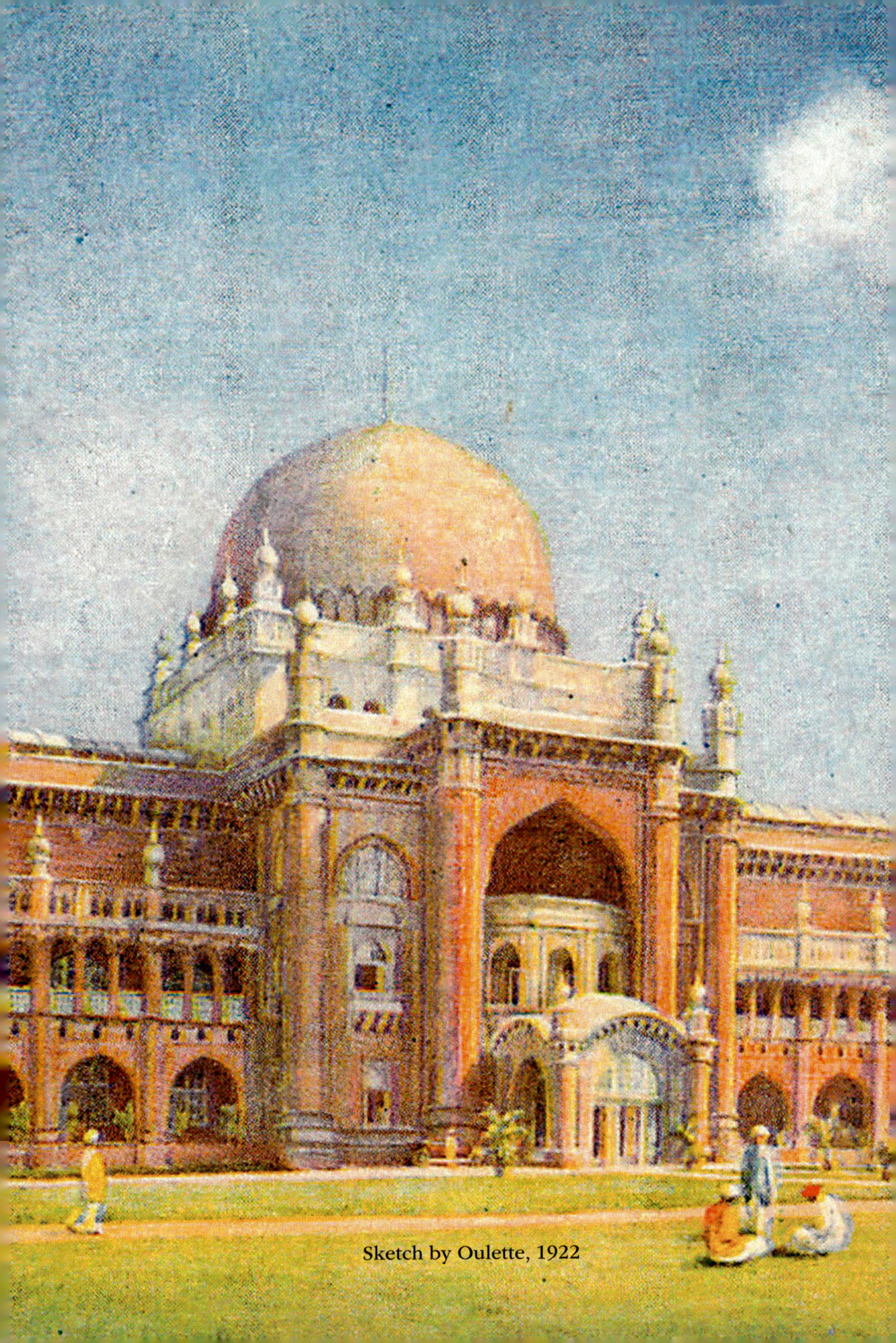

Sketch by Oulette, 1922

Musings in the Museum

Celebrating the Centenary of
The Chhatrapati Shivaji Maharaj Vastu Sangrahalaya
Formerly The Prince of Wales Museum of Western India

छत्रपती शिवाजी महाराज वस्तु संग्रहालय

1922–2022

HARSHA V. DEHEJIA

NIYOGI
BOOKS

Published by
NIYOGI BOOKS
Block D, Building No. 77,
Okhla Industrial Area, Phase-I,
New Delhi-110 020, INDIA
Tel: 91-11-26816301, 26818960
Email: niyogibooks@gmail.com
Website: www.niyogibooksindia.com

Images: Images are drawn mainly from the collection of the Chhatrapati Shivaji Maharaj Vastu Sanghralaya and Dehejia Collection of Art. Where an image is from neither of these sources it has been credited.

Editor: K.E. Priyamvada
Design: Shrinidhi Sridhar

ISBN: 978-93-91125-52-3
Publication: 2022

Printed at: Niyogi Offset Pvt. Ltd., New Delhi, India

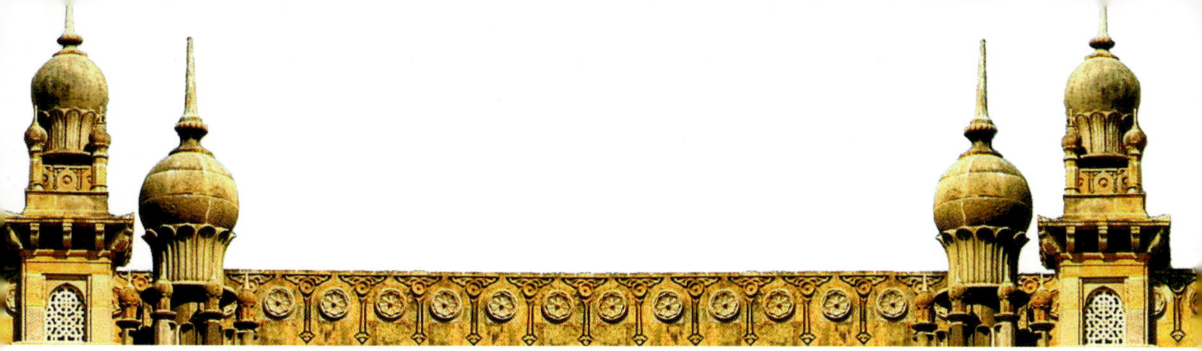

Salutations to the many unknown
sculptors and painters,
potters and weavers,
who gave shape and form to
our concepts of what is beautiful,
whose artistic creativity has flowed through
trackless generations,
so that we may be nurtured and embraced
by beautiful objects,
and in so doing discover beauty
within ourselves.

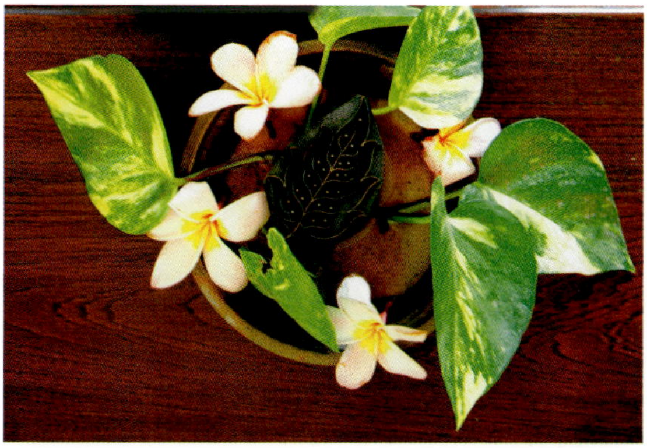

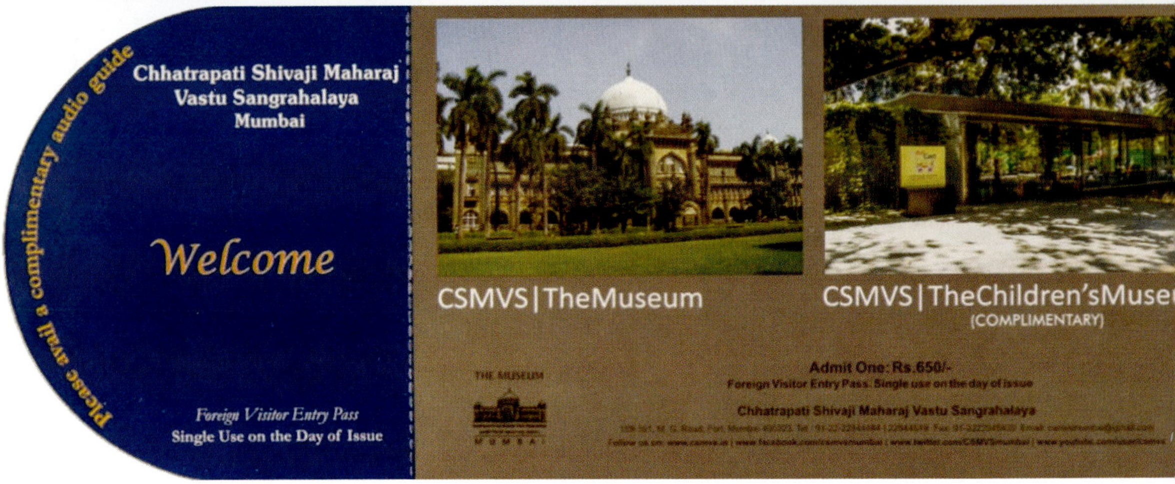

Let People of Taste Enter this Museum and Partake of its Objects of Beauty.

रसिकाः सङ्ग्रहालयमायान्तु रसयन्तु च
सुन्दराणि वस्तूनि ।।

The Museum

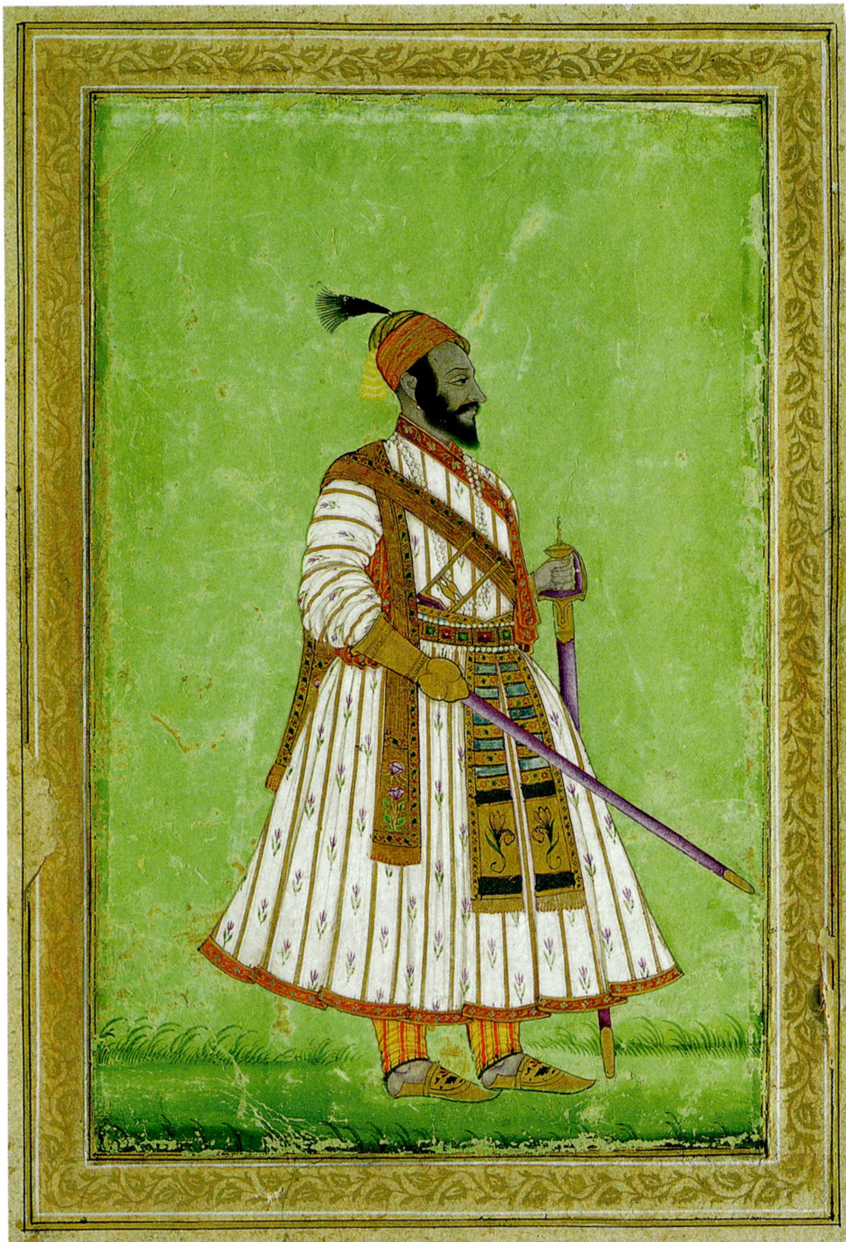

Chhatrapati Shivaji Maharaj, 1627–1680
Posthumous Portrait, 1685, Deccan

Chhatrapati Shivaji Maharaj,
a valiant Maratha
who stood up to our invaders and proselytisers
to maintain our dignity and integrity
and ensure that every Indian can hold their head high
whose footfalls are heard in the Sahyadri even today.
We in this Museum, pay our respects
to this great son of India.

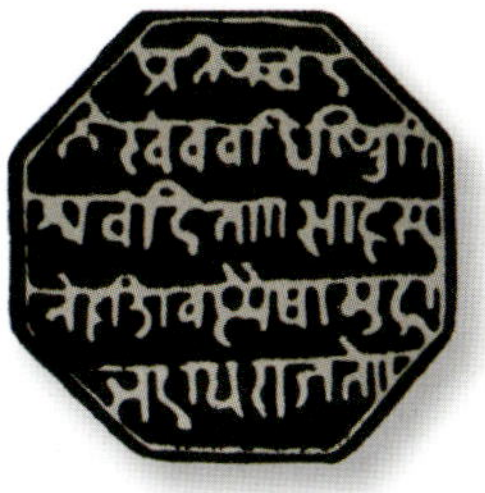

Seal of Shivaji Maharaj

प्रतिपच्चन्द्रलेखेव वर्धिष्णुर्विश्ववन्दिता ।
साहसूनोः शिवस्यैषा मुद्रा भद्राय राजते ॥

Everglowing in splendour like the Moon of the
First day of the bright half of the month and adored by the world,
this seal of Shivaji, the son of Shahaji, shines for the benediction of all.

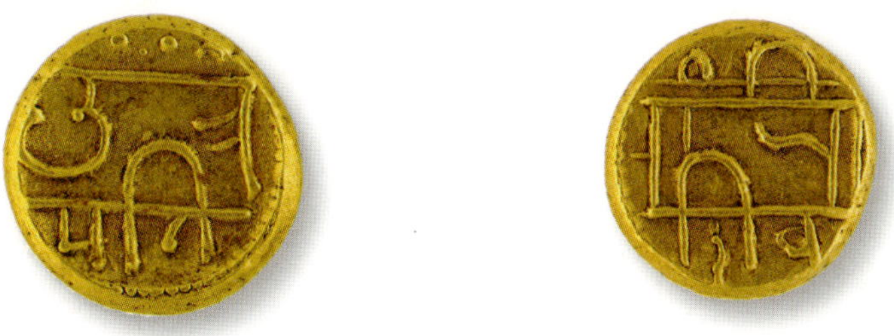

Shivaji Maharaj issued gold coins called Hon
at the time of his coronation on June 6, 1674.
The legend on one side says Chhatrapathi and on the other Sri Raja Shiva.
He also struck copper coins called Shivrai which were used in
Bombay Province till the 19th century.

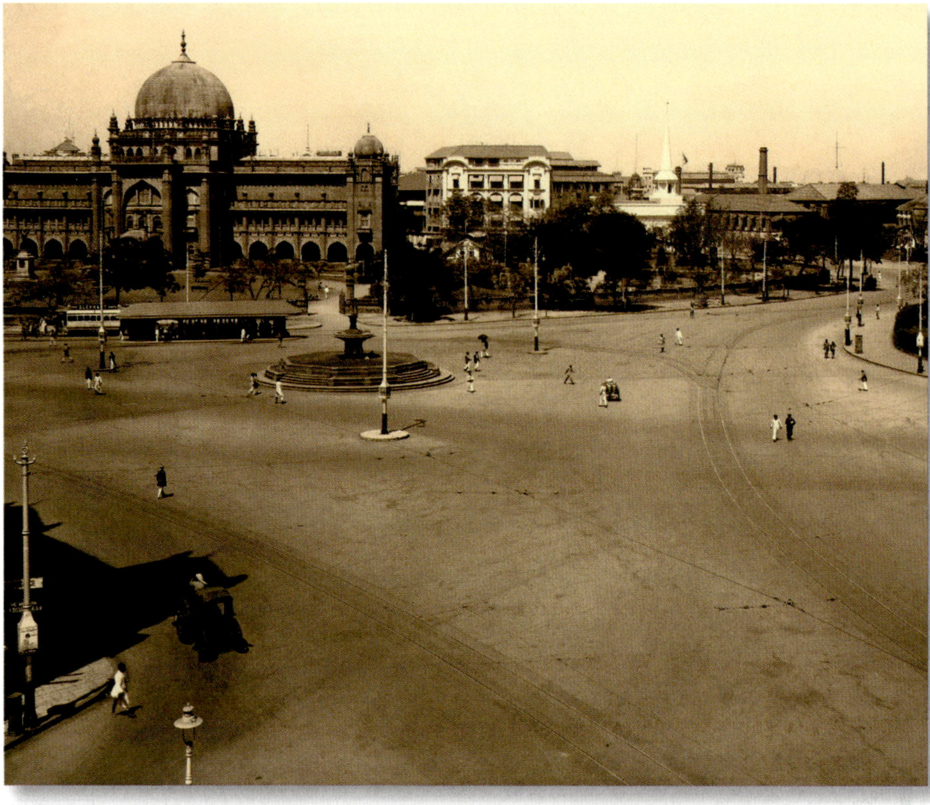

1920. Photo Courtesy: Phillips Antiques

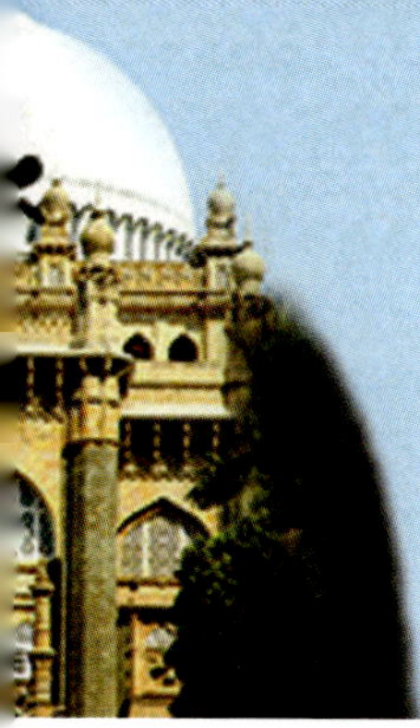

As we Begin

Meeting the Sutradhar

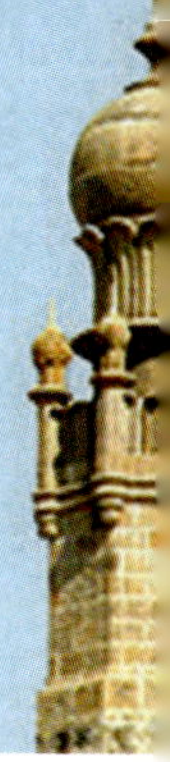

It is late at night and the last visitor to the Museum has left, and as we enter the grounds let us walk gently, lest we disturb the footfalls of the many visitors who have come here in the last hundred years, let us talk in whispers lest we disturb the hushed conversations of the many artists and artisans, painters and patrons, whose work is enshrined in the Museum, and who have gathered in the Museum, let us enjoy the grandeur and majesty of the Museum architecture in awed silence, even as we walk in the shadows of the tall trees with ancient memories. The roots of these trees go deep to a time when the Museum was first established, and they must know how stone by stone this magnificent edifice went up, and the artists and artisans whose work it preserves.

It was the early 20th century; the British Raj was in its full glory and our colonisers wanted to leave their stamp on India, and what better way than through architecture. The Indian establishment, while accepting their English masters, at the same time, wanted to maintain the Indian identity. The Prince of Wales, the future George V, was to pay a visit to India, and on 14 August 1905, a number of prominent people of Bombay gathered at the Town Hall and resolved to erect a memorial to the visit of the Prince of Wales in the form of a public museum on a plot of land called the Crescent.

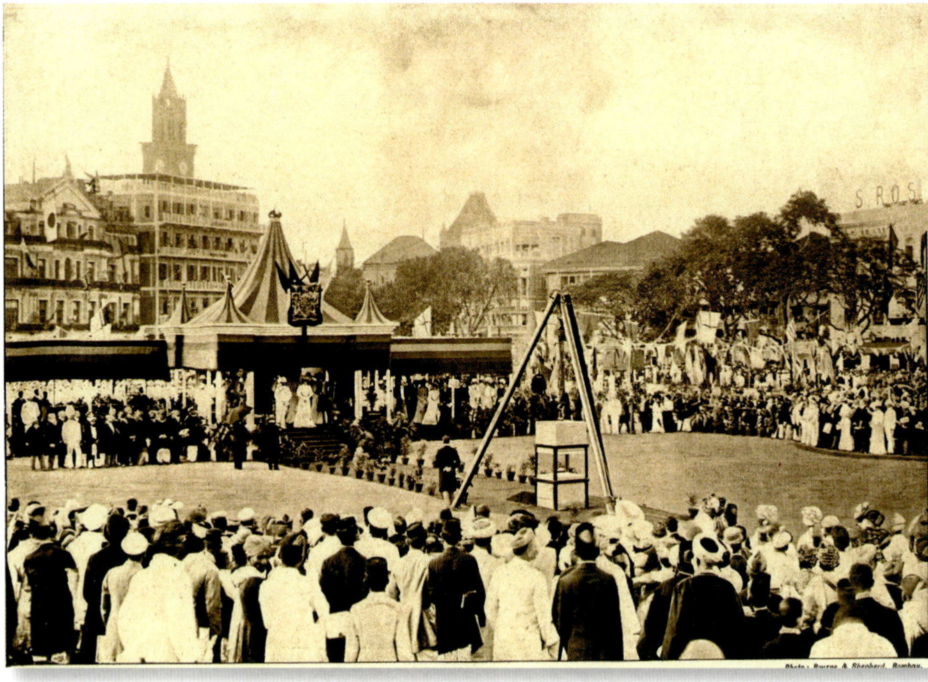

The Prince of Wales laying the Foundation

The meeting was attended by Sir Pherozeshah Mehta, Justice Badrudin Tyabji, Narotamdas Gokuldas, Justice Chandavarkar, Sassoon J. David and many other dignitaries known for their outstanding contribution in their respective fields, and also in the development of the island of Bombay. The Foundation of the Museum was laid by the Prince of Wales on 11 November 1905, and the Museum was named The Prince of Wales Museum of Western India. The building was completed in 1914 under the supervision of George Wittet, the architect. It was initially used as a military hospital and opened to the public on 10 January 1922, a day we observe as Museum Day. Mr Wittet was instructed to ensure that the design is Indian, and he therefore adopted the Indo-Sarcenian style of architecture. The Indo-Saracenic style of architecture is a hybrid style, with Hindu and Muslim elements of architecture combined with European finesse. Saracen was a term used in Europe until the 19th century referring to Muslim and/or Arabic-speaking people and regions of the Middle East and North Africa. The first Indo-Saracenic building is said to be

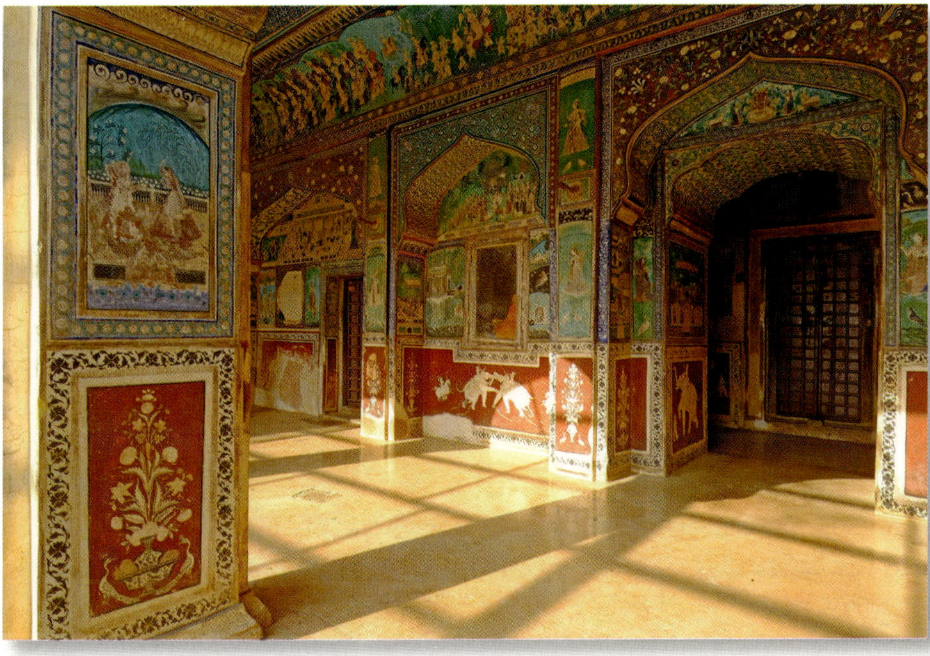

Rang Mahal, Bundi Fort

the Chepauk Palace, completed in 1768, in present-day Chennai. Bombay and Calcutta as the main centres of the Raj administration, saw many buildings constructed in that style.

The concept of a museum is alien to the Indian way of thinking and is essentially a European construct. *Chitrashalas* or a gallery of painting was known in ancient Indian literature. The dramatist Bhavbhuti in *Uttarramcharit* speaks of a picture gallery that was visited by none other than Rama and Lakshman; another dramatist Bhasa who flourished in the Kushan period speaks of *rajakula* or royal chapels that housed statues of ancestors. Kushan royal portraits are also known in that period. Murals pre-date even that, and temples and palaces were rich with sculptures and murals depicting generally Puranic themes. The *chitrashala* of the palace at Bundi is one of the finest picture galleries of its time. These palaces and temples were a virtual art gallery. Perhaps not open to everyone but certainly to the royalty and the nobility of society.

Early museums began as private collections of the royalty and the nobility who would collect objects from their travel or conquests, and they were often displayed in so-called wonder rooms or cabinets of curiosities. The Capitoline Museums of 1471, the Vatican Museum in 1506, The Royal Armouries in the Tower of London in 1660,The Ashmolean Museum in Oxford in 1677, the British Museum in London in 1753, the Louvre Museum in Paris in 1793 are some of the earliest museums in Europe. The word "museum" is derived from Latin which was, in turn, inspired by *mouseion*, the Greek term for "a shrine to the Muses." In Classical Greek mythology, the nine Muses are the goddesses of the arts and sciences, making them perfect patrons for these knowledge-based institutions.

This museum, like all others, was a turning point in the way in which Indian art was celebrated and understood by us. While we do not have a single word for art, the word *kala* which is commonly used, stands for *kriti* or the method of creating the art object. On the other hand, we have many words for beauty, such as *sunder*, *lavanya*, *charu*, *mohani*, *ramya*, *ruchika*, *shri*, *sundari*, *kamini*. It is important that even though we are entering a European style museum we keep an Indian *drishti* or point of view when we engage with the objects. The objects in this Museum are *vastu* or objects, not art, and this is important to keep in mind. These objects are not inanimate but have a life of their own. They have a history, they have been lovingly made and affectionately touched, they have relationships with the *raja* and the *praja*. Indian *drishti* puts life back in these objects as that *drishti* is synaesthetic, namely it is an enlightened visioning, which brings in a variety of modalities of vision, texts, tradition and imagination, and gives the object a context and a life, for without that the object lies torn from its source, fragmented from its surroundings, divorced from its creator, distanced from its creator and removed from its patron. It is almost as if the object in this Museum has a sense of separation anxiety, similar to that of the new born child. While we remain grateful to the many curators who have shaped and designed the Museum, we must entertain a disclaimer, namely that the chronology and order that has been imposed on the various objects is artificial and does not inherently belong to the concept or the inspiration that created the object. Only when we free ourselves from that clinically imposed order would we be able to experience the objects in the Museum in totality.

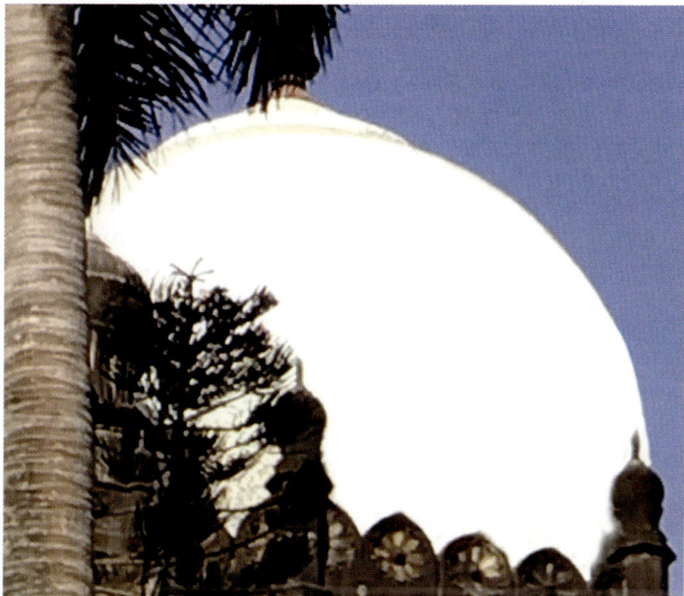

In today's India, art objects displayed in a museum, or published in a book, are totally taken out of context and from its origins in *sahitya*, and any engagement with them, without its underpinnings, can result only in a fragmented art experience. The creation of beautiful objects, whether in a temple, palace, *haveli* or home was to ensure that they become a part of our life and living. Anything that is worthwhile and beautiful nourishes and chastens us inwardly and revives our sense of what it means to be fully alive. At its finest, it quickens, refines and extends our sense of delight. It enlivens our senses and opens the door to a wider and more beautiful view of the world. And as we savour a beautiful note of music or take in a beautiful form, it quietens the mind, brings it to a state of stillness, creates serenity and transforms our sensuality into spirituality as we cherish that aesthetic experience. For us, *saundarya mimamsa* or investigation into beauty, is the object of art activity in a museum. This is aesthetic experience understood in modern and museum terms, and if thoughtfully and contemplatively carried out can become a transforming and transcendent experience.

India is more than a country, it is a civilisation where great metaphysical truths were enunciated, majestic art was created, there were multiple streams of intellectual dialogues and a constant search for truth through beauty. This message comes through loud and clear in our Museum. However behind all this, whether it was forest discourses or courtly soirees, temple dancing or itinerant singers, temple or household art, court and folk art, there was the constant quest for the beautiful, to make it a part of daily life and living, thinking and feeling and this is the whisper we hear in the Museum from one gallery to another, a whisper not found in the didactic notes accompanying the object. The beautiful for us moves seamlessly between the sacred and the secular, and despite the diversity and pluralism of our land we are united in our quest and experience for beauty. This is the signature of our Museum: That beauty for us is not just a esoteric concept or a far away ideal but it is an integral part of our life and living. And thus it is that in spite of invasions and colonisation, internecine conflicts, ravages of nature, the representation and experience of the beautiful defines the Indian civilisation, where we adorn with a passion, but even more, investigate the meaning of adornment, where through sound and speech we are not content with the apprehension of the beautiful but reach for the divine and the spiritual, where even silence is beautiful and the search for beauty is not just in the world outside but more in the serenity of the mind within. It is with this spirit that we enter the Museum.

The potter's wheel, the needle of the embroiderer, the mould of the textile block printer, the brush of the Kalamkari maker, the chisel of the sculptor, the *kalam* of the calligrapher, the spindle of the weaver, the adept hands of the flower seller making garlands, the tender hands of a young girl learning the first steps of handling cow dung and the bare hands of the housewife making *rangolis*, these are the basic tools of *akritis* and are a testament to human creativity. This creativity is thus a joyous process similar to cosmic creation, and it is this we must celebrate rather than invidual objects that we encounter in this Museum.

In these hands reside knowledge, an ancient memory, a beautiful energy, in them are bodily rhythms of trackless generations, from their movement will arise metaphors and motifs passed down from mother to daughter and above all in these hands is the living and pulsating desire, a deep delight of creativity to create a beautiful *akriti*. When we are in the Museum we will lose ourselves in their patterns and textures, their forms and shapes, their colours and hues, and in them we will hear hushed sounds of moving fingers, and we will discover hidden truths about life and living. Thus it is that *akriti* for us in the Indian tradition leads to Sanskriti, the form takes us to the formless, the limited to the vast and the embodied transforms itself into infinity. This is the unwritten insignia of our Museum.

Creating objects of beauty and giving them a centrality in our homes and lives points out, the importance of bringing grace and dignity into our lived lives, but it does not stop there. Even more it asserts the importance, nay sacrality, of human creativity. We beautify our surroundings and thereby bring a certain elegance and brightness into our homes, but it is more than that; we decorate our living spaces to give it grace and panache, but it goes beyond that; we adorn our own selves with the traditional sixteen adornments, but there is a higher purpose to creating beauty than mere adornment decoration or vanity. To be in the midst of the beautiful is to be assured of ancient racial memories and hoary archetypal symbols, of living myths and timeless metaphors, of well loved designs and traditional patterns, of evocative colours and cosmic shapes and let it work on us at many different levels, magical, religious and aesthetic assuring us of dignity and wellbeing.

An object in a museum is more than an object, for within it and around it, are vistas of human creativity, visions of beauty, chronicles of history and above all, a glimpse of what is ultimately real for us as enlightened human beings. For both the *raja* and the *praja*, the *rasika* and the *bhakta*, the artist and artisan, the philosopher and the historian, there is a *darshan* and a *drishti*, a vision and world view enshrined in these objects, that arises from that creativity. There is in these objects, an initial and immediate engagement, where, with both perception and inference, memory and stored knowledge, we are held spell bound and captive. It is at this point that various surface attributes of the object like colour and shape, form and texture, myth and narrative speak to us, and we are touched by its beauty and significance. This is its *shakshat artha* or the initial knowledge of the object. However, to the contemplative observer, there are layers and nuances of hidden voices in the

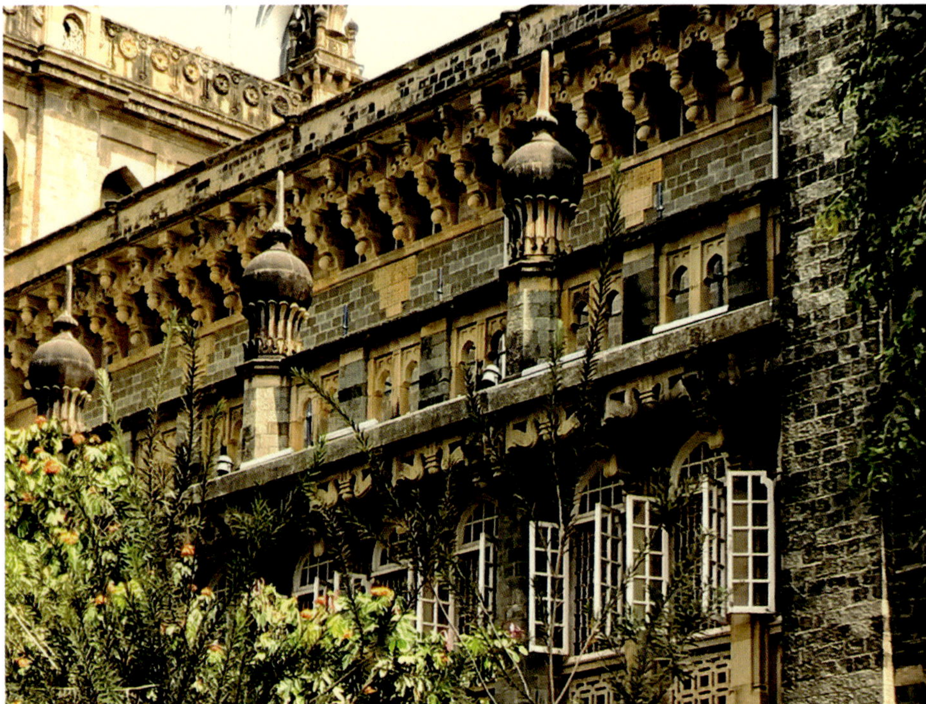

object. This is its *paroksha artha*, a deeper, more contemplative engagement with that object, which then opens up like a book, and layer upon layer, page by page, footstep by footstep, we create a world around that object, so that the object no longer remains an object but is the doorway to another world of a beautiful subjective experience of creativity. It is this other world, hidden and forgotten, but alive and inviting, that we want to remember and discover, when we visit this Museum. This is the musing that we want to create in this Museum, and not just the chatter and the noise. We do not want to be satisfied with a superficial apprehension of the artistic and historical attributes of the object, the captions and curatorial notes are important but not sufficient to take us to the source and inner voice of the object, for we want to be washed by the ocean of the creativity of the Indian civilisation from which these objects have arisen. It is as if we want to do a *samudra manthan* from which the ratnas emerged. We are as interested in the creative process as much or perhaps more than the created object. We have to begin a *manthan*, a churning, to fully appreciate the grandeur and majesty of these objects, for only then will we be able to drink from the *amrit kalasha* that will emerge. And when we do that, it will be like sitting on the banks of a river and thinking about the many streams of Indian wisdom that has flowed; it would be akin to sitting under a tree with a friend and chatting about the many dialogues and conversations that must have taken place about the concepts of what is beautiful for us in the Indian tradition, or sitting in a *durbar* as artists would present their creations to the king. We will hear voices of artists in many ateliers, be touched by the vision of enlightened patrons, be chastened by the deliberations of *rishis* about the meaning of *saundarya*. Paints and threads, chisels and brushes will speak to us as they were fashioning the art object, *shilpis* and *chitrakars* will tell us their stories, dancers and singers will recreate rhythms and melodies, and housewives will recount the chatter as they embroidered a fabric in the comfort of their *chowk*. And as we do this we will be transported into another world, and when we open our eyes the objects in front of us will become alive, there will be a fourth dimension to them, they will become our friends in our journey of understanding the five thousand year magnificence of the Indian civilisation and its creativity enshrined in this Museum. So, come with me, with open arms and bare feet, and let us hold a handful of earth and hear the footfalls of our *rishis* and kings, let us together walk the many paths of our towns and villages where these objects were created, let us listen to the hushed conversations of poets and potters, stone masons and carvers as they created these objects, and sit silently but holding hands in temples and courts, homes and *havelis* where we will understand the meaning and the purpose of life; and when we do that we will return again and again to this Museum, not to view objects or just walk through its corridors or visit the many galleries, but to meet objects that have become our friends and continue our conversation with the objects where we left off. Let us make this Museum a temple of knowledge, a theatre of our stories, a library of our artistic creations, a forum where we will have discussions and debates, a home where our past and present come alive. Our Museum is not merely a chronicle of the past but is as relevant in our life today as it was yesterday.

When we enter this Museum we are confronted by spaces that are created by walls and curated by history. We must leave behind these artificial divisions, for what we want to celebrate in this Museum is human creativity and central to it is the desire to transform the *arupa* into *rupa*, the formless thought and feeling into a beautiful form. Along with the desire there is the joy of creation and in the creative process, the joy of life and living, a life that fulfills itself like a seed that grows into a tree. The created form for us could be the spoken word, a chanted *mantra* or a lyrical song, a rhythmic dance and evocative sculpture, an idyllic painting or a beautiful household object. Speech is the foundation of human creativity and culture and is the first form that we create in a bubble of air. The evolved human being was not satisfied with the material aspects of life and therefore moved on to create through this bubble of air emotional, aesthetic and spiritual sounds, which are nothing other than *kavya* or poetry. This it achieves through devices like *rasa* or aesthetic deployment of emotions, *dhvani* or metaphor and *alamkara* or ornamentation. It is through poetry that we summon our gods and goddesses, celebrate romantic *nayak* and *nayika*s, venerate our royalty and nobility and recreate the many forms of nature with beautiful words. The next step in the creation of beautiful forms is the conversion of *shravya*, or what is heard, into *drashya* or what is seen, and thus dance was born. The dancer does this through *abhinaya* and *mudra*, *sangeet* and *tala*. Dance is the most beautiful transformation of *kavya* through the human body into artistic forms in time and space. The further evolution of dance takes us to sculpture which freezes anthropomorphic dance movements in stone and gives it super human attributes like many hands and heads. The painter then takes this, and with his *rekha* and *rang*, line and colour, makes colouful forms on paper and cloth. While all this is going on let us not forget the potter who, through his simple and unlettered way, takes a lump of earth and creates many beautiful forms which may not obey the many rules of formal art, but yet are rich with artistic creativity. The soil of India responds

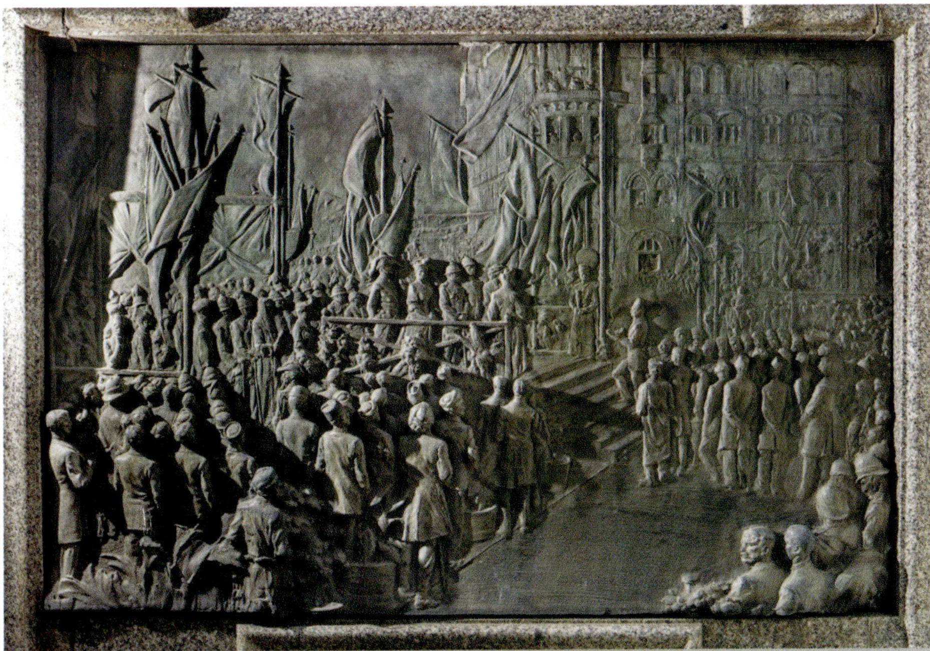

Engraving at the base of the statue of the Prince of Wales at the Museum

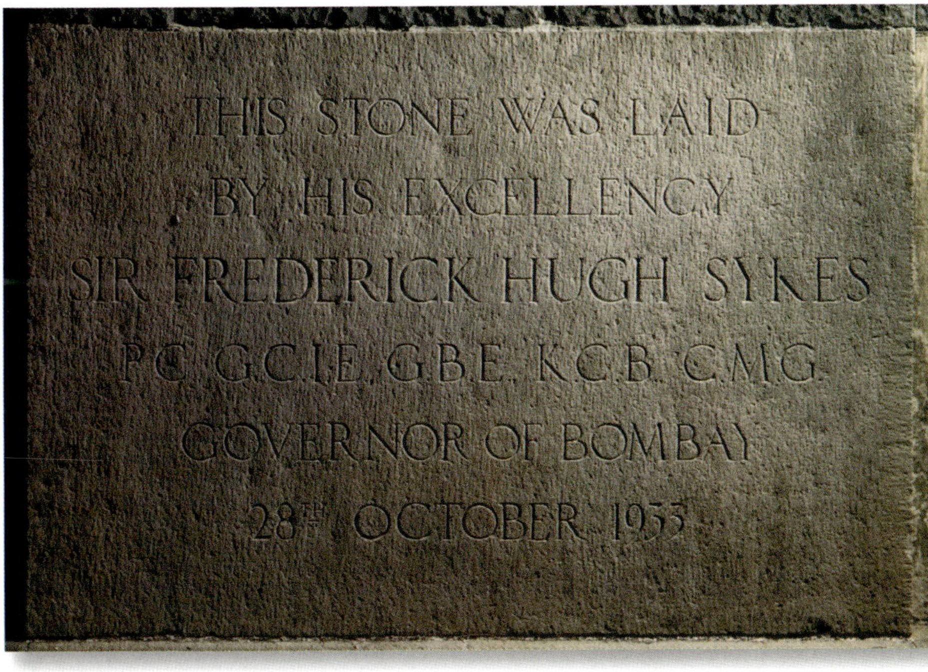

Foundation Stone of the extension of the Museum

to, and shapes in each of its parts, the urge of giving form to the unformed as an expression of the quest of the formless. Once these beautiful forms take their place in temples or *havelis*, homes or village *chowks*, the journey of these *akritis* is still not over for it is still imprisoned in a form. Even while asserting and celebrating the *sakar* or what has form, we must embark on another journey of transforming the form into the formless. The form is *nashvar* or what crumbles and tied to space and time, while the formless is *ishvar* that lives beyond space and time. However, the form has to be fully asserted and understood, its shape and texture, its *bindu* or central point of energy, its *karnas* and *bhangas*, its lines and colours, its landscape, and above all its message or meaning, have to be deeply understood. This is part of the aesthetic contemplation. The *rasika* or the committed aesthete then contemplates on these beautiful forms, remembers the trackless history and the many *shilpis* and *chitrakars*, sculptors and painters who created these objects, lets the various *sahitya* or literature that was the first inspiration of these forms resound in his mind, think of the many patrons who were responsible for this object of beauty. Slowly in their minds the form becomes formless again as the serene *rasananda* or blissful aesthetic experience sets in. At this point the form has disappeared from our mind and this is the final resting point of the beautiful form, and this is what we will carry with us when we leave the Museum and are away from the many beautiful forms that we have left behind. This then is the journey that we have to embark on, a journey that starts with our *kamana* or desire to enter the Museum and partake of the beautiful objects, undertake a contemplative engagement with the objects and then let it chasten our mind and lead us to *rasananada*. The transformation of *sunder* into *saundarya* is a yoga of beauty that has transpired in the Museum.

We need a guide to take us through the Museum for we have to negotiate many paths, multiple centuries of creativity, so many patrons and a chronology of many millenia, Let us make the *nayika* of our arts our *Sutradhar*. We need someone who can handle the many concepts and nuances of what is beautiful. It is not easy to define the concept of the beautiful in concrete terms. However Indian tradition has enshrined the beautiful in the woman more than in any other object and even among women, the woman in love, the *shringara rasa nayika* or the romantic heroine, is the most poetic and the most evocative in the tradition. In body and mind, through adornment and anticipation, in longing and belonging, in forest bowers and in opulent *havelis*, the *shringara rasa nayika* embodies and represents what we consider sensually beautiful. In her, we not only have the poetry and the sensuality of the beautiful, the throbbing emotion of romantic love but even more the inward serenity and spirituality of inner beauty.

The *shringara rasa nayika* is first and foremost an expression of *prakriti* or materiality, endowed with sensual beauty, and like *prakriti* she is also the abode of growth and fertility which she shares with the world of nature around her. The beautiful woman is also *saubhagya* or one that endows auspiciousness, and in representing her on temples and *havelis* she performs an apotropic function and confers grace and auspiciousness on them. As *salabhanjika*, or the tree nymph, she makes the Ashoka tree blossom with the kick of her left foot, and sensuous women are an integral part of temple architecture and the railings of stupas. In the *bhakti shringara* tradition the *atman*, whether that of a man or woman, in its quest for the *parmatman*, was considered female, for there could not be any greater or beautiful loving or longing than that of a *nayika* longing for her beloved. Thus the woman is central to much of Indian art and thought.

Even as we enter the garden of the Museum we are struck by the number of trees and the manicured lawns interspersed with icons set in the characteristic Mughal *char bagh* design. In creating this the architect asks us to recognise the contribution of the Mughals to Indian artistic creativity. The majestic Bao Bao tree, so tall and wide must have roots going down to a time even before the Museum was conceived, and it surely has an ancient memory. The beautiful Laburnum tree with its yellow chandelier-like flowers must remember the songs and stories of the many artists whose work is enshrined here as it welcomes us. The flaming Gulmohar must know how the many colours, that were used in the objects in this Museum, were created. The Frangipani with its soft and delicate white flowers must store memories of the fragrance and aroma that some of the objects must have contained. And of course, the Kadamba tree must remember the many romantic moments of Krishna that are captured in the Museum. There is more than botany in these trees, they are silent poets of the Museum.

After being touched by the majestic and ancient trees in the gardens what meets the eye is the magnificent dome of the Museum, 56.2 metres in diameter, reminiscent of the Gol Gumbaz of Bijapur. George Wittet was an apprentice working with John Begg who was then designing the GPO. Begg asked Wittet to come to Bijapur and study the Gol Gumbaz. It is interesting that Begg chose the Deccan, rather than the north dominated by Mughal and Rajput architecture. This speaks of the pluralistic culture of Bijapur in the time of Ibrahim Adil Shah II, who was a poet and a musician, author of the *Kitabe Nava Rasa*, where beautiful objects and structures were not defined by religion but by a culture where religions and languages, native and foreign, intermingled to produce a truly eclectic ethos. The Gol Gumbaz truly represents this pluralistic culture of the Deccan, and this is what George Wittet brought back to Bombay, the *urbas prima in Indes*, the first city of India.

George Wittet was born in Blair Atholl, Scotland in 1878. He studied architecture with a Mr Heiton of Perth, Scotland, and worked in Edinburgh and York before moving to India.

Wittet arrived in India in 1904 and became an assistant to John Begg, then Consulting Architect to Bombay. The two men were responsible for the evolution, and the subsequent popularity, of the Indo-Saracenic style of architecture which was different from both the neo-Gothic, an example of which is the Victoria Terminus, and the neo-classical style exemplified by the Cowasji Jehangir Hall that also prevailed at the same time. On 12 May 1917, Wittet, by then Consulting Architect to the Government of Bombay, was unanimously elected as the first President of The Indian Institute of Architects. Wittet's initial creations in Bombay, like our Museum and the General Post Office, were in the Indo-Saracenic style, and there is some suggestion that he was under pressure by his British masters to do this as they wanted to create a building that reflected the pluralistic traditions of India. However, as Wittet became a private architect, he chose the neo-classical style as is seen in the Institute of Science, the Small Causes Court at Dhobitalao, the Wadia Maternity Hospital, Bombay House, the King Edward Memorial Hospital, the Grand Hotel and other buildings at the Ballard Estate, by the Bombay Docks.

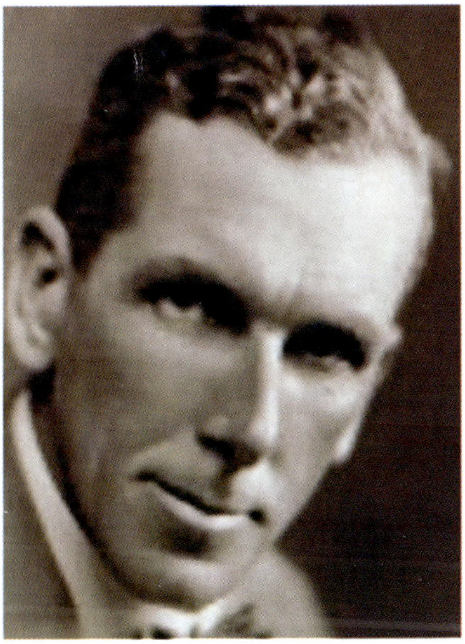

MR. GEORGE WITTET.

A correspondent writes:—By the death of Mr. Wittet, consulting architect to the Government of Bombay, announced by your Bombay Correspondent in *The Times* of Saturday, the Presidency suffers a very heavy loss. He went to Bombay over 20 years ago, and had the good fortune to find opportunities such as rarely fall to a young architect. During Lord Sydenham's Governorship the designing of several important buildings fell to his lot, among them being the Prince of Wales Western India Museum, the Royal Institute of Science, and the Gateway of India on the Apollo Bandar. Among his other important buildings are the Port Trust offices in Karachi, the Sassoon Hospital in Poona, the King Edward Memorial Hospital in Bombay, the new buildings of Bombay University, and the Custom House in Bombay, together with the adjacent railway station on the Ballard pier. The last two of the buildings named in this brief list confront the traveller on his first setting foot in Bombay from a mail steamer, and the first road to be passed on leaving the Ballard pier has been named after Mr. Wittet by the trustees of the port. It is his misfortune that he must for the present be judged —by the uninformed at any rate—by incomplete schemes. Financial difficulties have delayed the construction of the central building and gateway in the university scheme; the fine museum building still lacks its two wings, and the great avenue, which was to lead from the Gateway of India towards the city of Bombay is scarcely likely now to be built, so that the angle at which the Gateway is set does not appear wholly appropriate to its surroundings.

Six years ago Mr. Wittet left Government service and joined the Tata Engineering Company as a director. In that capacity he built the premises now occupied by the Central Bank of India and some adjoining houses, which have amazingly transformed an old part of the main thoroughfare in Bombay, and he also built the fine house on Malabar Hill, which was the residence of the late Mr. R. D. Tata. In 1926 he rejoined Government service, though at the time of his death he still had a good deal of private work in hand.

All Mr. Wittet's work is characterized by distinct individuality and great thoroughness, as well as by an intense love of beauty. Many an Indian architect owes much to him, for he was for some years a lecturer in the architectural class which Mr. Cecil Burns established in the School of Art in Bombay, and which proved a conspicuous success. Mr. Wittet was widely known in Western India, for, in addition to his professional genius, he had a fine gift for friendship and many attractive qualities. He struggled for long against ill-health, and had been suffering from acute dysentery for some weeks before his death. He was an Edinburgh man, was born in 1878, and was married to a French lady, who, with two children, survives him.

The Times of London

THE ROYAL TOUR.

THE PRINCE AND THE NEW MUSEUM.

SPEECH BY THE PRINCE.

BOMBAY, Nov. 11.*

The Prince of Wales laid the foundation-stone of a new museum this afternoon.

The museum, as explained in the address presented to his Royal Highness, is intended as a permanent memorial of the Prince's visit. It will consist of three handsome buildings forming a museum, library, and art gallery, occupying a commanding site in the crescent between the Sailors' Home and the King's equestrian statue, to which a pendant will be provided in a statue of the Prince of Wales through the generosity of Mr. Sassoon David. The buildings will be surrounded by ornamental gardens. The address further explained that the Governor had taken a warm and sympathetic interest in the project. The funds have been subscribed by the inhabitants of Bombay, and handsome contributions were received from the Bombay Government and corporation. The subscriptions included a munificent donation by Mr. Carrimbhoy Ibrahim.

The ceremony attracted a gathering of invited guests numbering several thousands, prominent among whom were the native chiefs and all official personages. The guests were seated in a vast semi-circle fronting the Royal pavilion.

The Prince and Princess of Wales, preceded by the Governor of Bombay, arrived at half-past 4 amid a tremendous demonstration. Their Royal Highnesses were received by Sir Lawrence Jenkins, the chairman, and by the other members of the committee. The Prince and Princess having ascended the dais, Sir Lawrence Jenkins advanced into the open space in front and read the address.

The Prince, in reply, said :—

"I wish to thank you all on behalf of the Princess of Wales and myself for the compliment you have paid us by commemorating our visit in a manner so useful and so lasting. If we had been asked to suggest an object for your warm-hearted and generous efforts we should have chosen an institution such as you contemplate, for we have heard of the pleasure which museums in other parts of India afford the people. You have with justice alluded to the sympathy shown by my dear father, the King-Emperor, in the educational and artistic progress of our people. It interests me to find that in this land, so strange at present to me, you are following ideas which are very familiar to us in Great Britain and throughout the Empire. Day by day we are grasping the importance of education by object-lessons, and I anticipate the happiest results from the museum, library, and art gallery which will one day stand on this spot. If, as you assure us, the buildings of which I am proud to lay the foundation-stone to-day are to be fully in keeping with the other architectural adornments of this beautiful city, then we shall feel that our visit has not only brought pleasure to ourselves, but permanent advantage and happiness to the citizens of Bombay and the thousands of strangers who visit this busy centre of commerce and government.

"To-day's ceremony is a practical proof of the public spirit of the people of Bombay about which I have so often heard. At the same time, you were fortunate to have in Lord Lamington a Governor quick to see the local want. I must also congratulate you on your corporation, which has been wise to recognize that a great capital like this has its intellectual as well as its material requirements, and last, but by no means least, on having in your midst such citizens as your Sheriff, Mr. Sassoon J. David, and Mr. Carrimbhoy Ibrahim. I hope that they and all you who have helped to bring this public-spirited idea to a fulfilment will live long to see and enjoy what, under wise and experienced direction, may prove to be one of the most important beneficial institutions of Bombay." (Prolonged cheers.)

The Prince and Princess of Wales then descended from the dais and advanced to the foundation-stone, which, with the usual ceremony, the Prince declared to be well and truly laid.

The Princess's reply to the ladies' address at the town-hall was as follows :—

"I thank you all most warmly for your kind and graceful greeting. I know the feelings which have prompted you in presenting this address to me, and you have certainly succeeded in making my first impressions of the women of India bright, happy, and hopeful. One of my chief objects on this tour is to see as much as possible of my Indian sisters, for I believe that the more I see of the reality of your lives the more I shall esteem those high qualities for which the Indian woman is renowned. If my first impressions, so charming and so powerful, become firm and fixed as I travel through India, then, to use the words of your address, I shall carry home an agreeable memory and a sympathy which will bring us into a closer bond of mutual esteem, regard, and good will."

In the evening there was a brilliant reception at Government House, attended by the native chiefs and an imposing throng of notabilities.

NOVEMBER 12.*

The Prince and Princess of Wales spent a restful Sunday. In the afternoon their Royal Highnesses went for a drive in a motor-car, and in the evening attended Divine service at the Cathedral.

The Times of London

The Indo-Saracenic Revival, also known as Indo-Gothic, Hindoo or Hindu-Gothic, Mughal-Gothic, Neo-Mughal was an architectural style movement by British architects in the late 19th century in British India. It drew elements from native Indo-Islamic and Indian architecture, and combined it with the Gothic revival and Neo-Classical styles prevalent in Victorian Britain. While the dome of our Museum is distinctly Islam, the arched windows and the lotus leaves at the bottom of the dome could be considered the Hindu elements.

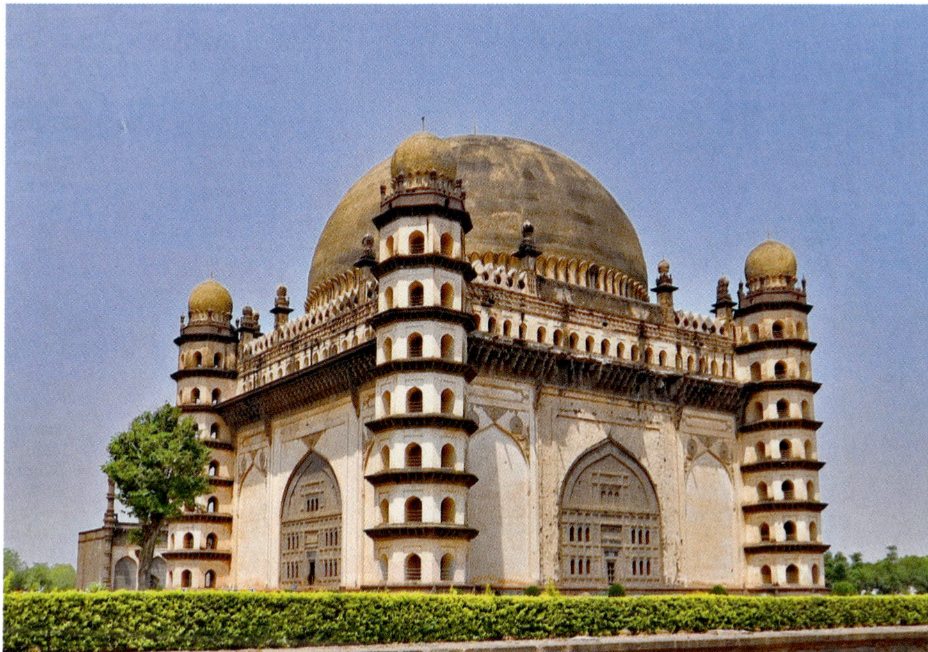

Gol Gumbaz, Bijapur

The dome of the Gol Gumbaz was the most technically advanced to be built in the Deccan, and exemplifies the flowering of art and architecture that occurred during the period of the Adil Shahi Sultanate's reign. This is Hindu-Muslim or north-south syncreticism at its best As the eye settles in over our dome, one sees lotus petals at the base of the dome and smaller domes which are copies of the main dome. The combination of the dome and the lotus petals is the most beautiful example of the Indo-Saracenic syle. The dome of our Museum was built with layers of mortar rendered on both faces, so that the dome acts as a concrete shell reinforced with bricks.

The dome as an architectural construct is prehistoric. In its early beginnings in the Vedic period the dome was a funerary mound. Later the dome was used to denote royal patronage, like a parasol. Medieval India saw the widespread use of domes by the Muslims as in the Humayun tomb, the Taj Mahal and the Gol Gumbaz, to name a few. Later the British used it extensively in their constructions in India as in the Rashtrapati Bhavan and the Victoria Terminus. Signifying the heavens or cosmic space, the dome became a standard architectural device in the hands of the British in India.

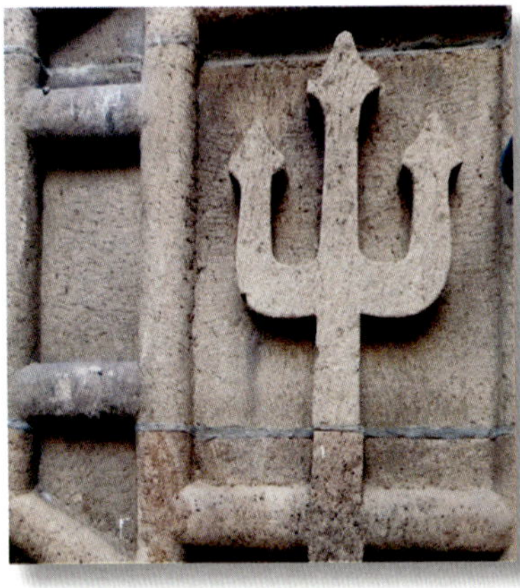

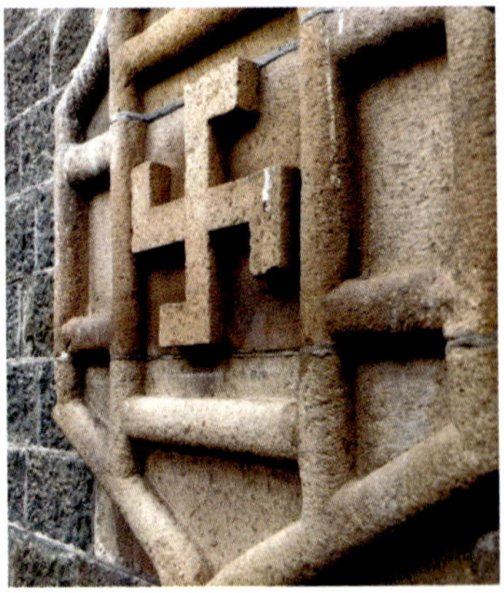

Symbols on the top of the Museum noticed during conservation by Mr. Vikas Dilawari.

However, it is important to note that traditional Hindu structures like a temple or a palace never have a dome. The answer to this lies perhaps in the concept that the dome is a man-made construct, and therefore alien to the Hindu psyche which prefers natural structures, like a mountain, which become the *shikhara* in a temple. Also, a dome represents a sphere cut in half, and this once again does not sit well in the Hindu mind as it prefers holistic forms. *Chhatris* or a canopy are dome-shaped structures that mark a memorial site. Such memorials usually consist of a platform ringed by a set of ornate pillars which support a stone canopy. The other known meaning is of small pavilions that adorn the corners and roof of the entrance of major buildings.

This imposing and magnificent building, although it was not built according to traditional *vastu shastra* or texts of architecture, nevertheless gives insistent hints of both its Indian and Sarasenic heritage. While the dome and the small minarets are obviously Islamic, there are plenty of hints of its Indian pedigree. The *chajjas* at the top of the building are very suggestive of wooden structures of yore. The arched and screened windows take us back to rock cut caves and Rajasthani *havelis*. The exterior of the building which features stones reminds us that stones are pre-historic and their very presence on the building gives it a certain character. Stones always take us away from the banalities of modernity to times ancient, for through them have flowed the footfalls of millennia of human civilisation, they have been witness to endless stories of kingdoms and dynasties, in them are echoes of political and religious triumphs and in their textures is written the story of human aspirations and endevaours.

Others features of the Museum building that demand our attention are the *chajjas* supported by brackets which are reminiscent of wooden structures of the past, like a *haveli* in Gujarat or a *wada* in Maharashtra; for this Museum is a place where the past will come alive through suggestions of architectural elements. Small minarets suggest a Mughal ethos chastening our mind that when it comes to beauty our mind is not going to be divided by narrow religious divisions. *Jalis* in windows is another Mughal feature which adorns the building. The British tried to encapsulate India's past within their new Indic hybrid buildings and our Museum, along with other buildings like the Bombay Municipal Corporation, are good examples. Let us tarry for a few minutes admiring and understanding the building and decoding its silent messages, for only then would we able to have a mind that is ready to receive beauty that is inspired by Hindu ideas and created by Muslim hands, and patronised by trackless generations of patrons cutting across political dynasties, objects that are both sacred and secular, creations which have touched both the *raja* and the *praja*, where adornment is not just to beautify but was a way of life, which we shall see in all of these beautiful objects that await us in the Museum.

The finding of enigmatic symbols by Conservation Architect Vikas Dilawari, like the *swastika* and the *trishul*, carved in stone on the back of the Museum, raises interesting questions. In the absence of any archival records in this Museum, about these symbols, one can only speculate and look for collateral evidence in other situations. The stone masons working for the Museum under the supervision of British architects, were most probably from Bombay and its surroundings, skilled in their profession but equally steeped in their faith, probably Shaivite, and would never make a distinction between a secular structure like the Museum from a sacred structure like a temple. For them every construct is a *vastu* and can never begin or conclude without divine blessings and concurrence of the planets. I have no doubt that astrologers must have been consulted, *bhumi puja* performed, and before they left the site at the conclusion of the project, wanted to ensure that the building be blessed; and that is why they left behind these symbols. Some temple inscriptions, and also paintings, do mention the names of the sculptors and painters; however our stone masons had the nobility and the grace not to leave their names but create cosmic symbols which stand even today, touching us who care to think of the unknown *shilpis* who must have toiled to make this building.

We shall bypass history and chronology and also the division of the Museum in specific galleries. We shall do this not just to be different but because our main concern is to celebrate human creativity, to venerate Vishwakarma the divine architect who inspires poets and patrons alike, to hear the silent voices, nay prayers, of the *sthapati* as he sets about to create a beautiful form. This is a magical, almost mysterious process, as the master sculptor is about to capture a divine essence in stone. He is not interested in creating transient emotions or textures of *samsara* but the abiding truths that underlie both nature and cosmos. We know from talking to tribal artists, like the painter of the mural of the Pithora Baba in Gujarat, that the artist would perform prayers and sleep by the wall which he was to paint the next day, so that even in his sleep he would be privy to divine visions, and the next day after his ablutions, he would again pray before starting his work. This is one of many examples that shows that creating a sculpture or painting was a sacred act no different from cosmic creation. We also know that some kings like Yashovarman were also sculptors. When the formless inspiration becomes a form, this is the pristine moment of creation and of joy, reminding us of the Upanishadic statement that from joy creation arises and into joy it becomes.

Ours is a tropical country, and filling the space from the earth to the sky is lush and fecund vegetation, luxuriant trees, colourful blossoms and verdant foliage. As we engage with various objects we must keep this at the back of our mind.

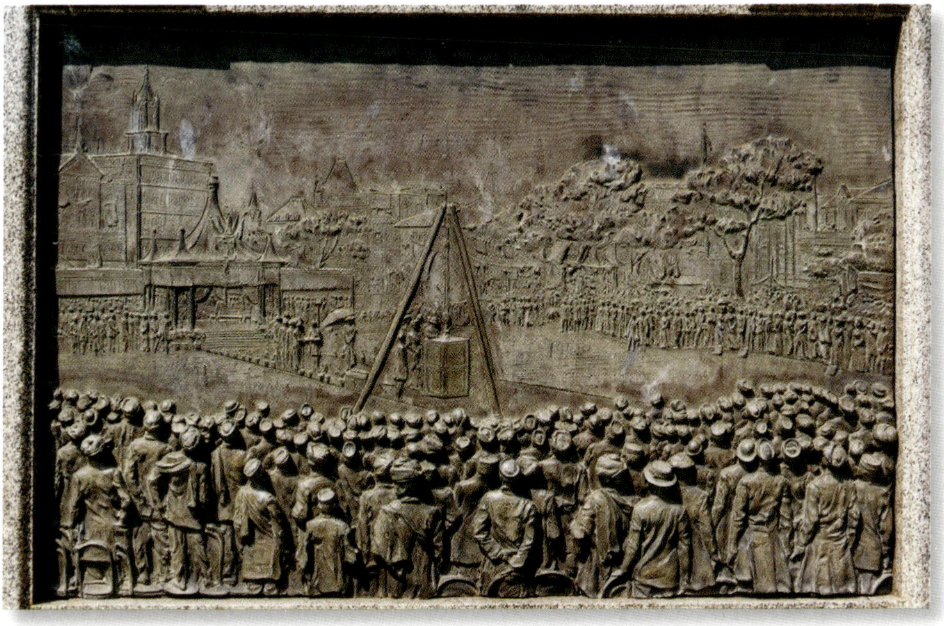

Engraving at the base of the statue of the Prince of Wales at the Museum

As Pratapaditya Pal states:

> The sculptural form itself often expresses vegetative abundance, and as we look at the the swaying, curvaceous figures with their surging sensuality, we are at once reminded of the lush vegetation of the tropical world. The forms expand like fruit laden branches, exuding a rhythmic vitality that is essentially organic.[1]

One reason why our journey has to be inter-gallery and not from gallery to another is because all art forms and artistic creativity for us are inter-related.

A dialogue between Vraja and the sage Markandeya in the *Vishnudharmottara* comes to mind:

> Vraja: Teach me how to sculpt so that I may express divinity on them.
>
> Markendeya: He who does not know the canon of painting can never know the canon of image making.
>
> Vraja: Teach me then the art of painting.
>
> Markendeya: To know the art of painting one must know the canon of dance.
>
> To this one can add that before dance comes music and even before that comcs *sahitya*.[2]

Poetry is the primal art form and everything merges from it. Kavya is the *kalpavriksha* and the *kamadhenu* of artistic creation. I believe the birth of my *kavya* takes place somewhere in the hidden and mysterious spaces of the mind where the voices of all our ancient poets flow in a stream, voices of Bhartrhari, Amaru, Kalidasa, Jayadeva, Keshavdas, Tagore and many more, where the hoary conversations of everyone in love are heard in whispers like those of Shakuntala, Kamakandala, Damayanti, Sohini and Radha and, chatter of *shilpis* and *chitrakars* of the past resonate. In those spaces, as the past comes alive and where the footsteps of poets and painters, singers and dancers are heard and then when in those dimly lit spaces the smile of my beloved shines brightly like the sun and softly like the moon. Just then my romantic feelings turn into thoughts of love and when those thoughts find a flower they go and rest within its petals and with the touch of the flowers my thoughts become words. Just then a bird sings and my words leave the flower and become a poem which I then offer to my beloved and when she places my words in her *odhni* those words once again turn into flowers and I pick one flower and put it in her hair and the rest of the flowers I offer to Krishna.

I take shelter in the wonderful and
beautifully ornamented house of poetry,
that has words as bricks, inflections etc. as mortar,
and meaning as its sanctuary!

Now that we are ready, like a devotee that enters a temple or a student steps foot in a place of learning, let us enter this sanctuary of beauty with a *sankalpa*, resolve, that we shall befriend and embrace these objects, give it our best and loving attention, provide a context to it, trace it to its roots and then come again and again till these beautiful objects become a part of our chastened mind.

We must recreate for us the *ananda* with which the artist began remembering the words of the Taitrriya Upanishad,

आनन्दाद्ध्येव खल्विमानि भूतानि जायन्ते।
आनन्देन जातानि जीवन्ति।
आनन्दं प्रयन्त्यभिसंविशन्तीति।
(तैत्तिरीय उपनिषद् ३.६.१)

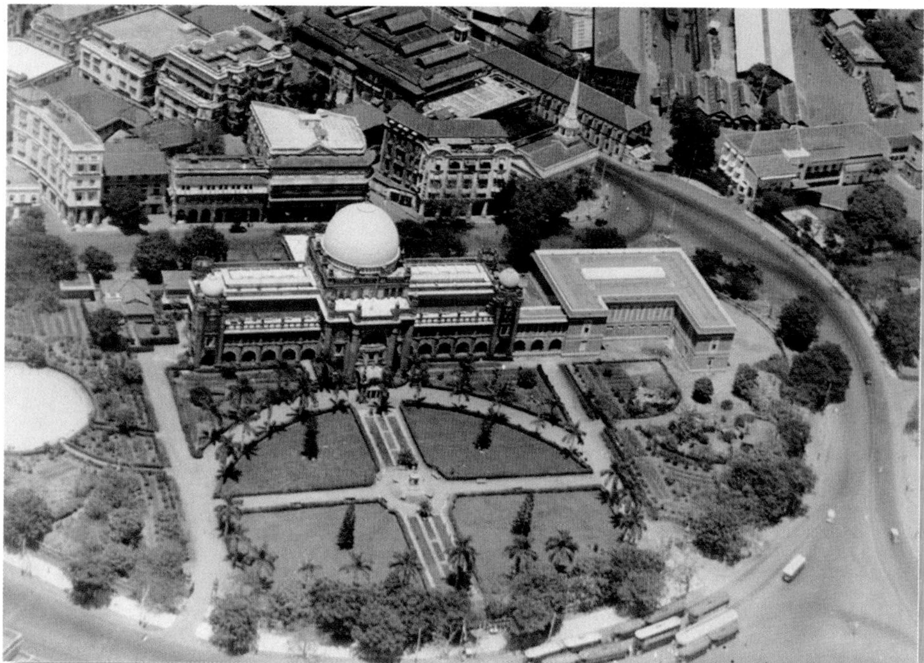

Photo Courtesy: British Library, London

Chronology of the Museum

Foundation Stone of the Museum
11 November 1905

Museum Building Completed
1914

Museum Formally Opened
10 January 1922

Foundation Stone of the Annexe
28 October 1933

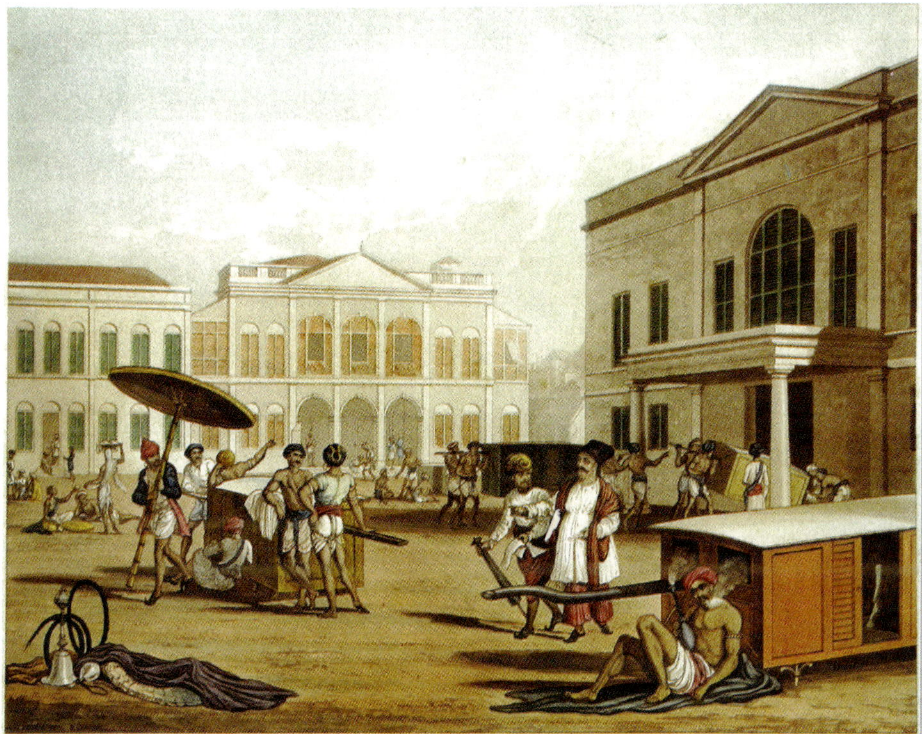

This lithograph give us a glimpse of what Mumbai must have looked like when the Museum was coming into being. Elegant British ladies riding in palanquins, men in sola hats trotting about and the Indian cognoscenti rubbing shoulders with our British masters. They came as merchants but became our masters and left behind institutions like our Museum as their legacy. While we attribute the building to them, the beautiful objects that the Museum houses belongs to the soil of India.

Photo Courtesy: Pheroza Godrej

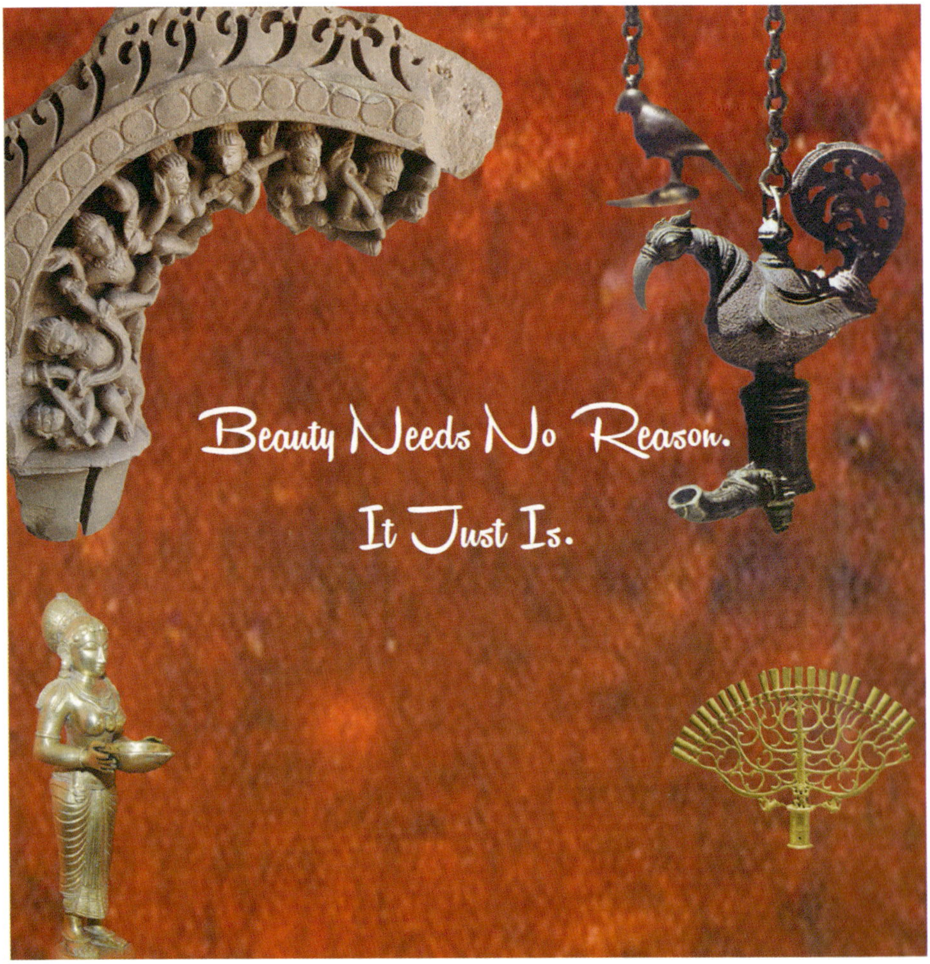
Beauty Needs No Reason.
It Just Is.

Alap

The First Notes

This Museum, like all others, was a turning point in the way in which Indian art was celebrated and understood by us. While we do not have a single word for art, the word *kala* which is commonly used, stands for *kriti* or the method of creating the art object. On the other hand we have many words for beauty, such as *sunder, lavanya, charu, mohani, ramya, ruchika, shri, sundari, kamini*. It is important that, even though we are entering a European style Museum, we keep an Indian *drishti* or point of view when we engage with the objects. The objects in this Museum are *vastu*, not art, and this is important to keep in mind. These objects are not inanimate but have a life of their own. They have a history, they have been lovingly made and affectionately touched, they have relationships with the *raja* and the *praja*. Indian *drishti* puts life back in these objects as that *drishti* is synaesthetic, namely it is an enlightened visioning, which brings in a variety of modalities of vision, texts, tradition and imagination, and gives the object a context and a life, for without that the object lies torn from its source, fragmented from its surroundings, divorced from its creator, distanced from its maker and removed from its patron. It is almost as if the object has a sense of separation anxiety similar to that of the new born child. While we remain grateful to the many curators who have shaped and designed the Museum, we must entertain a disclaimer, namely that the chronology and order that have been imposed on the various objects are artificial and do not inherently belong to the concept or the inspiration that created the object. Only then would we be able to experience the objects in the Museum in totality, for our lens, our *drishtikon*, is human creativity as it creates beautiful objects and not so much its history.

All great civilisations have created works of art which embody their concept of beauty, and we in India have not only an ancient but equally a growing and evolving artistic tradition and culture. We have entrusted our deepest thoughts and cherished visions to our artists, be they poets or potters, *shilpis* or *sangitkars*, dancers or designers. These objects of beauty and the discourse around them have endured, as the enjoyment and contemplation of the beautiful is a hall mark of the *rasika*, and is an essential value for us in the Indian aesthetic tradition, and further it defines what it is to be cultured and cultivated. The *rasika* or the cultivated connoisseur, not only engages with objects of beauty but undertakes a contemplative understanding of that object. The beautiful is not only worthy of contemplation but we associate *sunder* with *saubhagya*, the beautiful with what is auspicious, and even more we equate *sunder* and *ishvarya* or beauty and divinity. It is quite clear then that representing and understanding what is beautiful is an important part of the celebration of what it is to be an Indian and becomes the credo of Indian aesthetics. That should be our watchword as we celebrate the *vastu* or the objects in this Sangrahalaya.

Paints and threads, chisels and brushes, will speak to us as they were fashioning the art object, *shilpis* and *chitrakars* will tell us their stories, dancers and singers will recreate rhythms and melodies and housewives will recount the chatter as they embroidered a fabric in the comfort of their *chowk*. And as we do this we will be transported into another world, and when we open our eyes the object in front of us will become alive, there will be a fourth dimension to them; they will become our friends in our journey of understanding the five thousand year magnificence of the Indian civilisation and its creativity enshrined in this Museum. So, come with me, with open arms and bare feet, and let us hold a handful of earth and hear the footfalls of our *rishis* and kings, let us together walk the many paths of our towns and villages where these objects were created, let us listen to the hushed conversations of poets and potters as they created these objects, and sit silently but holding hands in temples and courts, homes and *havelis* where we will understand the meaning and the purpose of life, and when we do that we will return again and again to this Museum, not to view objects or just walk through its corridors or visit the many galleries but to meet objects that have become our friends and continue our conversation with the objects where we left off. Let us make this Museum a temple of knowledge, a theatre of our stories, a library of our artistic creations, a forum where we will have discussions and debates, a home where our past and present come alive. Our Museum is not merely a chronicle of the past but is as relevant in our life today as it was yesterday.

Ours is a tropical country and filling the space from the earth to the sky is lush and fecund vegetation, luxuriant trees, colourful blossoms and verdant foliage. And the energising principle or *shakti* of this is the *Yakshi*. She is the tree spirit that imparts its fertility to the tree and the tree in turn resonates

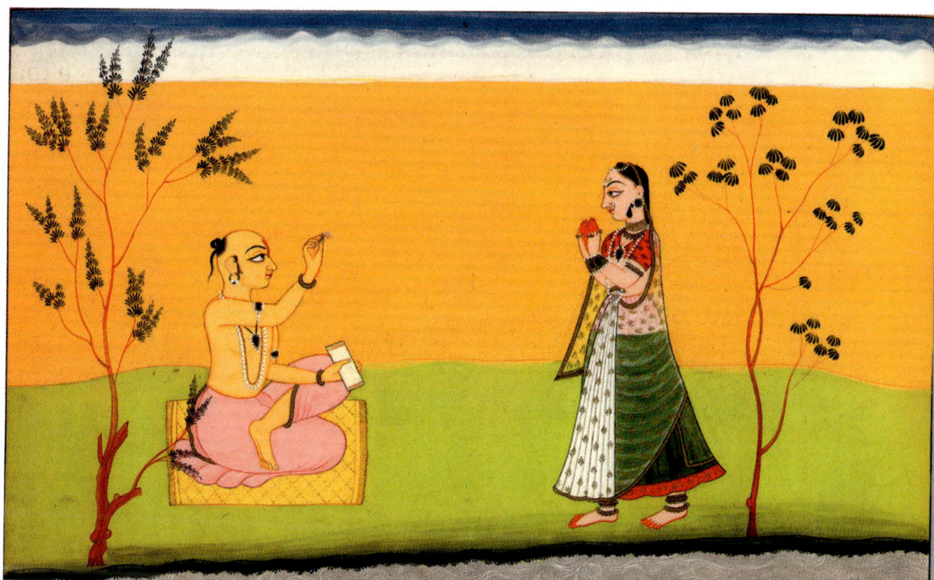

Guru Shishya. Painting by Vijay Sharma

with her. It is not surprising therefore that one of the first images to be sculpted was that of the *Yakshi*, the tree nymph which is seen in Buddhist stupas as in Bahrut.

The *sutradhar* reminds us that that one must bring a number of artistic disciplines to bear when we are celebrating an art object. This is the hall mark of our aesthetics, our *saundarya mimasa*, our inquiry into beauty in this Museum, remembering that the basis of what is beautiful is *kavya*.

Our concern is artistic creativity and once we have known the poet and the painter, the patron and the potter, all of them recede in the background and we stand in awe of that magic moment of artistic creation.

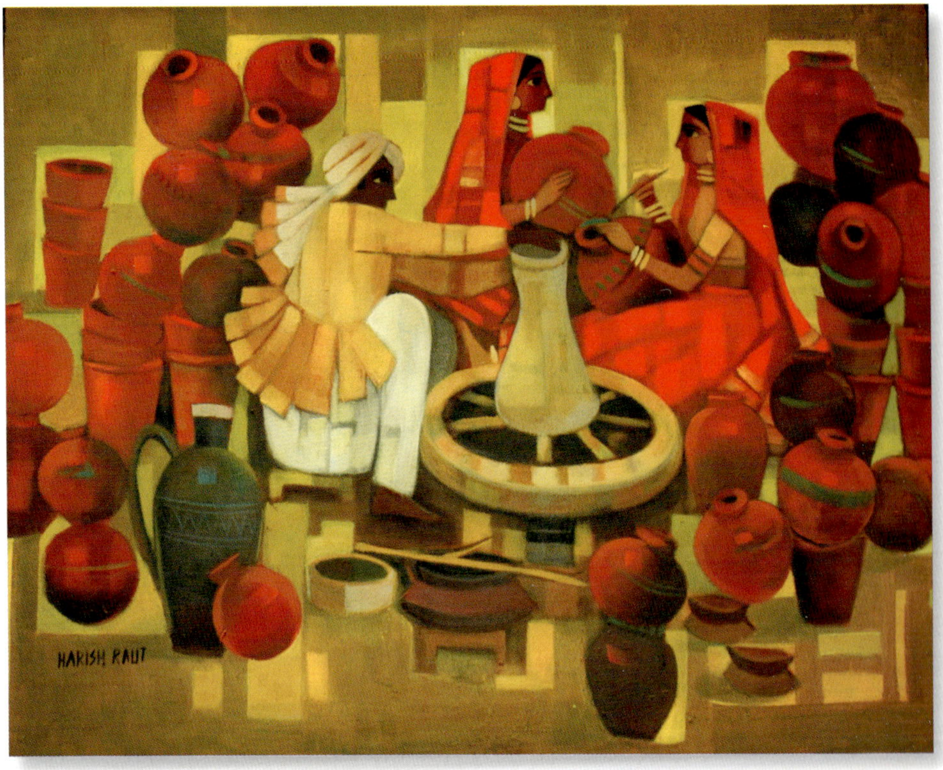

Potter. Painting by Harish Raut

'एकः शब्दः सम्यक् ज्ञातः सप्रयुक्तः
स्वर्गे लोके च कामधुग् भवति॥'

If just one word is properly
understood and properly
spoken it becomes a wish
fulfilling cow in this life
and the next.

Bhartrihari, 4th century CE

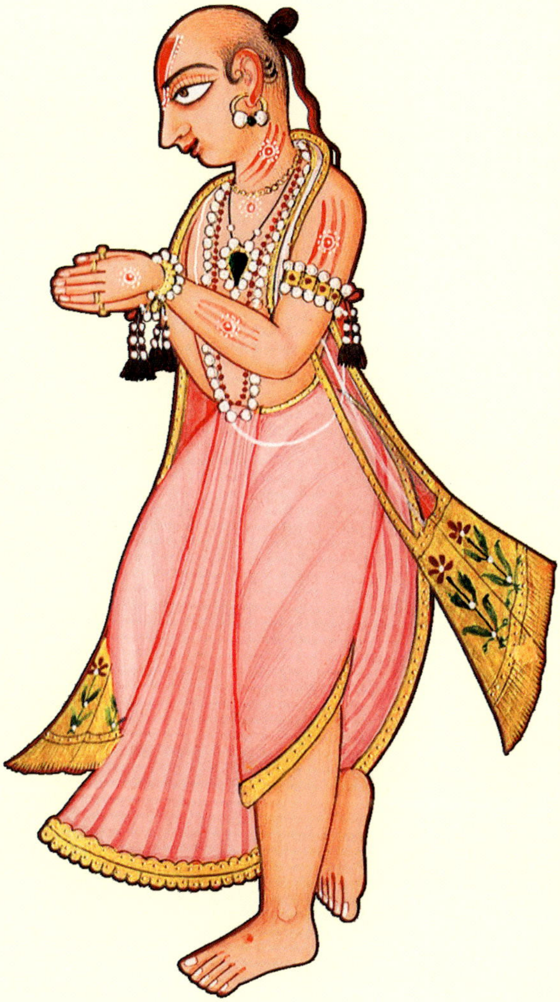

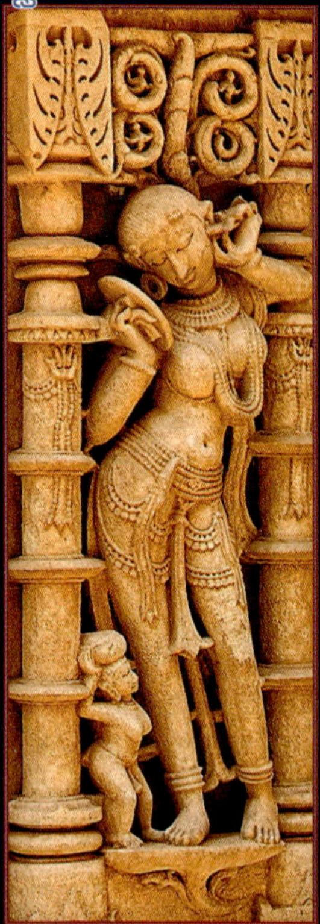

कोहम्

Who am I?

अहम् इदम्

I am This

किम् इदम्

What is This?

इदं भारतीयं सुंदरम् ॥

That which is Beautifully Indian

Sanskrit words for design, *akriti* and *rachana*, both imply a creative process and signal an exalted human activity, an activity that requires not only skill but creativity, not just *sadhana* or moral discipline, but a spiritual outlook and an aesthetic sense. The Upanishadic dictum *purnam adaha purnam idam purnad purnam udachyat*e, asserts that it is only out of the fullness that something full can arise. Applying this to beauty, one can say that it is only out of a total sense of beauty that the beautiful can arise.

Creation in its best sense stems from a sense of *kama*, joyousness, hence it comes within the purview of *dharma*; it is born from a desire to produce something in the likeness of the Creator, a desire also to replicate the cosmos in smaller terms. Creativity, therefore, arises from a need to give form to the formless, from *nirakar* to *sakar* and thereby give shape to something beautiful so that it can then take its rightful place in the world we inhabit.

Design for us is not just ornamentation or arrangement, but it is an expression of a world view, where to be surrounded by beautiful objects is an act of noble living.It is thus that an object that is created by Indian design is not just an object, but something more than itself. It has been correctly observed that in India, all forms have a hint of the formless, all sounds lead to silence and all movement has in it the seed of stillness, for has it not been said *rupam rupam pratirupam babhuva,* all forms are a replica of the primal form. An essential feature of Indian design is the use of robust and evocative colours, colours that are not just ornamental but speak of emotions and states of being. We see this especially in miniature paintings, fabric such as saris, and homes which feature *rangoli* and *mandana*. Every colour is associated with a deity, for example blue with Vishnu. Colours signify states of being such as the red with fertility and yellow for auspiciousness. For miniature artists, colours are a visual language especially in paintings of *shringara rasa*. For example, red is passion, yellow denotes young love, black is the night in which the *abhisarika nayika* goes stealthily to her beloved.

Indian design has a close rapport with the world of nature, trees and blossoms, creepers and leaves. In connecting with this world, Indian design makes a statement that the human being is not alone in this world but resonates with the world around, and the rasa that flows within them is not different from the sap that animates nature. Most saris would have a leaf, the *aam butta* or a creeper in their design. The Indian mind abhors emptiness and we, therefore, avoid empty spaces in our designs. Another feature of Indian design is that lines are not just linear but lyrical, not just straight but wavy, not static but alive with motion, they almost dance. A feature of Indian design is that beauty exceeds utility.Objects of daily living like a toilet box or container are made beautiful, and even more, feature religious motifs like Kurma and Vishnupadas, which suggest that the sacred and the secular are not dichotomous but seamless. And when the design is complete, we always make a border around it, to contain the beautiful forms in a limited space and prevent it from being lost in the infinite space around it.

Indian design is welcoming, beautiful, evocative, animated and meaningful and is an expression of our *drishti*, gaze, our way of looking at the world and our life within it.

While artistic skill is innate and inborn and repetitively passed down from father to son and mother to daughter through centuries of artistic creativity, we also have shastras or texts that describe the process of artistic creation. The first in a long list is Bharat Muni, who in his *Natyashastra*, lays out not only prescriptions for the dancer, but in his foundational sutra defines *rasa*. *Rasa* has remained the quintessence of beauty and aesthetic discourse even after a lapse of two millennia. Bhartrihari's Sphotavada, Anandavarsdha's Dhvanyloka and Abhinavagupta's Abinava Bharati takes the concept of *rasa* further through meaning and metaphor. Likewise the Vishnudharmattora Purana, Shilpaprakasha and Vastusutra Upanishad offer advice on the making of icons. These and other texts do give the technique of creating art objects, but in the end, artistic creativity remains a mysterious and unknown process that requires both *sadhana* and *dhyana*.

Sadhana or spiritual discipline starts with the desire or *kamana* to create something beautiful; this is then followed by rigorous and dedicated training and practice, there has to be a commitment to one's gurus and to all who have gone before, it requires adhering to tradition, and obeying the context into which the art object will be created, it needs a knowledge of the material that will be required, and finally a respect for the entire artistic *parampara*.

Tradition or *parampara* can sometimes enslave the artist and thereby there is a certain repetitiveness in our objects of beauty. But as Bhartrihari reminds us even when there is repetition, the human eye delights in this, and yet finds something new every minute.

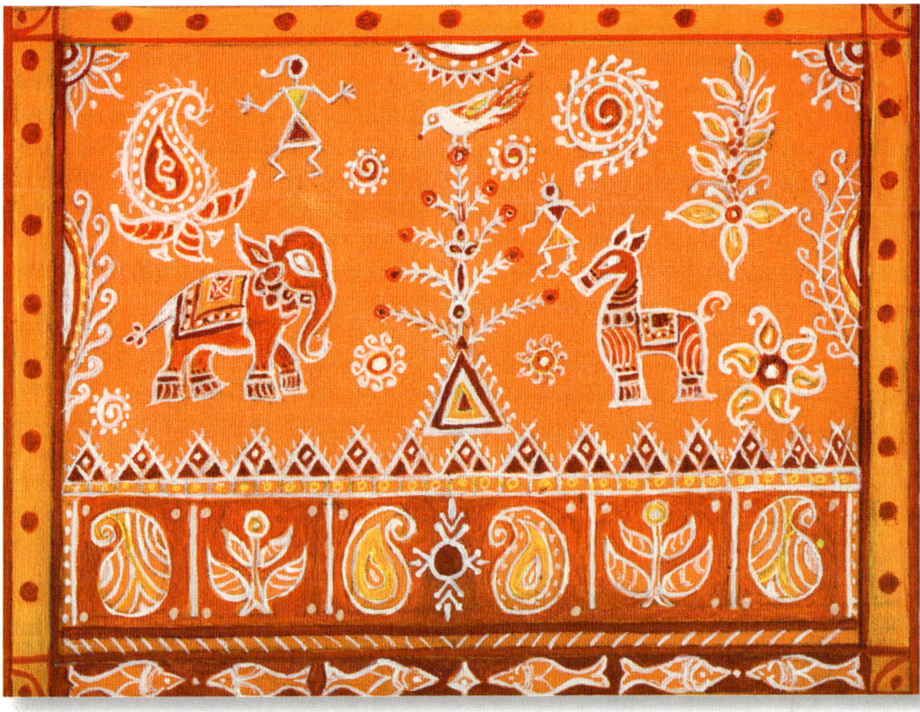

Painting by Varsha Mehta. Inspired by Jamini Roy.

Dhyana on the other hand is to enter a serene and inner creative space, crossing the *buddhi* or intellect and overcoming the *ahamkara* or ego, but at the same time retaining *asmita* or an enlightened self-awareness. This the artist or artisan does by being clean in body, cleansing the space in which he will be working, worshiping the tools that he will be using, thereby sanctifying the environment.

A space in the home of the artist or the artisan, that is the womb of creativity, is the *mandapa* or pavilion. While the *rangamandapa* is the ornate chamber of the temple where the *bhakta* raises his awareness before the final religious experience in the sanctum, the *pranaya mandapa* is the pavilion for the pleasures of love where *shringara* is transformed into *shrinngar bhakti*. In its basic form a *mandapa* has a floor and a ceiling and four pillars and recreates cosmic space, where the floor is the earth and the ceiling is the sky. When an artist sits in a *mandapa*, howsoever simple, he is creating an axis mundi, connecting the earth to the sky through him. A common space for the artisan is to sit under a tree while he is working, which then becomes the *mandapa*.

While *sadhana* and *dhyana* are paramount in artistic creation the choice of material is also equally important. All our beautiful objects that are traditionally created use organic material. Whether it is fabric for our textiles, palm leaf for our pothis, stone for our icons and paint for our paintings, they are natural products from plant and soil. Therefore they bring with it the sacredness of the earth, the aroma of flowers, the textures of rain beaten stone, the pattern of leaves on embroidery, the undulating movement of a creeper. Nothing is artificial, no material is made by machines, there are no man-made chemicals. Even the instruments that are used are from the world around us, the naturally occurring stone that chisels, the camel hair that paints, the cotton threads that create patterns in the fabric, the precious stones that are used for our ornaments, all are products of the earth. Just as the joy of the creator comes from within himself, so do the materials come from the world around us. There is a harmony of everything that comes together in the creation of the beautiful object, only then will we hear the *raga* of beauty. This *raga* is heard by the *sahradaya*, the prepared aesthete, the trained *rasika*, who hears the subliminal music that emerges from these objects.

The potter and the weaver are considered primal artists. The potter is a poet of the earth and the weaver a poet of threads.Weaving is a very ancient tradition in India, and weaving and philosophy share many common words, words such as *sutra* and *tantra*. It is in the growing, spinning, weaving, dyeing, printing and embroidering of cotton that the Indian craftspeople found their richest expression. Threads or *sutra* are an important part of Indian traditions, both religious and secular. There is a sense of wonder in creating a thread from a cotton pod and then weaving a fabric from it. Wrapping a thread around the trunk of a tree is done for the granting of a wish. In certain tribal villages a continuous thread is tied around the periphery of the village, and this is to contain the good and ward off the evil from the village. Coloured threads serve as a *vastra* for the deity in a *puja*, and the devotee ends the *puja* by tying a thread on his wrist. Some of the deepest sentiments such as between a sister and brother are expressed by tying a thread as in a *rakhee*. And it is from threads that fabric of all kinds are woven.

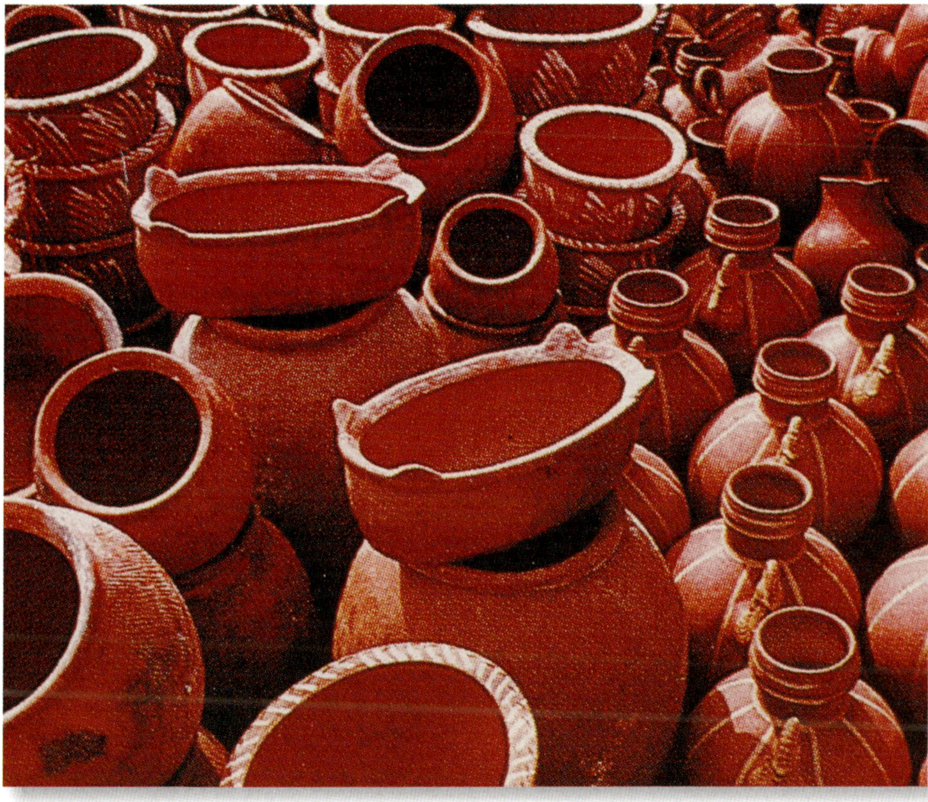

Pots

Weaving has often been compared to music, both are fine arts and done with a dedication and *latifa* or pleasure. To fully understand a certain piece of textile, its colour and texture, design and motifs, one must bring to it not only one's sight but touch as well. Just as music begins with a single note, textile begins with a single thread. And like the many notes of the musical scale there are many types of threads, and they can be combined in many different ways to produce a fabric. The loom is the weaver's instrument and he adjusts and sets it, like a musician tunes his instrument. When the weaves fills his *bani* or weft and throws his shuttle it is as if the musician has started the *alap*, and like a *raga* weaving has a certain rhythm or *laya*. And just as a *raga* has a certain *rasa* or *rang* the weaves, infuses a certain feeling in what he weaves, and each fabric like each *raga*, requires a different technique. The environment in which the weaver lives filled him with wonder: green leaves, the bark of a tree, roots of a date palm, fruits like the mango, birds and blossoms, the feather of a peacock and the fine thread of a spider web filled him with wonder, and he incorporated that in his fabric. And then there are colours which the weaver derived from the world around. Truly has it been said that weaving is like music.

Artistic creation is a sacred act, whether the object being made is a *kalasha* or a *murti*, an everyday object or a religious icon. In trying to find a home for aesthetic experience it is important that we pay equal attention to the artist and the aesthete alike, to the art object and the experience it generates, to the object and subject equally. It therefore places a responsibility on us who come to the Museum as visitors but must leave as *rasikas*.

The Rg Veda while not formulating aesthetic doctrines hints at an aesthetic approach when it says:

> Penetrate deeper to know the truth, know the physical first and then the spiritual. He who knows the first vital thread, binding all the things formed in shape, colour and words, knows only the physical form of the universe, and knows very little. But he who goes deeper and perceives the thread within the thread knows the real entity.
> Rg Veda 8.58.2

Although many objects that we will see and encounter in this Museum have a religious origin, that is they come from a temple, we must maintain a distance from religious dogma and doctrine and let aesthetic experience be self-standing. The one image that comes to mind that gives hints of artistic creation is the Sheshashayi Vishnu. Lying recumbent, with Lakshmi tending his feet, his eyes half open and a lotus emerging from his navel upon which sits Brahma. One can probe artistic creation only up to a point but in the end it must be understood as a mysterious and beautiful process, where the artist and artisan from the joyousness within him, creates an object which is joy giving to us.

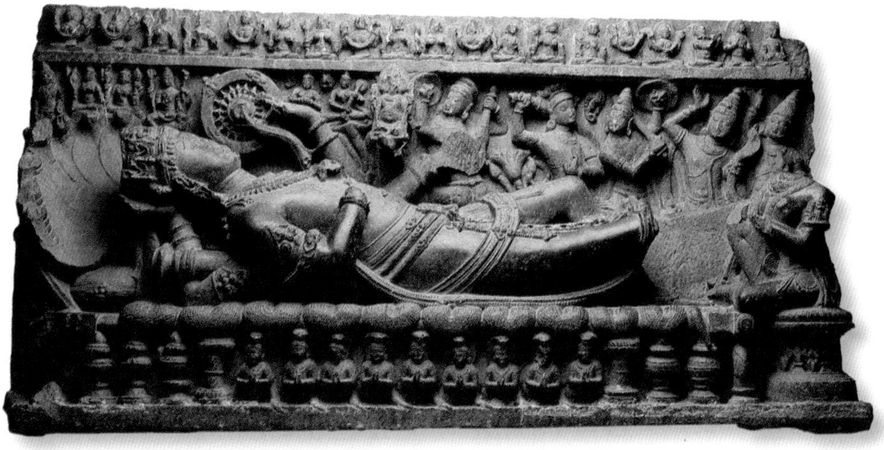

Sheshayi Vishnu, Eastern India, 15th–16th century

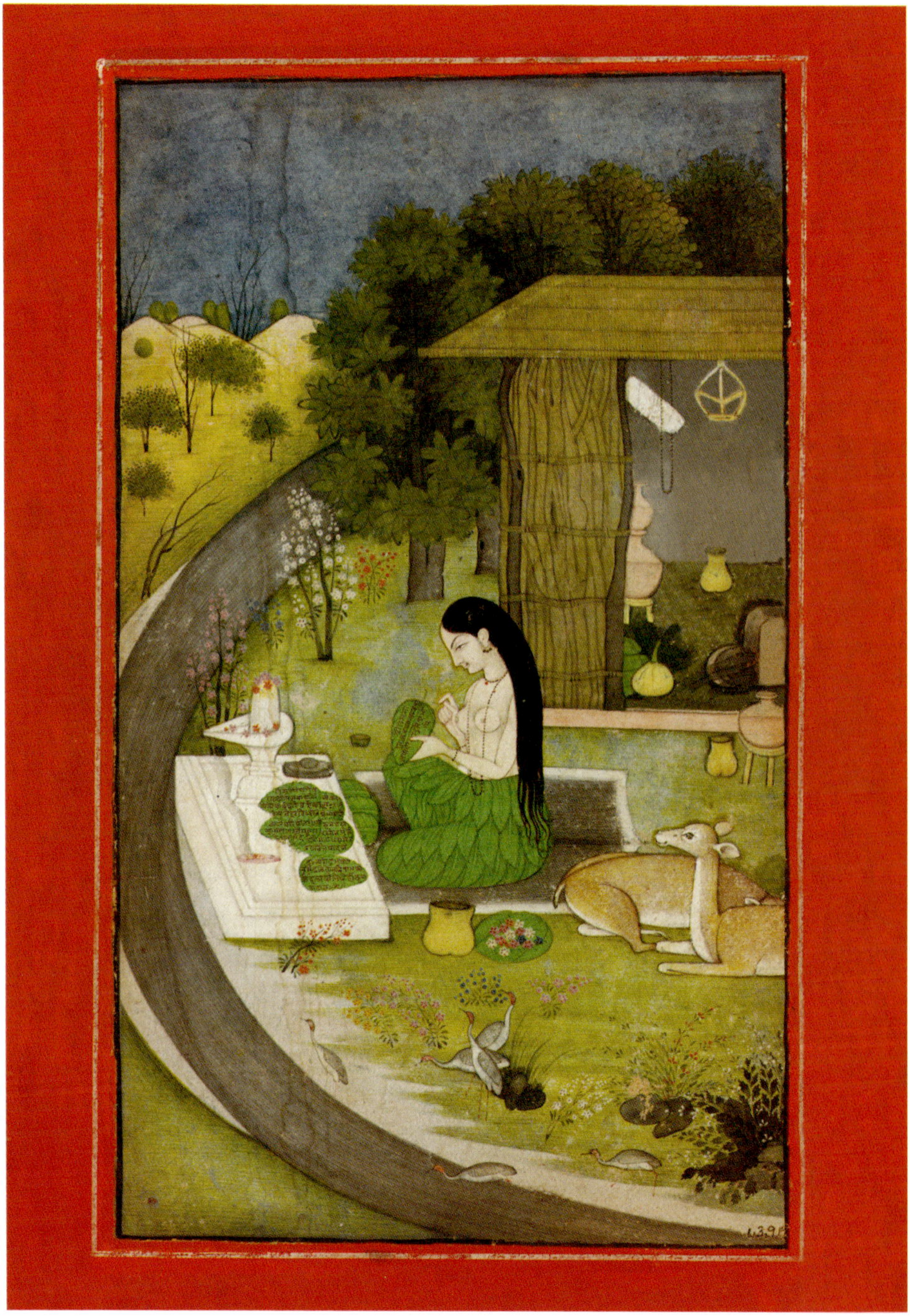

Shakuntala Writing a Love Letter, Kangra, 19th century

The Sensuous Feminine

Yakshi to Nayika

The Indian tradition has enshrined what is sensuously beautiful in the woman more than in any other object, and has ensured that in celebrating her sensuality we do not lose sight of her spirituality, for the two in the Indian context are indivisible and not dichotomous, and it is in the woman that the two meet seamlessly. *Sunder* or what is beautiful is only a starting point in our quest, and as we explore that we must not forget this is only a doorway and that our ultimate destination is the experience of *saundarya* or inner subjective beauty through the woman.

The woman is first and foremost *prakriti* or materiality, endowed with sensual beauty, and she is also the abode of growth and fertility which she shares with the world of nature around her, and in representing the *surasundari* or the beautiful woman on temples and *havelis,* she serves an apotropic function as she confers grace and auspiciousness on them. As the *Yakshi* or the *Salabhanjika*, or the tree nymph, she makes the Ashoka tree blossom with the kick of her left foot, and in becoming a symbol of fertility she is an integral part of temple architecture and the railings of stupas. As *kamini*, or the one that is desired, she is the embodiment of desire and equally of *shringara* or love, and she becomes a romantic *nayika* in plays and poetry. As the embodiment of artistic skills she is the *ganika* the consummate courtesan. As the paradigm of music she is a *Ragini*, a picture of a *raga*. Finally, it is the same woman who renounces all materiality and becomes a *yogini* as she searches for life's ultimate freedom. Our journey is that of the sensuous feminine from times pre-historic through the pages of history and the corridors of political dynasties.

In one of the Indus Valley seals 5000 years back a woman is shown standing within a stylised Pipal tree. This is one of the first visual statement of the Indian world view of the celebration of *prakriti* or materiality and woman as the paradigm of that. Possibly this is the first *Yakshi*. *Prakriti* is the fecund and luxuriant world of nature that goes from the earth to the sky, and of which the most evocative representation is the woman. *Prakriti* is sensuous and beautiful, charged with colours, resonating with emotion and the *rasa* that animates a woman resonates with the sap that flows through the trees. This firmly establishes the connection between a woman and a tree in Indian thought and art, which remains an inspiration for millennia, and which is

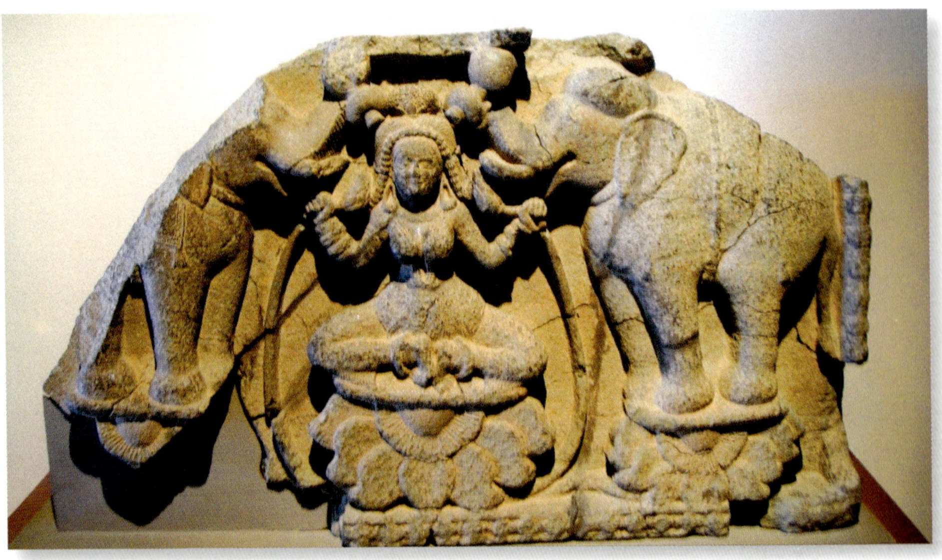

Gajalakshmi. Basalt, Pitalkhora cave no. 4,
Aurangabad district, Maharashtra, 2nd century.

robustly epitomised by the *Yakshi*. *Prakriti* is the *garbha*, the womb of life, where creation begins and thrives, for it is only when we plant a seed in the earth that it grows into a tree. However, *prakriti* does not exist in isolation, it is interconnected in all its varied manifestations and it creates a web of life where there are no loose ends. Even though some systems of philosophy, and Advaita Vedanta in particular, does not grant *prakriti* any ultimate reality, the world of nature frames and embraces our life and remains central to our life and living and our world view. It is important to note that one of the first deities to be represented visually is the *Yakshi* on the railings of the Buddhist stupas. Mythologically *Yaksha*s and *Yakshi*s are semi-divine beings whose work was to guard over Kubera's treasures and gardens in heaven. One of the duties of the *Yaksha* was to bring fresh flowers to Kubera for the worship of Shiva. One day, unwilling to leave the company of his wife early in the morning, he brought lotus buds instead, gathered the previous night. While Kubera was offering this to Shiva the next morning, a bee lurking in one of the buds, stung his fingers. Angered at this, Kubera cursed the *Yaksha*.

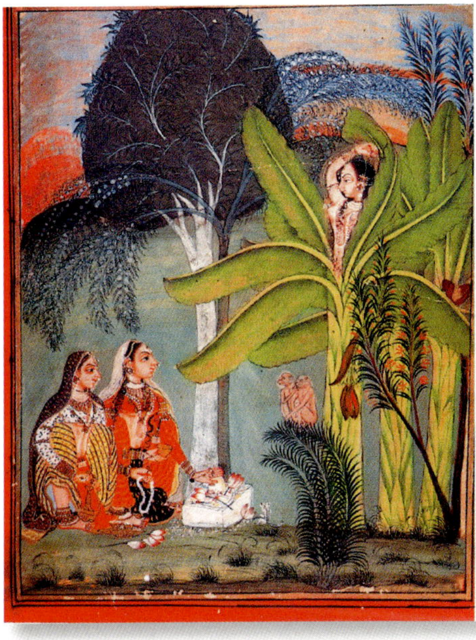

Yakshi, Bundi, c. 1775

*Yaksha*s are therefore separated from their wives, and *Yakshi*s who were banished from heaven reside in trees on earth. *Yakshi*s are considered tree nymphs and confer their fertility to the vegetative world. It is believed that it is because of them that trees acquire fruits and vegetables, flowers get their colour and fragrance, and the world of nature its verdant qualities. In a tropical country like ours where agriculture defined our world view *Yakshi*s were important and developed a cult of their own.

One of the oldest Indian sculptures in stone is the Didarganj *Yakshi*, dating to the pre-Christian era. As early as the 2nd century BCE, sensuous female figures in the form of *Yakshi*s and *Salabhanjika*s were depicted on Hindu, Buddhist and Jain monuments at Bharhut, Sanchi, Bodh-Gaya, Mathura, Chandraketugarh and elsewhere. *Yakshi* figures are also seen in coins of Ujjain of the 2nd century BCE. Terracotta *Yakshi*s come to full fruition in the Kushana period.

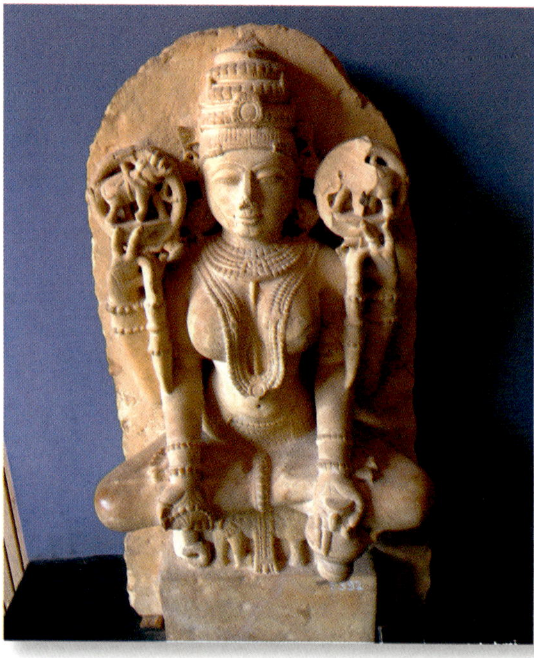

Gajalakshmi. Gujarat. 12th century

The potter was the *adi shilpi* for it was he who made terracotta images of the *Yakshi*. Potters were organised in *shrenis* or guilds, and settled in suburbs or *nigamas* or market townships outside the gate of towns. The making of *Yakshi* figures in terracotta gained prominence in the Maurya period, c. 320–200 BCE, especially in Magadha in present day Bihar and Mathura in present day Uttar Pradesh. There is some suggestion that in these hand-molded terracotta *Yakshi*s there was a Hellenistic influence. It was in the eastern part of India that the *Salabhanjika* festival was observed, where women plucked flowers of the Shala trees and wore them in their ears. Buddha's mother delivered

Gautama, the future Buddha, while holding the branch of the Shala tree. This firmly established the cult of the *Yakshi*s celebrated as fertility figures, and from about 200 BCE to 50 CE the production of terracotta figures reached a high art. With the rise of mercantile communities the creation of terracotta figures of Lakshmi was popular. Lakshmi, the future consort of Vishnu, was also considered a *Yakshi*. This was the period when Panchachuda *Yakshi*s, *Yakshi*s with five hair ornaments, was also popular.

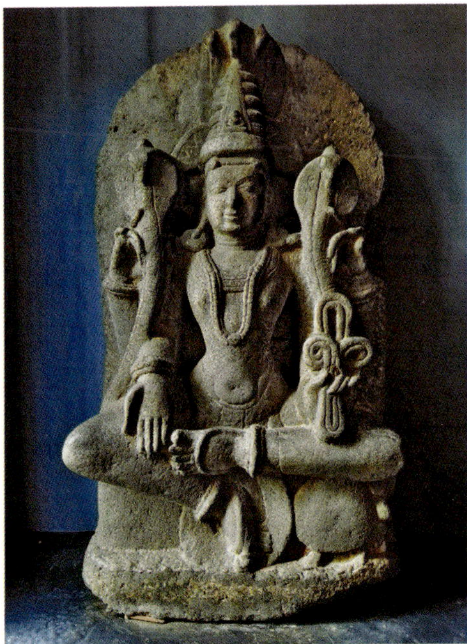

Jain *Yakshi* Padmavati. Karnataka. 12th century

These *Yakshi*s are sensuously beautiful, but equally they confer auspiciousness and fertility by their very presence, signifying not only earthly fertility but the generative force of the divine. It is said that when a *Yakshi* touches a Ashoka tree with her left foot, the tree comes into bloom which again underscores the living connection between a woman and a tree, and in a larger sense ensures the oneness of the world of humans with that of nature, a world that grows and prospers. It also makes the *Yakshi* a living symbol of one who fulfils the *dohad* or longing of a tree. The *Yakshi* then becomes the intermediary between the world of humans on the one hand and the verdant world of Nature on the other.

Kalidasa uses the trope of a *Yakshi* separated from her beloved in Meghadutam and introduces a human and emotional content in the *Yakshi*'s sensuality. This was a seminal creation by Kalidasa as now the *Yakshi* evolves into the many sensuous females of the Indian tradition. Occupying an intermediate place between the human and the divine, *Yakshi*s negotiate the twilight zone between them. It is important to note that *Yakshi*s are positioned on the railing of the stupa assuring the world of the humans on one side, a world of material fertility and fecundity, and on the other side the spiritual world of *nishkama* and *nirguna* reality of the Buddha.

*Yakshi*s were worshipped in ancient India, and in some parts of the country there were shrines dedicated to them. It is interesting to note that when the farmers in Bihar rescued the Didarganj *Yakshi* from the Ganga they built a ramshackle temple for it, and it has the British who removed it to the National Museum. Placed generally at the border of the world of mankind and that of the gods, at the border of stupas and on the outer wall of temples, *Yakshi*s provide the bridge from humanity to divinity, from the *nastika* to the *astika*, from material to spiritual. *Yakshi*s are not just emblems of feminine sensuality or of the longing that throbs in mankind and nature alike of the immediate for the ultimate, but they are symbols of the living connection between everything that lives and loves in our world, and which aspires fulfilment in a higher cause.

In ancient India Lakshmi, even before she was considered a goddess and consort of Vishnu, was also considered to be a *Yakshi* performing the function of material plenty and prosperity. Sitting on a lotus and flanked by two lustrating elephants Lakshmi fulfils all the roles of a *Yakshi* once again emphasising the importance of *artha*, understood as material abundance, as a *purushartha* or an ideal of human life. Whether she is a *Yakshi* or Mahalakshmi, one fact stands out like a beacon of wisdom, namely that material abundance and the fecundity and fertility of nature, is only an intermediate step in our journey and cannot be the sole end of life. However, at the same time, these celestial beings also assert that the proper understanding of sensuality is a pre-requisite in the experience of ultimate reality and cannot be bypassed. This foreshadows the development of the *devadasis* of the 19th century who were intermediaries between the devotee and the deity.

The concept of Lakshmi is the greatest glorification of the feminine aspect of the almighty. Lakshmi is a mirror of multiplicity, her aspects are many. As Gajalakshmi she is in glory, flanked by elephants, token of rain and creativity who lustrate her with gentle sprays of water. As Mahalakshmi she is the immense divinity who embodies the characters of all the gods. To *grahasthas* she is Grihalakshmi, the goddess of the house. To kings and statesmen she is Rajalakshmi. To men of courage and valour she is Veeralakshmi and Vijayalakshmi. To merchants and traders she is Dhanalakshmi. To the farmer she is Dhanyalakshmi. To people at large she is Bhagyalakshmi, and to the spiritual seeker she is Mokshalakshmi. These aspects and more are significations of the pervasiveness of a culture in which inauspiciousness, *alakshmi*, were abhorred. Lakshmi is the consort of Vishnu in all his manifestations and incarnations. She was Padma or Kamala for Vaman, Dharini when Vishnu was Parusharama, Sita when he was Rama. The *Mahabharata* explains that Lakshmi lives in rivers and mountains, lotuses and elephants in spirit only, but she lives with Narayana in her embodied form. She is represented as *srivastava* on Vishnus's breast. Lakshmi in inextricably linked with the lotus. Like the lotus, Lakshmi is always connected with water, for it was from the *kumbha* that she emerged as one of the nine jewels. She is seated on a lotus, she is of the colour of a louts, she holds a lotus in her hand and wears a garland of lotuses. Lakshmi is venerated even in the Rg Veda, for in the Srisukta she is described as radiant as gold and is called Isvari, the lady of all creation, the signifier of fortune, beauty, cattle wealth, crops, vegetation. She is perceived as the fragrance of fertility.

It was in the Jain tradition that *Yakshi*s were given a prominent role. From about the 6th century onwards *Yaksha*s and *Yakshi*s evolved from the older nature nymphs into attendants and protectors of the Tirthankaras. A Tirthankara being himself freed of worldly attachments could not be approached for fulfillment of mundane wants of people. *Yaksha-Yakshi* pairs were assigned to each of the 24 Tirthankaras. However it was Ambika who accompanied all Tirthankaras, and is prominently displayed.

Kalidasa's *Meghadutam* was a landmark in Sanskrit poetry, for not only did it give the *Yakshi* an emotional underpinning by making it human but it marked the beginning of the evolution of the *Yakshi* into the *shringara rasa nayika* in varied arts. If we are to accept Shakuntala as the *adi shringara rasa nayika* of *natya*, she is the trail blazer of centuries of the woman in love, dignified in moments of longing as well as belonging that were to follow. In the *Abhijnana Shakuntalam*, Kalidasa gives Shakuntala many of the attributes of a *Yakshi*. Listen to this dialogue:

Anasuya
Kashyapa has appointed you, who are tender like the blossom of Jasmine
to water the trees of the hermitage.
Shakuntala
For me these trees are like my sisters.
Kashyapa addressing the trees in the hermitage
when Shakuntala is about to leave
She does not drink water unless she has watered you,
she though fond of ornaments
never plucks your leaves through affection for you,
she for when there is a festival when you put out blossoms.
Shakuntala
My love letter is in my mind but I do not have any materials for writing.
Priyamvada
Incise with your nails your letter in this lotus leaf
which is as tender as a parrot's breast.[3]

In *Malvikagnimitram*, Kalidasa transforms Malavika into a *Yakshi* as she touches a Ashoka tree which then bursts into bloom.

The *Shatakatrayi*, the anthology of 300 verses of Bhartrihari, is one of the earliest contributions of early classical Sanskrit to romantic literature. Although the anthology was compiled around the 4th century CE Bhartrihari probably lived in an earlier century of the Christian era, which was also the time frame of Bharata of the Natyashastra. Bhartrihari in his poetic creations gives equal space to ethics, romance and renunciation. Shringara Shataka,which is part of the Shatakatrayi, the 100 romantic verses, bears some resemblance to

Gathasaptasati and does raise the obvious question of how much Bhartrihari was influenced by the idioms and metaphors of Prakrit love poetry. Notice how he talks about the joy of being with one's *priyatama* or beloved, lines which are reminiscent of the Gathasaptasati:

White jasmine about to bloom in her hair
sandal paste mixed with saffron on her body
my beloved languorous in her intoxicating youth
resting on my chest
this is nothing but heaven paying me a visit.[4]

Bhratrihari's *shringara* has an unmistakable undercurrent of *vairagya* or renunciation and this becomes the hallmark of *shringara rasa kavya* in early classical Sanskrit. Even when Bhartrihari speaks of the pleasures of the moon and the beloved's face, he says *sarvam ramyam anityam upagate citte ne kinchit punah*, once the mind has sensed impermanence nothing at all is the same. In another *muktaka* he reminds his listeners that if one is surrounded by songs, accomplished poets and the sound of jingling bracelets of fanning maids, one may as well enjoy the delights of the world, but if this is not the case then one must plunge at once into a state of meditation. While there are many handwritten manuscripts of Bhatrihari's Shatakatrayi we do not have any paintings.

Amaru, also called Amaruka, is believed to have lived in the 7th century, and wrote a number of *muktakas* or miniature romantic verses which were later compiled under the title *Amarushataka* or the centenary of Amaru. The benedictory verse of *Amarushataka* captures the essence and ethos of Amaru's centenary, for it invokes the blessings of Ambika, whose sidelong glances are as beautiful as the bees that hover over the blossoming twigs that adorn her ear and resplendent as the nails of her hand held in the *khatakamukha* gesture. Amaru prepares us for the feast, both for the eyes and the ears that is to follow, for the *muktakas* create an emotionally-charged world where every nuance of romantic love is explored, where the pangs and pleasures, pathos and poignancy of amorous dalliances are sensitively portrayed, where neither the restraint of dharma nor the restriction of society is allowed to interfere with a glorious celebration of love, for he clearly says:

May the face of the fair lady, her languid eyes, the slightly fluttering hairlocks, the moving ear rings and her *tilaka* partially effaced by tiny drops of perspiration protect you. Gods like Shiva and Skanda serve no purpose.[5]

Unlike Bhartrihari, Amaru is committed to the primacy of love. He paints the varied moods and nuances of love with words that evoke vivid colours and lines that are sonorous with music.

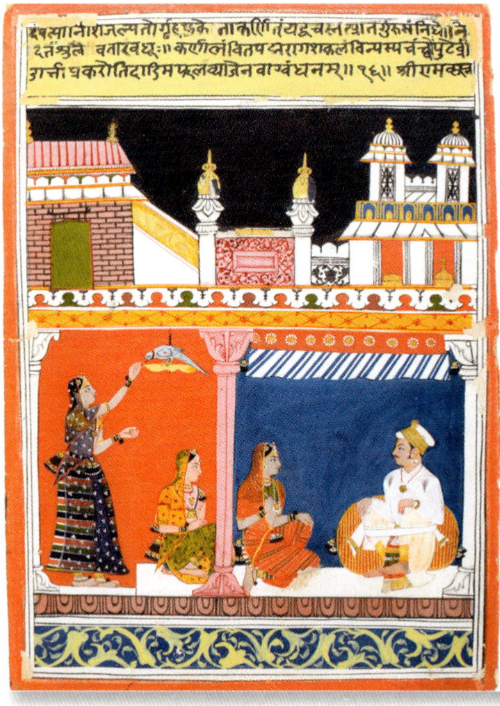

Amarushataka, Malwa. 16th century

Give up your sulking for your beloved waits outside drawing lines on the ground, your friends who weep ceaselessly have swollen eyes and have gone without food, the parrots in their cages laugh or speak no more.[6]

Amarushataka basks in a sunlit space, fragrant with the aroma of love, brilliant with the hues of a throbbing heart and within the minute compass of a verse we are privy to a universe of romance. Amaru's lovers are driven by desire, devoid of guilt, finding their fulfillment in a passionate embrace or a loving gaze. Amaru taps into traditional Prakrit romantic idioms of the anguish of separated lovers, such as the rumbling of rain clouds, the fragrance of blooming jasmine flowers, bangles that slip from an emaciated arm and bodies weakened by the anxiety of long separation.

Amaru's *nayikas* have languid eyes, fluttering hair, moving earrings, eyes that betray longing, and tear-filled eyes that speak of the pangs of separation. In his verses we are privy to passionate embraces and coquetry that undermines the desire for an embrace. Amaru's world of romance is inhabited by mischievous parrots that threaten to reveal intimate conversations and lamps that are extinguished by flower garlands to create spaces of intimacy, of mango blossoms and summer winds, of jingling anklets that destroy the secrecy of clandestine meetings. In his imitable style Amaru laments the gods who churned the oceans to obtain the ambrosia of immortality when, he says, a passionate kiss would have yielded sweeter nectar.

The *shringara rasa nayika* was now firmly established as a poetic trope. However, it was not until the coming of the *Bhagavata Purana* and Jayadeva's *Gita Govinda* that none other than Krishna became the presiding deity of *shringara rasa*, a seminal development that was to change the texture of the *shringara rasa nayika*. *Shringara* now was to be read at two levels, at one level it was the love of Radha and Krishna and at another it was the love of the *nayak* and *nayika*. It was both sacred and secular at the same time. More importantly *shringara* was not just a *rasa* but was *bhakti shringara*, in other words Krishna's *madhurya* was a form of knowledge or truth and not just emotional or sensual gratification.

The post *Bhagavata* period saw a thousand years of the creation of beautiful Krishna poetry and painting. We shall bypass the *gopis* of the *Bhagavata* and Radha of *Gita Govinda* and explore the *nayika* in the post-Jayadeva period.

The next step in the evolution of the sensuous feminine in Sanskrit literature was Bhanudatta's *Rasamanjari*. Jayadeva had brought romantic poetry in classical Sanskrit to a climax, and none was to rival him in this genre of poetry. Bhanudatta in the 15th century continued the tradition of romantic

Sanskrit poetry and built on the traditional *nayikabheda* or classification of romantic heroines, but went on to provide an elaborate taxonomy, not only of romantic heros and heroines, but of the many and varied romantic situations. *Rasamanjari*, far from being an arid and prosaic document, shows a deep poetic awareness and sensitivity of the many moods and seasons, the changing colours and resonances of the mind of the *nayika* and the *nayaka,* which bring into play *saroja sundara chatmakara*, or the wondrous arts of love. The poetry of the *Rasamanjari* leaves no doubt that romantic activity was no idle pastime or a trivial sport, but was a sincere commitment and a lifelong dedication of the romantic persona, who totally believed in their love and defined their lives in its pursuit and fulfillment. To such a person the celebration of romantic love was the raison d'etre for life and living. This is the central message one derives from the *Rasamanjari*.

Bhanudatta recognises that romantic exchanges rarely need words but are even more beautifully conveyed by suggestive signs and gestures. The hero desirous of having a romantic rendezvous, is asked by the beloved to meet her at sunset:

When the lover holds in his hand the golden lime fruit
the moon faced *nayika* puts a dot on the sun that is painted on the wall.

Bhanudatta while providing an elaborate taxonomy intersperses his *nayikabheda* with descriptions of beautiful, romantic moments like:

The modest *nayika* who is in a dilemma. To fall asleep is to lose sight of the adored one, to remain awake is to risk physical possession.

The *nayika*, lest the morning should bring the love play to a close, hastily covers the lotuses in her ears with the hem of her garment so that their opening may not announce the dawn of day.

O traveler the sun being piercingly hot today it is proper for you to rest on the bank of the river adorned with rows of jasmine creepers entwining Tamala trees.

The sweet eyed *nayika* turned pale like the leaves of a Palmyra tree when she learnt that the clove creepers which grew at her trysting place had shed their leaves with the advent of the month of *chaitra*.

The deer eyed *nayika* adorned herself with flowers and ornaments, scented her curly hair and put betel leaves beside her bed. Her fair body bedecked with gold and *ketaki* flowers lighted up the chamber.

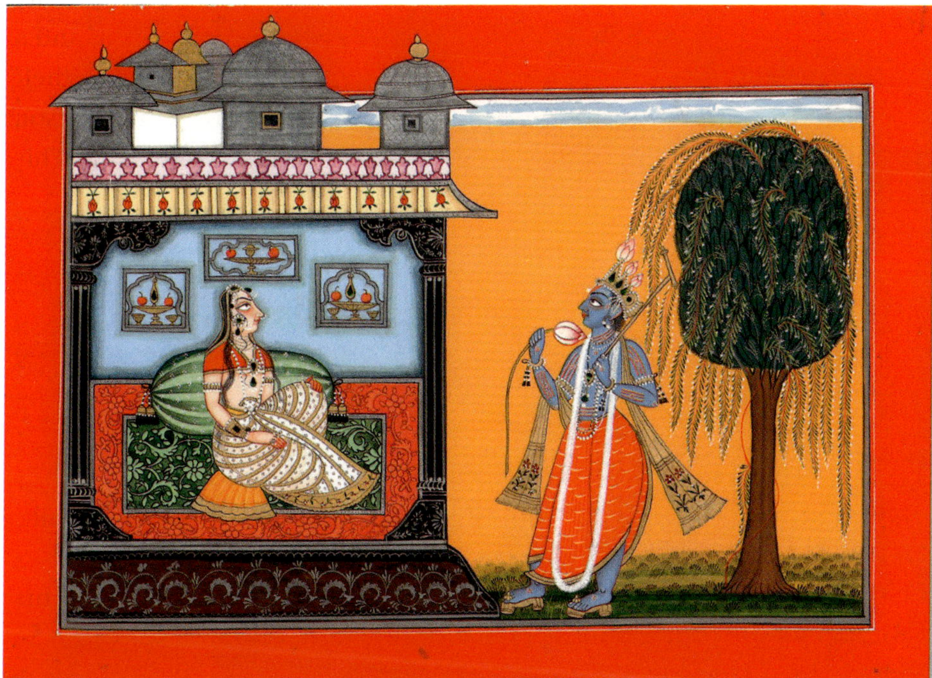

Shringara Rasa *Nayika*, painting in Basohli style of Rasamanjiri by Vijay Sharma

By sweet trickery she puts her mother-in-law to sleep, covers the flame of the lamp and by producing sounds like the cooing of pet doves makes a sign to her lover to come.[7]

While it was none other than Bharata, who in his Natyashastra had touched upon the subject of *nayikabheda* and provided a typology of the different types of romantic heroines, it was left to *ritikal* poets to give substance and enlarge it to a delightful taxonomy. Such a taxonomy was not merely an arid compendium of people and places, neither an album of romantic events but it was like a bouquet of flowers from the garden of love. It helped in not only underscoring the many sides of romantic love and highlighting the delicate and tender facets of the mind of the heroine, but importantly it led to a beautiful and deep understanding of the various shades and nuances of the romantic emotion itself. A defining feature of the romantic emotion is that it is uncertain, fleeting and transient, the beauty is in the present moment as

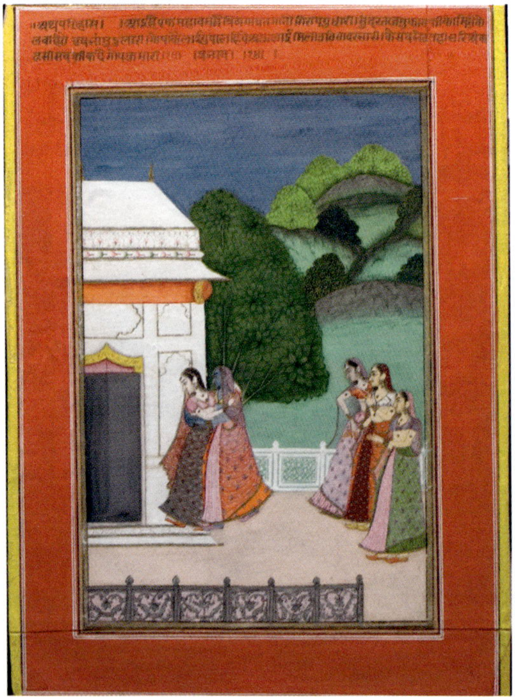

Rasikapriya, Bikaner, 18th century

there is no promise of the future. It is this uncertainty, as much as the various types of heros and heroines, that creates the endless situations and moods of romantic love and leads to elaborate taxonomies. The romantic emotion was the living *rasa* of the heroine that animated her like the sap of the tree, and just as a tree responded to the whisper of the winds and the rhythms of the earth, the changing of the seasons and the loving care of the gardener who tended it, the *nayika*'s persona was equally alive and sensitive to the smallest change in the ambience, circumstance and moods of love. This is her connection to the *Yakshi*. For many indeed are the colours of romance, variegated its varying hues, various are its responses, and numerous its manifestations, and the poetry of *nayikabheda* takes us inside the mind of the *nayika* and forms an important part of the treasure of *shringara rasa kavya*.

Keshavdas (1555-1617) is the prototypical *riti* poet. He was the court poet of an Orchha prince Indrajit, and it was there that he produced his monumental work *Rasikapriya*. It is an encyclopedic compendium and taxonomy of *nayaka*s and *nayika*s, their moods, meetings and messengers, and is considered a *lakshan grantha*, foundational work in Ritikavya. While rooted in Sanskrit rhetoric, Keshavdas makes a significant contribution to romantic literature in choosing to express himself though Brajbhasha, a language which is ideally suited in conveying the earthiness and sweetness of romance. Using variable metres and appropriate metaphors, through enunciation of romantic theory and demonstration of how it can be put into practice, Keshavdas makes every nuance of romantic love come alive through melody and meaning in his verse. Keshavdas clearly enters the mind of the *nayaka* and the *nayika* for he expresses the hidden as well as the manifest features of every nuance of love. His is an enchanted world of the joys of dalliance and the pangs of pathos, the muted voices of messengers and the whispers of lovers, the arrogant heroine and the truant hero, of clandestine meetings in groves or in the comfort of a *haveli*, of words on Champa leaves and the sanctity of Tulsi groves. In describing the *ashtanayikas*, the eight types of romantic heroines, Keshavdas uses the inflections of Brajbhasha to great advantage. While painting the variegated and tender emotions of the *ashtanayikas*, Keshavdas not only shows an understanding of feminine sensitivity, but beautifully connects that pulsating love of the heroine to the world around the *nayika*, for the love that pulsates in his lovers is no different from the sap that enlivens the world around them once again taking us back to the *Yakshi*. Romantic love for Keshavdas is not a trivial or titillating emotion, not just a psychological state but the animating principle of life itself. He offers this taxonomy of the *ashtanayikas*:

The *svadhinapatika*, who is greatly loved by her beloved, gets her soles scrubbed by pumice stone and painted red by her beloved who keeps her in the mirror of his heart as betel leaves in a basket.

The *ukta*, who is troubled because her lover is absent, worries about his health or the rain in the middle of the night which has kept him from coming.

The *vasakasajja*, who adorns herself and waits expectantly around sandalwood trees, entwined by clove creepers and yearns for her beloved with every sound of the breeze and leaves and looks like Rati in a *tulsi* grove.

The *abhisandhita*, is the heroine who is arrogant when approached, does not glance at him even when he falls at her feet but thereafter sorrowful without him, and finds that even sandalwood, lotus and moon burn her body.

The *khandita*, who reproves her beloved when he misses his rendezvous and arrives only in the morning, and whose eyes reddened by the henna of another raises suspicions of unfaithfulness.

The *prositapatika*, whose beloved is away on business but who will return, but whose heart is hard like a log of wood which does not burn even with the fire of separation.

The *vipralabdha*, whose beloved does not come in spite of a tryst arranged by her *sakhi*, finds her 16 adornments are like embers, and flowers have turned to darts and gardens to fearful forests, and inscribes some words on a *champa* leaf.

The *abhisarika*, who sets out to meet her beloved. When driven by love she is *premabhisarika*, by pride *garvabhisarika* and by passion *kamabhisarika*. Adorning herself with sandal paste and a garland of flowers she makes the chakors forget the pain of parting, ignoring snakes entangled around her feet and the thunder of clouds, she is driven to him.

The strength of *Rasikapriya* lies in its encyclopedic presentation of lovers, a treasury of their emotional states, a taxonomy of their meetings and messengers, an atlas of their joyous togetherness and their painful separation, and a veritable anthology of variegated amorous situations and states. Thus it was that it became so popular with kings and nobility, and provided an inspiration for miniature painters who found in it endless themes and countless motifs to depict the many facets of romantic love.

Following in the footsteps of Keshavdas was another notable *ritikal* poet. Matiram, who lived in the mid-17th century. He was a court poet of Rao Bhav Singh of Bundi, and among his works are *Rasraj*, *Lalit Lalam* and *Alankar Panchashika*. Matiram continues the style and tenor of his predecessor and

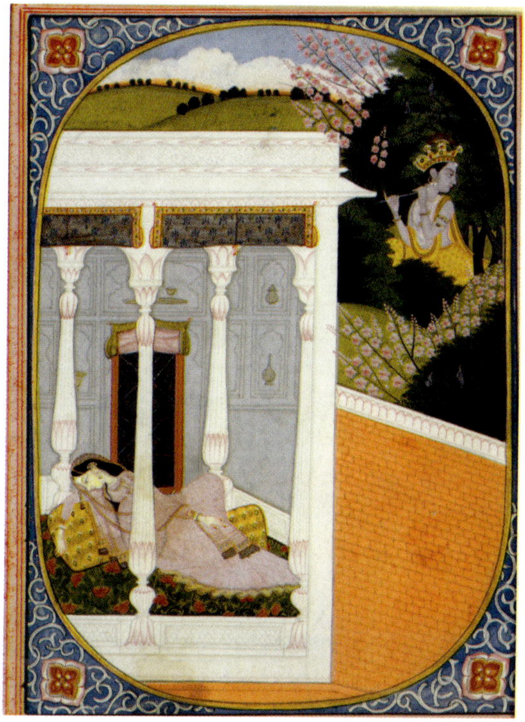

Matiram's *Rasraj*, Kangra, 1830-40

outlines, in a taxonomic fashion, the various *nayaka*s and *nayika*s. In a beautiful passage he describes the beauty of Radha's face thus:

it was none other than Brahma who has created the face of Radha
a face so beautiful that it caused the moon to feel jealous
one night the moon spread its rays to steal Radha's beauty

but having been caught committing piercingly theft was arraigned in
Brahma's court
and was punished with black spots on its face.[8]

Another significant *ritikal* poet whose gem-like verses shine in the repertoire of Ritikavya was Bihari. Born towards the end of the 16th century in Orchha and having spent his creative life at Agra and Amber, Bihari's couplets may

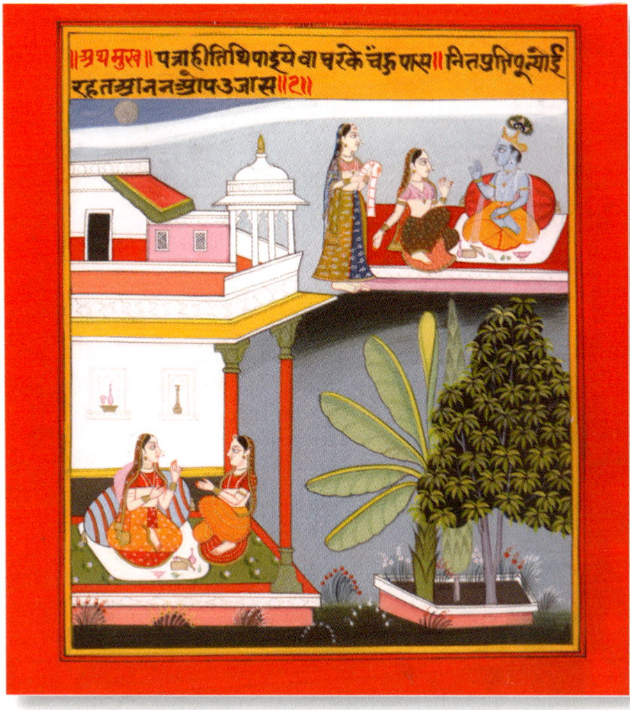

Bihari *Satsai*, Mewar, 18th century

appear insignificant but inflict a deep wound, like the arrow of a hunter. For Bihari, love was not mere sensual gratification but a spiritual outpouring for, as he says: The spoken words are of no account for they are false. That is why Brahma has made eyes for expressing what lies in the heart. In another *doha* Bihari says:

I never saw such eyes with glances more piercing
than Kama's arrows;

O Krishna their loveliness indeed surpasses
the eyes of a gazelle.

And then again:

Though without collyrium the coquettish eyes of that girl
adept in the art of love making
have put to shame those of the *khanjana* bird
even the lotus pales before their loveliness.

Colours were important to Bihari for they conveyed more than words could speak:

Her pink cheek is so tender and fragrant
that the rose petal that got stuck to it
could not be distinguished.

Also:

How perfectly the yellow Champa garland blends with your hue, dear girl
It can be seen only when its flowers fade.

And in this invocatory verse Bihari brilliantly uses the language of colours to pay homage to Radha:

Radha, take away the pain of existence, the cycle of the world, from me
you whose golden reflection turns Krishna's blue complexion into a
glowing green.

In other *dohas* Bihari uses words as a painter would use colours and says that the radiance of her limbs makes the while Malati flowers grow golden, and the crimson-streaked eyes are like twilight, the river turns a saffron yellow whenever she plunges into it, her limbs glisten like yellow Jasmine, her feet are redder than lacquer dye, her ruby red feet shed dust as a Dhupariya flower has blossomed at each step and her ravishing eyes are as dark as black bees. Bihari follows all the usual conventions of Ritikavya to describe the beauty of a *nayika*, but for Bihari sensuality was never far from spirituality as the human body was only a reflection of the world around it:

Her dazzling splendour shining through her flimsy drress
is breathtaking as a Kalpa tree
reflected leaf and branch in the waters of the placid ocean.[9]

Bihari wrote in Brajbhasha and he colours his words, ornaments his phrases and imparts a certain fragrance to his verses and his *dohas*, brief but elegants are sheer music to our ears as they weave through every situation and mood of romantic love. His *Satsai* was a landmark in romantic poetry for not only was it copied, translated and commented upon, but it inspired miniature artists to render them into paintings, and it can be said that if Keshavdas' *Rasikapriya* gave painters endless romantic situations, Bihari's *Satsai* provided inspiration for lyrical representations of romantic love.

Equally evocative are the sensuous females of the Ragamala tradition. To understand, capture and comprehend the divine qualities of music, its practitioners believed each melody to have besides *nadamaya* or sound form a *devamaya* or deified form, and thus it was that a link between *raga* and a deity was created. The Ragamala painters sought inspiration from the romantic Krishna lore, the Barahmasa genre of poetry as well as the precincts of the princely courtyards, and created a sensuous Ragini. While the principal figures are the *nayaka* and *nayika*, of equal importance are the objects which enhance the mood and symbolise various aspects of her sensuality. Two earthen jars hold cool water and represent the sensuous beauty of a female. Buzzing bees symbolise the passion of lovers and lotus blossoms are an epitome of beauty. Rain is the season when the Rajput warrior as well as the merchant return home, and it is therefore the season of love. With rain comes lightning which becomes the expression of passion. The peacock with its display of colour evokes the mating dance of the male. The bed chamber with its empty bed and bolsters further suggests the joy of love making. A platter of *pan* and other condiments, garlands and sandalwood paste are useful accessories in a romantic rendezvous A lady at her toilet adorning herself with jewellery is a sign of anticipation and depicts *raga* Bilaval. A *nayika* feeding a deer is a lovesick woman singing a lonely tune and is reminiscent of *raga* Todi. A thunder storm with the cry of peacocks and birds gathering for shelter in trees evokes the fear and longing of a *nayika* as she finds comfort in feeding a peacock, and this is suggestive of *raga* Madhumadhavi. When evening ends and darkness descends, the *nayika* lights a lamp and waits for her beloved, it is the setting for *raga* Dipak. To lessen the pangs of *viraha*, a *nayika* plays on the veena and composes a song, and it evokes Gurjari Ragini. When she makes a bed of flowers for her lover it creates the mood of Ragini Gormalar. A woman startled by the cry of the cuckoo and deriving comfort by the company of peacocks is the mood of Kakubha Ragini. And when the hero discharges a flower arrow at the sleeping heroine to instill her with renewed passion at the end of a night of love making, it is the mood of Ragini Vibhasa. While Ragamala paintings may not be the most perfect visualisation of music it did create a beautiful, warm and lyrical visual form and a unique idiom in Indian art.

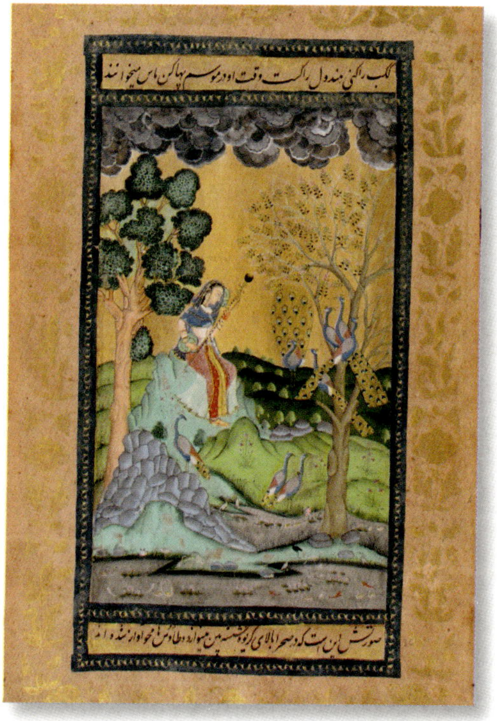

Todi Ragini. Deccan. 18th century

A Ragini that is both sensually evocative and spiritually inspiring comes from the Deccan. While the northern Ragamalas had more fidelity to the written text, the Deccani Ragamalas were less so. The Kakubha Ragini from mid-

18th century Hyderabad is reminiscent of the Deccani *yogini*, the foliage is wind swept and the colours are surcharged and saturated. The inscription in Persian states "Its form is such that in the jungle she plays the *been* and due to its sweet sound peacocks are attracted to her." Looking at this Ragini-one cannot but help recollecting the times of the Ibrahim Adil Shah II and realise that music and painting in the Deccan were two petals of the same flower. The Deccan is a kingdom of sated nostalgia, abandoned to scents and dreams, lingering in flowers, glowing in colours, calm and deep. There is both magic and mystery in the Deccani female form, and when one is admiring this one cannot be far away from the Deccani Yogini which was such a favourite of the artists and patrons of that region.

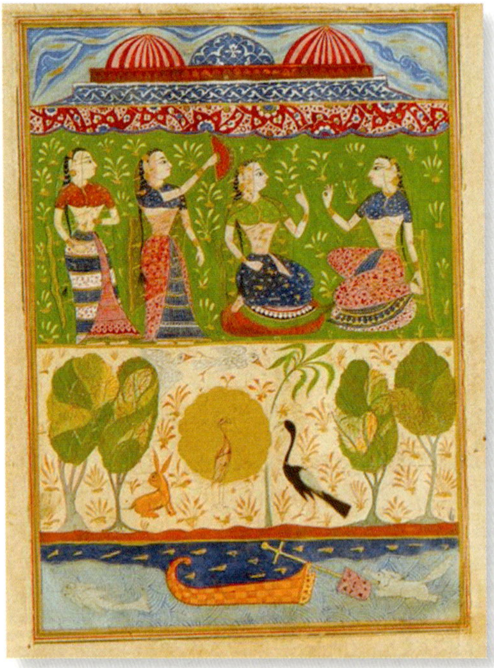

Laur Chanda, Delhi-Jaunpur. 1525–1575 CE

Thus, romantic poetry and the paintings that arose from it, in the Indian tradition, are a rich storehouse of the heart throb of the *nayika*s and the *nayaks* and a chronicle of their beautiful moments, be they of longing or loving, of ecstasy or anguish. It is a charmed world of the sighs of the love, torn heroine and the cries of the Chakravaka bird as it seeks its mate, of the footfalls of the *sakhi* as she carries love messages and the song of the peacock as it heralds the advent of the rain, of the perfume of sandalwood paste and the music of the bangles of the *nayika* as she awaits her beloved. It is poetry that is richly sensuous and equally spiritual, and takes us not only into the charmed spaces of a *haveli* but to the hushed ambience of Vrindavana, where Krishna and the *gopis* dally. In its lyrics we see the colours and the seasons of heartfelt emotions, we participate in the games and *lilas* of love, through its words we hear the music of Krishna's flute and the footsteps of romantic dalliance. Romantic poetry leads us into Vaishnava theology and Sufi mysticism, through it we learn of *shringara* and *prema*, and read poetic creations not only in ancient Prakrit and classical Sanskrit but equally in the Bhashas. A survey of romantic poetry is a journey into the minds of our poets from Amaru of the 4th century to Jayadeva of the 13th century and beyond, into the courts of Hala and Bhartrihari, into the kingdoms of Rajasthan and the foothills of the Himalayas. And as the music of romantic poetry resonates, we are lifted from the everyday mundane world to the realm of *ananda*, where love is not just passion or superficial excitement but an exalted state of living and being, celebrated for its own sake, and we are soaked in its aesthetic creations we cannot but exclaim *raso vai sah hyevayam labdhva anandi bhavati,* He is Rasa and leads us to *ananda.*[10]

As our journey of the *shringara rasa nayika* in the Kangra painting progresses, we are justified in asking who and where then is the *shringara rasa nayika*? Is she only *kavyamaya* in the mind of a poet like Keshavdas or Bihari or Matiram or the countless *ritikavis*, or is she only *chitramaya* and in the charmed space of a painting, by noted artists like Sahibdin or Nainsukh or Devidas, or is she only a *nartaki*, a dancer or an actor who entertains? She is all this but much more. She is a *kamini* and a *sundari*, she is *ashta rasa dharini*, the carrier and proclaimer of all the eight *rasas* of Bharata, but this is not all. She is the heart throb of *Ritikavya* like the *Rasikapriya* and *Satsai*, but she cannot be limited by that. She presides in ateliers of love, whether in Mewar or Kangra and emerges from the *kalam* of the artist in manifold colours and costumes, in *pranay mandapas* or sylvan meadows. She talks to birds, clings to trees, sends messages through clouds, weaves garlands. She adorns herself and waits for her beloved, or complains when neglected, or sets out in the middle of the night in search of her beloved. She is the ultimate *virahini*, languishing in longing when even moon beams scorch her body.

Yes she is all this, but to the contemplative *rasika* she is the paradigm of charged matter and a radiant mind, fertile feelings and fecund imagination, inviting the dormant Purusha to romance with itself. This is not a ordinary romance or a dance of the body but an *atmarati*, a romance of one's inner being, a dance of Purusha with the sensuously adorned Prakriti. The *nayika* is that Prakriti, now throbbing and now elusive, she invites and ignores, she is radiant and is dark, joyous and petulant, sometimes sensuously charged and at others self effacing. These are multiples faces of the *nayika* as she seeks the *nayaka*. Is she not the metaphor of our mind as it seeks fulfilment through the pleasures and passions of *shringara*? And when she is joyously together with the *nayaka* in a state of *ananda*, *shringara* has moved to *shringara bhakti*, and we who are witness and privy to the many splendoured vistas of *shringara* are also chastened, and we move from the thrill of romance to the serenity of *atmarati*.

The journey from *Yakshi* to the *shringara rasa nayika* has been a recognition of the centrality of the sensuous feminine both as an icon and as a generative principle in the Indian world view. She goes through philosophical systems, political dynasties, aesthetic theories but despite that stands proud and steadfast, resisting any attempt to denigrate her. Affirming and asserting sensuality but going beyond it, recognising that *shringara* is a central emotion for the human condition, acting as an intermediary between the world of human and that of the divine, resonating with the world of nature and its fecundity, and above all elevating the romantic emotion and making it a transformative experience, the sensuous female throbs with life and love, and ensures that while remaining on the earth we, as we celebrate her, raise our head and hands to the sky and go from the earthly to the celestial.

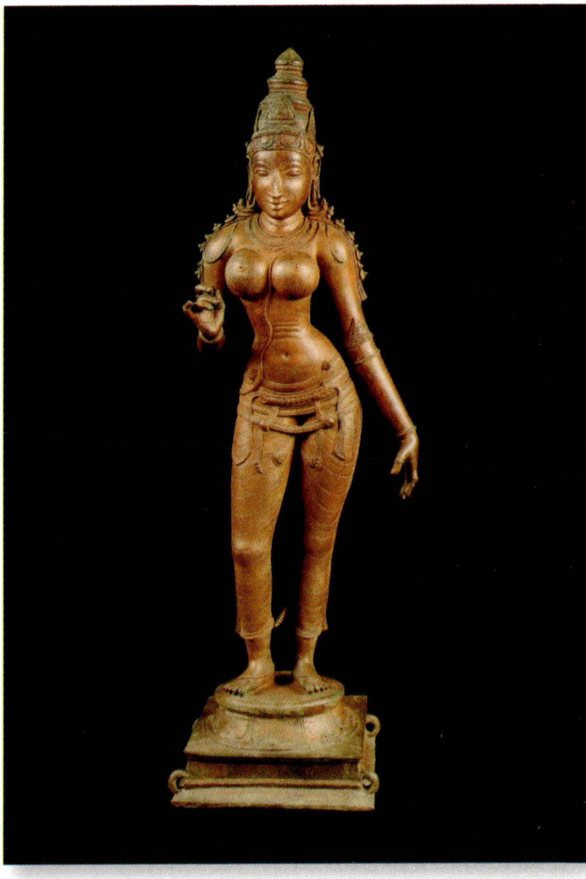

Parvati. Chola. 12th century

If one were to pick just one being who epitomises both sensuality and spirituality it has to be Parvati. Daughter of Himavat and Mena, Parvati through arduous penance becomes Shiva's consort. None other than Adi Shankara has described her beauty from tresses to the toes. Sculptors and dancers, poets and painters have depicted her but perhaps the most aesthetically pleasing representation of her is in a Chola bronze. Exuding grace from every limb, standing in the *tribhanga* position, love radiating from her eyes and holding a *darpana* in her left hand, Parvati is both *kamini* and *tapasvini*, *bhogini* and *yogini*, of unsupassed beauty and unflinching devotion, wife and mother, she remains steadfastly by the side of Shiva and is the greatest glorification of the Indian female.

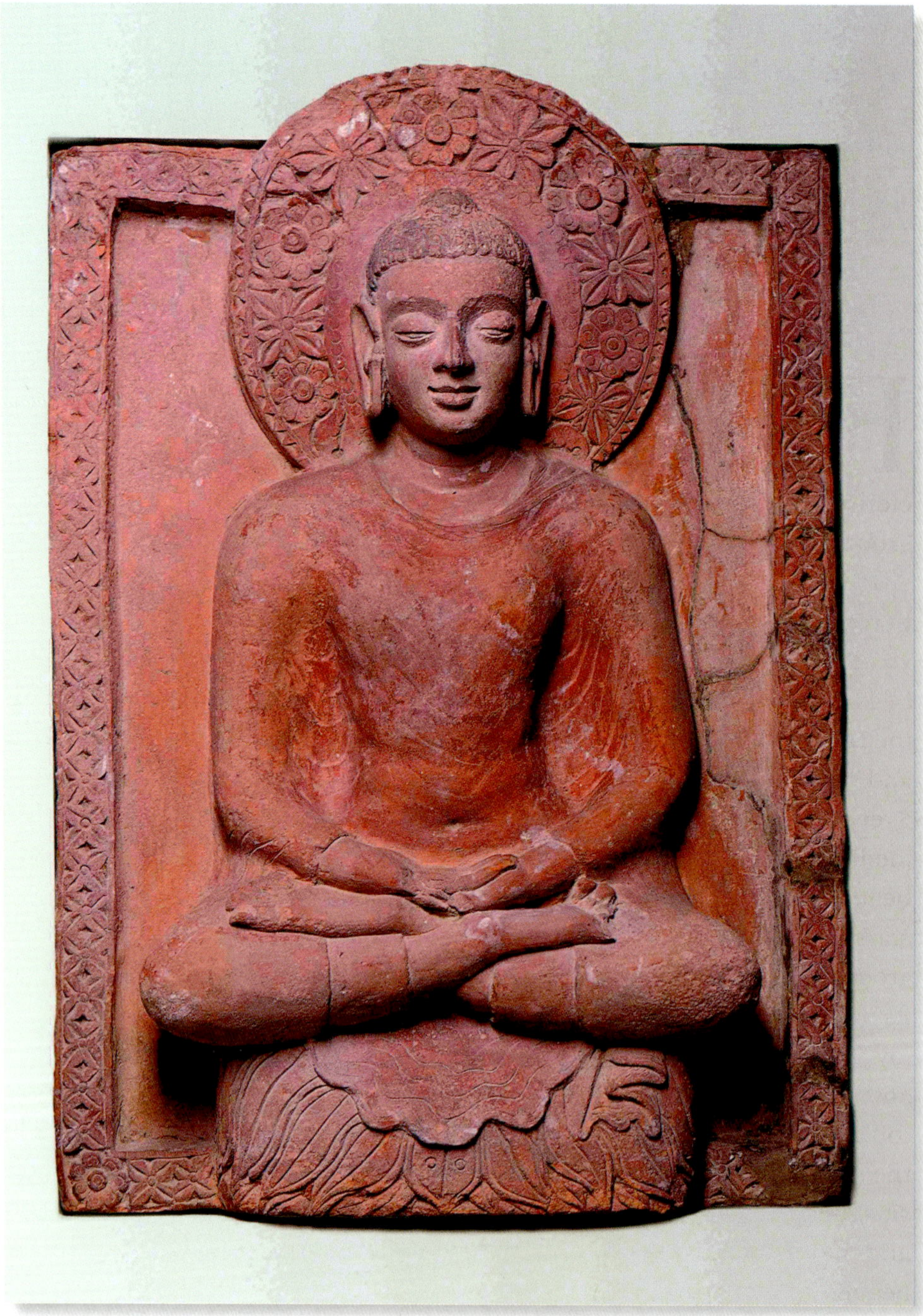

Buddha, Mirpur Khas, 5th century CE

The Journey of Our Icons

The Beauty of Sharira

For the Hindu, the *sharira* or the body, is not only the repository of the beautiful but equally, through its sensuality, it becomes the doorway to spirituality. Though time-bound it is capable of expressing the eternal, though *nashvar* it can point to *ishvar*, even though it is *mrinmaya* or grounded on earth it can point to the sky, even though it is defined by finite space it can reach towards the infinite, though limited it has the potential to represent the vast. It does all of this through its gestures and movements, voice and emotion, postures and adornments, attitudes and activities, and becomes the insignia of the Hindu view of life. One of the cornerstones of the Hindu view of life and its representation in the various arts is the *sharira*, and the image of the human being and its relationship to the world around. Every part of the human body becomes the source and the substance, the medium and the messenger of the expression of what is sacred, divine and beautiful. Through it even while standing on the earth we reach out to the stars, with it we embrace and touch the world of the trees and creepers around us, using it we express our deepest feelings of longing or fulfilment, its mute but eloquent movements bring out our inner sentiments, be they of joy or sorrow, through its sounds and rhythms we capture the joyous *nada* and *nritya* of the cosmos that surrounds us, through its *karmendriyas* we toil and labour but equally climb mountains, it is with the body that we hold the *kalam* and the chisel to create enduring beautiful objects, and when we sit still in *yogasana* we are in tune with the serenity within. It is the *sharira* and the *pratima*, the body and its image, that expresses our concept of the beautiful, and it is the same *sharira* that takes us to our *manas* or mind which then gives us an experience of the serene and majestic beauty which resides in our *atman*. Therefore it is not surprising that we chose the human body to express our vision of the sacred and the divine.

It has been said that India is a civilisation of images. For millennia we have made, worshipped, celebrated and adored icons, in word and song, paper and stone, wood or metal. We have given our deepest emotions and sentiments a palpable and visual form, and it has rightly been said, *rupam rupam pratirupam babhuva*, every image is a replica of the primal or pristine form of the Purusha. However it is important to note that there is an equally strong aniconic trait in the Indian tradition, a form that was whispered in the Purusha Sukta of the Rg Veda. The spoken word therefore, was the first expression of a image. However it was to take several centuries before the

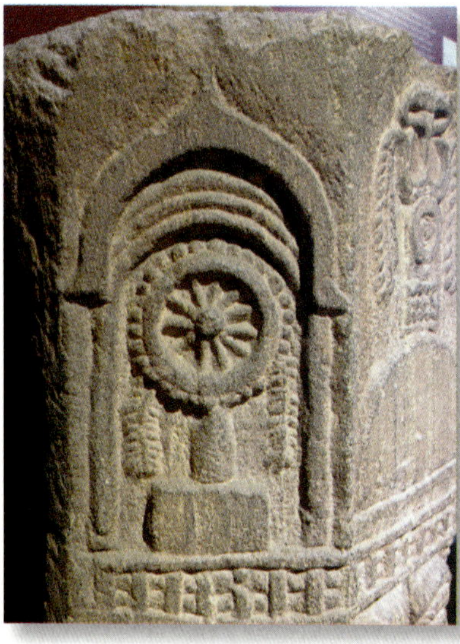

Buddhist Railing Pillar. Pauni, Bhandara District, Maharashtra.1st century.
The Dharma Chakra within a Chaitya window is an aniconic symbol of the Buddha.

spoken word was transformed into a visual and palpable icon. In this lies the story of our icons or *pratimas*. The Vedic tradition was strongly aniconic and no visual images were made in the Vedic period. The early Buddhist also showed an inhibition for image-making and the Buddha was represented by aniconic symbols such as the tree or foot prints or a riderless horse. The *sthanakvasi* Jains made prayer halls without any images. Some 19th century movements like the Arya Samaj sought inspiration from the Vedas and shied away from images. There has been an ongoing tension between those who celebrate images and those who would rather not represent any higher or transcendent idea in the form of an image. The aniconic Indian tradition finds its philosophic basis in the Vedantic *nirvikalpa*, *nirguna brahman* or the *brahman* without any attributes, or the Buddhist *sunyata* or emptiness. A basic Vedantic principle is that what we construct we also deconstruct, and *brahman* is no different. We build the majestic Purusha and give him radiant and beautiful attributes, but then in the end we realise that no attribute, no words, can suitably describe the grandeur of the Purusha, and at that point the image that we have built crumbles. During the Ganesha and the Durga

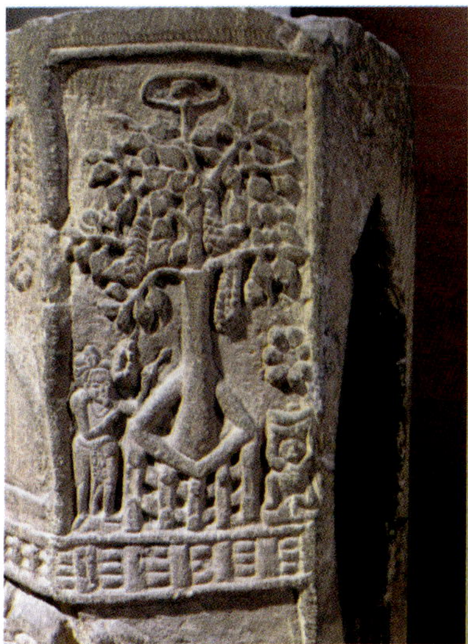

Buddhist Railing Pillar. Pauni, Bhandara District, Maharashtra.1st century.
The Bodhi Tree is a pervasive symbol of the Buddha.

festival we venerate the images of Ganesha and Durga, but at the end of the festival lovingly deposit them in the river. We will return to the concept of impermanence despite the apparent permanence in stone sculptures later.

Terracotta was the first medium in which we expressed ourselves and the potter, therefore is the *adi shilpi*, the first sculptor. We have evidence of this in the objects from the Indus Valley Civilisation, but it is not until the 3rd century BCE of the Mauryan period that terracotta images were produced, but these had a distinctly foreign flavour and it was not until the Sunga dynasty, that *Yakshis* and mother goddesses were created. The making of terracotta images was not confined to political dynasties, and housewives and potters in villages must have created a variety of images, plaques and toys all over the country. What they lacked in classical finesse they more than make up in their emotional content.

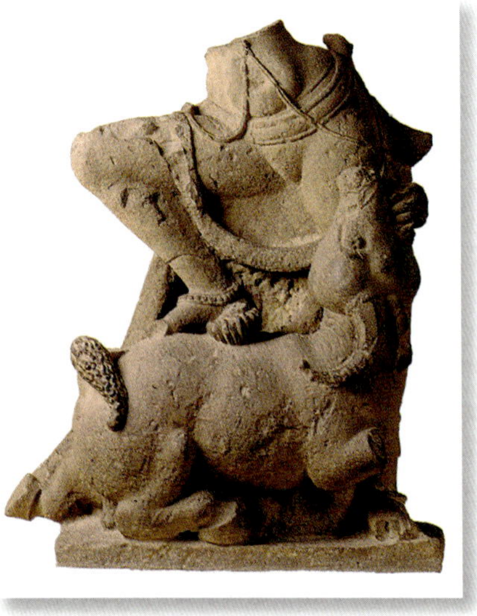

Mahishasuramardini, Elephanta, Maharashtra, 6th century

There were no stone sculptures in India till the time of the Mauryas, the first imperial dynasty founded by Chandragupta Maurya in 323 BCE. A good example of this is the Chandragupta *sabha*. However, let us not forget the *shilpis* of this architecture, who created a polished stone appearance, were Persio-Greek in origin and that there was no indigenous creativity here.The first major stone sculpture took place at Bahrut in the 2nd century BCE under the Sungas, and even there it is clear that it was their first attempt to carve in stone as they were essentially wood and ivory workers. Importantly the Bharut Yakshis have a native beauty of their own. It is in the Kushana period of the first few centuries of the first millennium that sculptors at Mathura were able to create sensuous figures in stone like *Yakshi* which can be called truly Indian.

When one enters the Sculpture Gallery there is a hushed silence, but in the distance one hears of the conversations between the *sthapati* and the *shilpi* and the noise of a stone being chipped away. It is in sculpture that one sees and feels the basic Indian penchant of giving a form to the formless. Let us not forget, the Sutradhar reminds us, that the first form of anything beautiful is *shabda*, understood as *kavya*. It is from *kavya* that most forms emerge. The Indian form is such that it gives insistent hints to something beyond itself, namely, of the formless. One of the first impression one gets is that the Indian sculptor consistently defies gravity, either by having the sculpture stand on a lotus pedestal or flying in the air. Also the icon occupies, not banal but cosmic space, going from *bhu*, *aap*, *tej*, *vayu* and ending in the *akash*, thereby suggesting that although it is in a human form the image is macrocosmic. Even as we touch the images and enjoy their visual and palpable texture, one is wonderstruck that one is in the presence of stones that are very ancient. What voices lie hidden in them, whose footfalls reside there, what cosmic events did it witness, where was it when the *Mahabharata* and the *Ramayana* took place? It is but appropriate that stones with hoary memories were chosen by our ancient sculptors. While most of these objects were painted in their day, the texture and the surface must have played an important part in the selection of stones, and in it also lies its aesthetic charm.

Even before we enter the Sculpture Gallery our eyes fall on the many sculptures in the verandah which we will visit. Here the stones speak, the noise of chisel and hammer is heard even as we envision *shilpis* creating a beautiful form from stone. In times ancient these sculptures were painted so that even as we are moved by their presence, one is reminded that one is admiring images that have deteriorated over time. Deteriorated perhaps, but still alive in many different ways. Ancient eyes would have looked upon these images very differently from what we do now. Every sculpted god had a specific colour, and the *shilpis* were well aware of that. Not only are we seeing weather-beaten stone sculptures, but what is more important to note is that these sculptures are being seen out of their original context. These images generally belonged to temples and have now found their way through circuitous routes to our Museum. Do we dare ask how they got here for fear of raising eyebrows? The least we should do is to mentally provide the original context and meaning of these images. These images were never seen in isolation but as a part of a larger whole. Which temple did they come from, who was their patron and *sthapati*, what tools did they use in crafting these images, whose eyes fell on them over trackless centuries, were they worshipped or were they only ornamental, were they hidden to save them from marauding invaders, were they broken or damaged to desacralise them? These questions of the Sutradhar must be raised even as we are walking through the Sculpture Gallery, for we are not just Museum visitors but contemplative viewers. One more time we are reminded that museums are a western construct and for Western eyes these questions are not that relevant. Very often I have felt like disobeying the 'Do Not Touch' signs, and feel and touch the images, not just for tactile pleasure but as my token of veneration, not just to the deity that is being portrayed but to the *shilpin* who created the image.

When it comes to creating icons, what is as important as the image is the material out of which it is fashioned. The oldest material is, of course, the earth or terracotta which is the primal womb out of which arises the entire creation. The earth is the mother which gives birth to trees and the plants, on it flow our rivers and in its dark and hidden depths are our springs of water. When a village potter makes a horse for the *adivasi* for their ancestral worship or a plaque of the mother goddess or a local hero, he takes a handful of earth from under the tree where the horse was placed the previous year and which had crumbled into dust. In doing this the potter is making a metaphysical statement of impermanence, of birth, death and rebirth. Images and objects from the Indus Valley carry this message although they rest on museum shelves today. The pre-Christian period saw a proliferation of terracotta images from Mathura and Bengal which carry the imprint and the fragrance of the earth. Wood as a medium for the creation of images carries the same metaphysical significance as terracotta, although in a tropical country like ours no ancient wooden image has survived. Which brings us to stone as the preferred medium for the making of images which started with Mauryans and persists even today. It has withstood ravages of time, in its textures are carved narratives of a period long forgotten. For centuries we have seen divinity in a hewn stone, and when to such a stone placed under a tree we apply a dab of vermillion it becomes a shrine.

Let us welcome Naman Ahuja into our conversation. He says: "Images of terracotta or even bronze are prehistoric and we find them even in the Indus Valley Civilisation but we do not know whether they were worshipped. Image worship in India started around the 2nd or 3rd century BCE and images of the mother goddess from Chandraketugarh come to mind. At that time exemplars like Mahavir and Buddha were celebrated as heroes but not as gods and there were narratives about them in stone. Hindu gods and goddesses began to be carved in stone just before the millennium and then they began to be worshipped religiously and we sought their *darshan* and the magico-religious energy that they imparted."

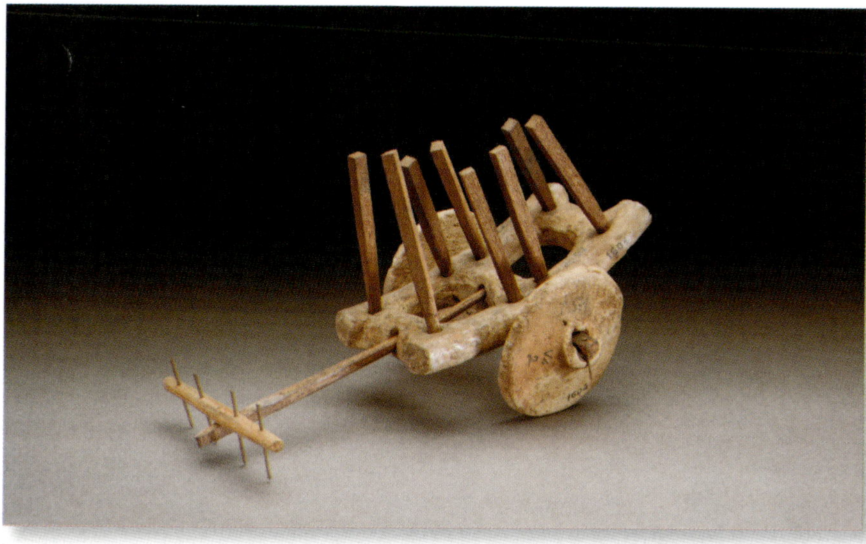

Reconstructed Miniature Cart, Indus Valley

Naman emphasises that the penchant for image worship was not inherently a Hindu concept, for we were essentially a non-iconic tradition. In the Vedic period the religious idiom was the *yajna*.

The impetus for creating images in stone came to us from Gandhara, present day Afghanistan, where images of the Buddha were made in profusion, and this prompted the Hindus to follow suit. Once images were made, the native Hindu mind preferred to worship it. In one of Ashoka's edicts he criticises the mindless rituals of image worship. In case we have missed to state it is obvious that the Indian sculptor enshrined both the divine and the beautiful in the human body which then becomes the expression of every emotion, from the sacred to the secular. And the *sharira* was the perfect repository of beauty. The Sutradhar brings up another important observation that for us, the sacred and the secular are a continuum and not a binary. Even a casual look at this Gallery affirms that.

While the *padmasana* is universally adopted as the posture most conducive to *dhyana*, it is the Buddhist tradition that used it extensively in creating the many *akritis* of the Buddha. Folded legs, arms drawn in and palms

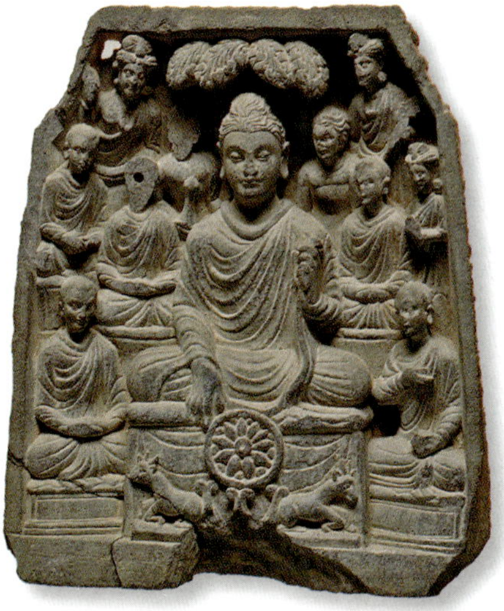

First Sermon of the Buddha, Gandhara. 3rd century CE

facing upwards, sitting upright and with eyes closed, the *padmasana* is undoubtedly the most dignified human *akriti*. Expressing neither regal power nor militant aggression, staying away from emotional indulgence or religious veneration, withdrawing gracefully from the demands and dictates of the world, converting movement into serenity, action into stillness, speech into silence, the *padmasana* as an *akriti* is a visual expression of the most exalted human condition, a condition where it is totally established within Prakriti, with complete mastery over not only the body and its energy but even more the mind and its *citta vrritti* through the *buddhi*, *ahamkara* and *manas*, so that just as the lotus remains untouched by water, the in-drawn mind in a state of *dhyana* stays in its beautiful pristine state, a mind that rests in a condition of effortless being. That state of being is best described as *atmarati*, *atmanishtha*, the mind established and romancing in and with itself. It is a state of freedom where the mind is not imprisoned or fragmented within narrow walls but enjoys the vastness and fullness of space, where arid dictates of earthly rationality are eclipsed by supra-rational vistas of the unlimited sky, where time is not linear and profane but circular and sacred, where the objectively grounded *sunder* is transformed into the pure subjective *saundarya*, where the objective melts into pure subjectivity and the human is not far from divine. *Padmasana* is part of the 32 *mahapurushalakshanas* that were given to the image of the Buddha and it was this that established the norm for sculptures of our divinity.

Once images of the Buddha were made and temples in tarracotta and stone began to be built, we started making images of our gods and goddesses and gave them a human form, and from a non-iconic tradition we became a robustly iconic civilisation. These images in their original location were worshipped religiously with appropriate rites and rituals. Worship in Hindu temples started in the 5th–6th centuries and involved bathing of the image, application of sandal paste, flowers, lighting of oil lamps and performance of vocal music and dances. However, in our Museum we must celebrate them aesthetically as they are not religiously fit, neither are they meant for worship. To contain the deity in the temple, the cult image in the *garbagraha* in particular, had to be made with exact measurements for the god could reside only in a perfectly-made image, and following this the deity had to be invited to reside in it, by a process called *pranapratishtha*.

Sculptures have both a racial and cultural memory for they arise from a bedrock of archetypes, Puranic and folk narratives, and motifs and metaphors drawn from the world of plants and animals. When a deity stands on a lotus, or a *surasundari* holds the branch of a tree, it suggests and it assures us that the sculpted form is part of the living world around it, which is a world of plants and animals, rivers and the sky.

There are Buddhist, Jain and Hindu sculptures in the same gallery, and this is a shared space reflecting the largely harmonious interplay of the major religious traditions in the country which integrated individuals and communities into a beautiful social fabric.

Unlike our Western colonisers, who imposed a monotheistic religious identity, the cultural and religious space of the past was pluralistic, a tapestry with many strands and fibres coming together.

The earliest surviving temples in the North are from the Gupta period at Deogarh, Nachna and Ramgarh. The Sutradhar asks us to fast forward three centuries and go to the temple town of Aihole in present-day Karnataka as we have three large ceiling panels from the Hucchappaya temple in our Museum. Aihole sits in company with temple towns like Pattadakal and Badami. Of Aihole, Mulk Raj Anand wrote:

> Temples have always been built at sacred sites, places where the gods reveal themselves to mankind. As one goes beyond the Malaprabha river and see the ochre-coloured shrines of Aihole, one is lifted from the ordinary self to the euphoria of happiness and one exclaims: What beauties! What splendours! What marvels! One feels more and more that is the felt experience of these ancient monuments which is more inspiring than their exact dates.[11]

The Chalukyan genius lay in moving away from rock cut structures to temples where they were able to experiment with different styles, and this period belongs to one of the most creative phases in the history of Indian architecture where a new style was being forged, but the memory of village architecture like open timber porches was not lost. What the Chalukyan *sthapatis* did was to have a profound influence on later temple architecture in south India. As we look at this panel we are transported to the 7th century. This was a time of the Chalukyan empire asserting its power in this part of the Deccan. The Chalukyans inherited temples built in this area by the Satavahanas, but they brought the carvers of the Vindhyas and the craftsmen of the Deccan along with the prevailing myths and symbols. With this they created a mixture, if not synthesis, of temple building, by taking the style of the Northern *shikhara*, and that of Ajanta and Ellora, and meld it into the first layers of the Southern style, thereby making Aihole a gateway to the south. Not only did they have a unique temple style but their uniqueness lay in having flat-roofed *mandapas* with gods carved on their ceiling. Ceilings in the *rangamandapas* of the temples represent the cosmic sky but the flat-roofed temples of Aihole were very special. These ceilings also had a number of geometric motifs which felt almost like a hanging piece of textile, and also flying couples emerging out of foliation which give us the impression of the sky. The panel of Brahma, Sheshashayi Vishnu and Umamaheshvara from the Hucchappaya temple in Aihole are a testament to their skill.

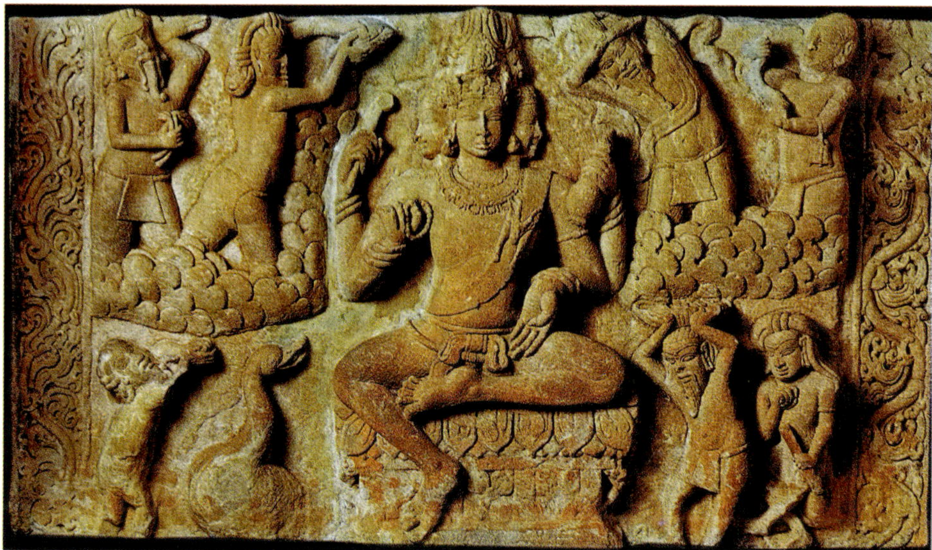

Brahma. Ceiling Slab, Aihole, Karnataka. 7th century CE

The Chalukyans, with their capital at Vatapi, especially under the patronage of Pulekeshin II, dominated the 6th to the 8th centuries and became the most powerful monarchs of the Deccan.The Sutradhar suggests that we should deconstruct the image into its geometrical components, each shape carrying a specific meaning, each shape arising from a central *bindu*. Look at the hands of the image, they are never empty, but they carry *ayudhas* or weapons, specific to each god. If the dancer, according to Bharata's Natyashastra was *rasa brahman*, or a carrier and conduit of *rasa* that was capable of taking us to *brahman*, the properly made sculpture or *pratima* or *murti* was *rupa brahman*, an image that purely on its sensual or aesthetic merits could take us to *brahman*, but in order to do this we must be contemplative *rasikas* and not mere voyeurs. The Sutradhar closes her eyes suggesting that it is time to view the sculptures with our inner eye.

Even though the North and the South of India have different temple designs the various sculptures have a pan-Indian uniformity, which raises the question as how did the various techniques of image-making spread from one part of India to another. Texts of image-making such as the Shilpaprakasha, Vishnudharmottara and Vastusutra Upanishad came much later. It is fair to

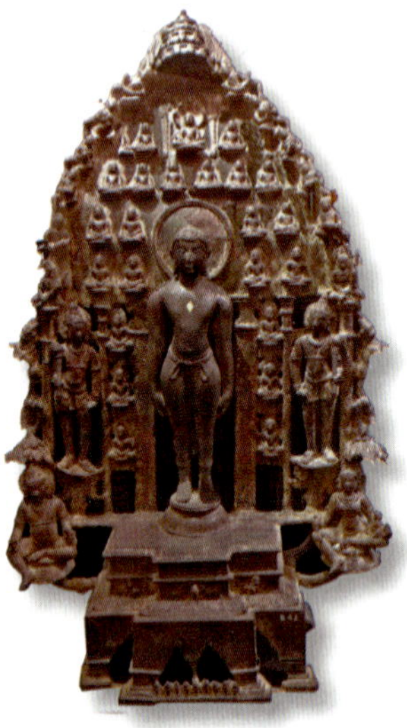

Chovisi of Rishabnatha, Khandesh, Maharashtra. 8th–9th century CE

speculate then that *sthapatis* travelled along trade and caravan routes and shared the techniques of image-making with each other, creating a vibrant oral tradition which was later written.

It is important to state that the various arts in India are interrelated. Our Sutradhar takes us now to the Jain *parampara* of beauty. A beautiful object from the Jain tradition which brings together art and ritual, piety and pleasure, is the *ghar derasar* or the home shrine of the Jains. It were the Shvetambaraa Jains who were *murti* worshippers who created beautiful domestic shrines to house the icon. John Cort points out it was because of the prevalence of wood carvers in Gujarat that these shrines had a special wood aesthetic to it. In its simplest form it had four pillars and a roof which was dome-shaped and intricately painted and the structure looked like a *mandapa*. The shrine speaks not only to the craftsperson who lovingly made it, but equally to the patron who commissioned it, and then to the householders who gathered around it to honour the Jina enthroned in it. The names Hemachandra (1088–1172), Nemichandra and Thakurra Pheru are important when it comes to the ritual practices of the Jain community. They made a number of prescriptions

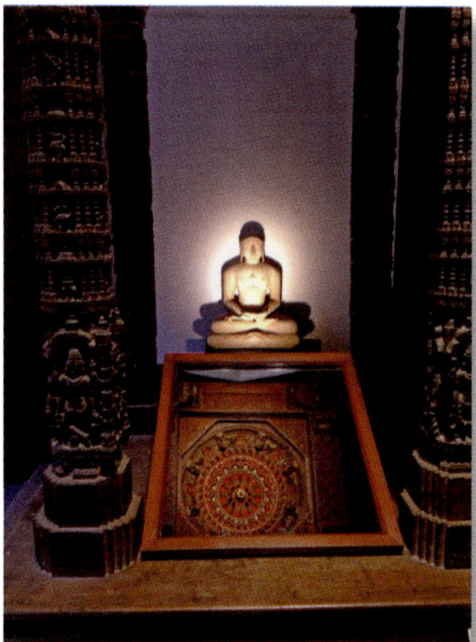

Ghar Derasar. 20th century

for the lay devotee for the worship of the Jina in their *ghar derasar*. These included the height of the icon, the position of the *derasar* in the home, preparatory ablutions, the chanting of songs valorising the Jinas. An icon in a properly carved *derasar* is considered a *arhat* or an embodied teacher, but without the carving the Jina is considered to be a *siddha* or a liberated soul. One of the main task of the worshipper is to renounce either an activity or possession as part of the ritual. On another important note there is a significant difference between a Hindu and a Jain icon. A Hindu icon by the ritual of *pranapratishtha* actually resides in the icon, but this is not the case in a Jain icon. Therefore the Jain worshipper has to imagine that he or she is standing in front of the Jina as he teaches. This is called *samasvarana*. Standing in front of the *ghar derasar* in our Museum takes us back to a ritually active Jain family in Gujarat offering their morning prayers to the Jina; and those of us who are touched by this are enriched by the many aspects of Jain theology, the concepts of *ahimsa* and *anekantavada* ring in our ear, and we thank scholars like John Cort for enlightening us about an important part of the Jain culture.

When a icon becomes the insignia and the signature of an entire civilisation it speaks volumes about that object. The reference is to the Chola Nataraja. It would not be wrong to say that this beautiful expression of Shiva as the cosmic dancer is a visual expression of the Hindu world view. This brings us to a discussion of Chola bronzes and its place in our iconography. The enigmatic bronze figure of the dancing woman, sometimes referred to as the common working woman, from the Indus Valley Civilisation, attests to the presence of the technology of bronze casting at that time. We must also acknowledge that folk bronzes may have been made throughout our history, but it was in the 9th and 10th centuries that the aesthetics and technology of bronze icons comes to a high point. The penchant of the Cholas for Shiva, the availability of metals like copper and tin in the Tamil country and neighbouring Sri Lanka, the strong presence of Bharatanatyam dance in the temples, and the underpinning of the Shaiva Siddhanta philosophy, all came together to lead to the creation of these wonderful bronzes. Made up of more than one metal, including gold and silver, Chola bronzes arose from the perfect lost wax process of metal casting. The Nataraja in particular is not only, aesthetically, the perfect icon but equally the metaphysical message it sends sums up the human condition. The four arms representing creation, protection, absorption and transcendence, the right leg suggesting the recognition of ignorance, and the uplifted left leg expression freedom, the Nataraja is also at the same an androgyn figure because of the presence of the *kundala* in His left ear signifying Parvati. Rising from the earth to the sky, holding the Ganga and the crescent moon in His matted hair, Shiva as Nataraja brings the dichotomies of life into an organic whole. Shiva dances a thousand dances, but it is in Chidambaram that He performs his *anandatandava*, and to the contemplative aesthete Chidambaram is both the temple and the *cidakasha* in our inner being. The Shiva temple in Chidambaram shows Shiva as Nataraja in 108 different poses. Dance and sculpture share common aesthetic principles and also laws of execution. Many of the terms too are common to both arts. In sculpture, space measurements are called *talas* and the deviation from the vertical median, *bhangas*. In the Kailasa temple at Ellora the inert mass of volcanic rock is quickened and brought alive, pulsating with figures that fly effortlessly through the air in a glorious homage to Shiva. There are a number of images of Shiva but the most

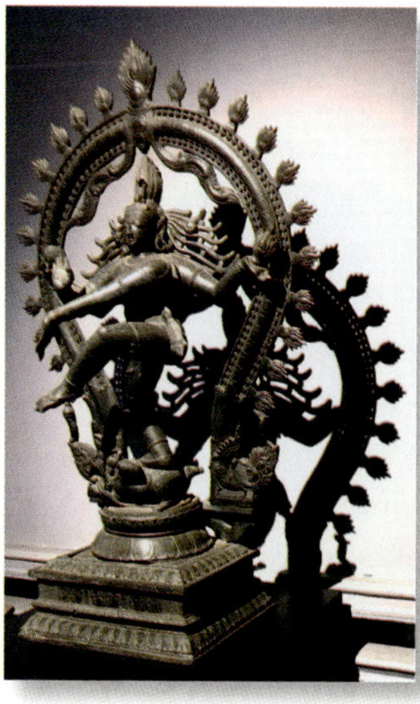

Nataraja, Late Chola

powerful is, perhaps, that of Nataraja, where Shiva is magically transformed into fluid movement, radiating dynamism through his many arms. Here at Kailasa, Shiva is rendered in all his diverse manifestations, in as many moods as he could be conceived.The period of the imperial Cholas (c. 850 CE–1250 CE) was an age of continuous improvement and refinement of Dravidian art and architecture. They utilised their prodigious wealth earned through their extensive conquests and trade in building long-lasting stone temples and exquisite bronze sculptures. Most of these still stand proudly articulating those glorious days. The Chola period is also remarkable for its sculptures and bronzes. Among the existing specimens in the various museums of the world and in the temples of South India may be seen many fine figures of Shiva in various forms, Vishnu and his consort Lakshmi, Shaiva saints and many more. Though conforming generally to the iconographic conventions established by long tradition, the sculptor worked in great freedom in the eleventh and the twelfth centuries, and the sculptures and bronzes show classic grace, grandeur and perfect taste. The best example of this can be seen in the form of Nataraja, the divine dancer. While the stone sculptures and the inner sanctum image empowering the temple remained immovable, changing religious concepts during the 10th century demanded that the deities take part in a variety of public roles similar to those of a human monarch. As a result, large bronze images were created to be carried outside the temple to participate in daily rituals, processions, and temple festivals. The round lugs and holes found at the base of many of these sculptures are for the poles that were used to carry the heavy images. Chola bronzes are admired for the sensuous depiction of the figure and the detailed treatment of their clothing and jewellery, Although bronze casting has a long history in South India, a much larger and a much greater number of bronze sculptures were cast during the Chola period than before, further attesting to the importance of bronze sculpture during this period. It should be noted that when in worship, these images are covered in silk cloth, garlands, and jewels, and would not appear as they do outside a religious context. Decorating the bronzes in this way is a tradition at least a thousand years old, as such decorations are referred to in tenth-century Chola inscriptions. If the Nataraja comes alive in the temple at Chidambaram, the real Chidambaram is in the minds of the devotees for whom Shiva dances forever. This is a form of *purnatva* or the human mind and body at its enlightened best.The Nataraja becomes an image of *purnatva* or totality in its richest aesthetic sense by the integration of the microcosm and the macrocosm into a meaningful whole, the depiction of the infinite and the eternal in a finite form, the representation of the temporal and the timeless together, the evocation of the continuum between the sacred and the secular, and creating a bridge between bipolar opposites in form. It is this *purnatasya akritihi*, or visual expressions of totality in the Nataraja that points to the exalted possibilities of the human condition, and is an assurance that as humans we are not condemned to what is time-bound and limited by space but can be privy to the experience of the infinite and the eternal.

An ancient form of painting was painting on cloth also called *patachitra*, or *patravali chitra*, and belongs equally to the Hindu, Buddhist and the Jain traditions. Although no examples of *patachitra* prior to the 14th century have survived due to the perishable nature of cloth in tropical climates, considerable evidence exists for such early *patachitras* in texts. The ancient Buddhist text Vissudhimagga speaks of canvas as the perfect background of painting. Both coarse and finely woven cotton and linen were used for painting religious as well as secular subjects. The cloth is first primed with wheat or rice flour paste to fill up the pores of the textile. Use of tamarind seed paste is also recommended in certain cases. After the primer is completely dry, the surface is burnished with an agate burnisher to ready it for painting. The outlines are drawn first, usually in red and then the colours are applied. Additional decoration in gold or silver, and the incorporation of a *mantrakshara* and identification labels in black and white are completed at the end. *Patachitras* can be narrative or didactic and also include *vijnaptipatra* or letters of invitation, *khamapana patrika* or letters of pardon and *chitrakavya* or pictorial poetry. *Patachitras* are used by itinerant story tellers. There are traditions of narrative scroll painting in Bengal, Bihar, Orissa, Rajasthan, Andhra and Gujarat. The story tellers unscroll the *patas* as they tell a story with the accompanying of drums and cymbals. The *patas* are held sacred and are passed on from one generation to another. When they are not in use they are rolled in fabric and stored in the attic. When a new scroll is acquired a ceremony akin to the birth of a child is performed. And when the scroll is frayed it is immersed in the river. *Patachitras* are an important part of the social and religious life of ancient India.

Kalamkari or pen work refers to textiles that are printed or painted using a particular technique. Although painted textiles have been recovered from the Indus Valley civilisation, modern Kalamkari can be traced to the 17th century Andhra Pradesh. Kalamkari, like most other Indian arts, owes its birth to temple rituals. Kalamkari textitles were used as aids to story telling in temple precincts. While the motifs of Kalamkari are drawn from Hindu mythology, Kalamkari owes a lot to Persian influences which came into this area when trade links were established between Safavid Persia and Qutub Shahi dynasty in Golconda. The two centres of Kalamkari are Masulipatnam and Shrikalahasti. Kalamkari textiles were used to decorate temples and palaces as well as for narrative scrolls, but over the years they have been used for household purposes like furnishings and even clothing. In British India Kalamkari fabrics were particularly popular as bed covers, and came to be called *palangposh* or *palampore*. The procedure for producing a *Kalamkar* starts with preparing the cloth which is first bleached, then soaked in myrobalan solution mixed with fresh buffalo milk. The outlines are then drawn in red and black. The cloth is then washed in running water before sunrise, then starched and waxed. The pen or *kalam* is made of a bamboo stick at the end of which a thick pad of human hair is attached and figures

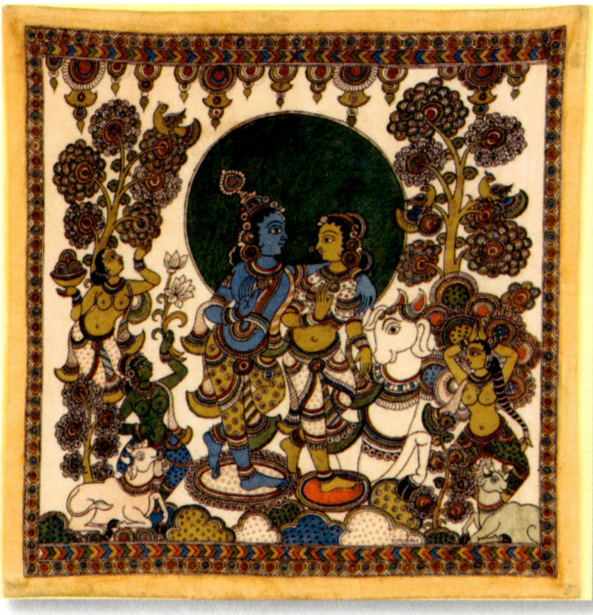

Kalamkari. Andhra. 20th century

are drawn with this pen on a wooden block. Red, blue, yellow and green are the main colours, and the Kalamkari artists worked with the techniques of a mural painter and the usual themes were taken from the Puranas as well as from the *Mahabharata* and *Ramayana*. The *kalamkars* were able to produce two-dimensional figures that equalled temple sculptures and murals. Kalamkari textiles thrived on Muslim court patronage, Persian trade and the markets of Europe, and remain even today an important part of the artistic repository of India.

The Deccan is known for its Kalamkari paintings on textiles and for its wall paintings at Lepakshi. Recently, scroll paintings from the Deccan have come to light. Scroll paintings have been recorded in Buddhist and Jaina literature where they were called *patachitras* and also in Sanskrit literature where they were referred to as *yama patas*. The tradition of scroll paintings has continued right up to the present day. In Bengal, Bihar and Orissa the paintings carry a mythological theme, while those in Gujarat and Rajasthan carry Tantric themes and the deeds of local heroes like Pabuji. While the Deccani scrolls depict Hindu mythological stories, a narrative of special interest to these

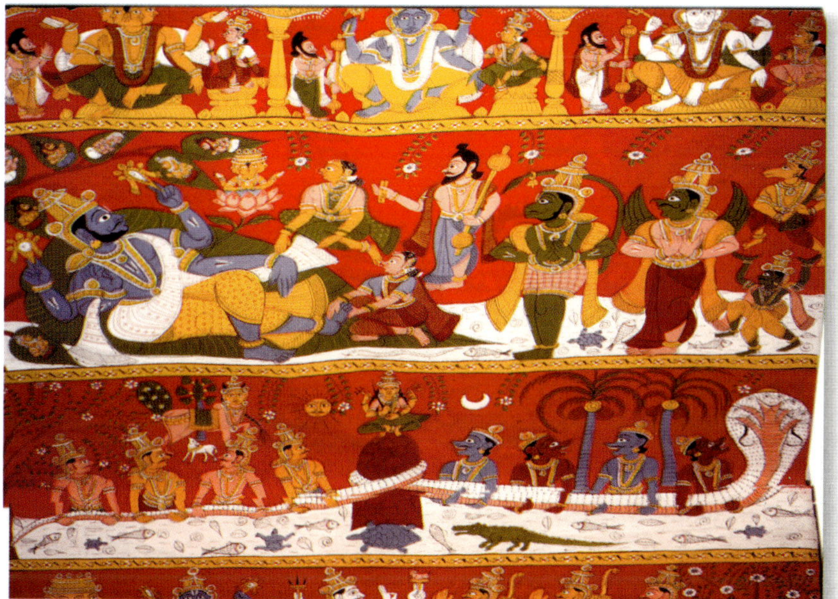

Vaishnava Telangana Scroll, 20th century

painters is the story of Markandeya and Bhavana *rishis*. Rishi Markandeya performed a *yajna* to provide clothing for the gods. From the sacrifical fire arose Bhavana *rishi* who pulled a fibre from the lotus stalk that arose from Vishnu's navel and made a ball of thread from it and under Vishnu's direction used this thread to make clothes for the *devas*. Bhavana married Bhadrava, the daughter of the sun, who bore him hundred and one sons from whom came the Padmasalis and the Pattusalis, who were the original weavers from Andhra. The Telangana scrolls of the 18th centuries were strongly influenced by the Vijayanagara styles of painting, while the scrolls of the 19th centuries show features of Nayaka art and were produced under the patronage of Hindu *zamindars*. The fabric for the scroll is prepared by applying several layers of white kaolin to which starch and gum were added. The fabric is then burnished with a polished stone. The gum of the *tirman* tree was used as the binding medium for colours. Red is the predominant colour for the background. The Telangana scrolls are characterised by the vigour of the figures and the persistent regard for a certain rhythm which linked the entire scroll. When completed, the scrolls were given to itinerant singers and performers who narrated the story painted in the scroll. The scrolls had a strong caste orientation, and each caste governed the general layout of the scroll.

Perhaps the oldest form of human expression of beauty are murals, prehistoric in its time line and primitive in its style. The murals of Bhimbekta in present day Madhya Pradesh going back 30,000 years come to mind and speak of the need and the desire of these pre-historic people to convert their feelings into designs and forms on the walls of caves which they would inhabit. From this to the frescoes of Ajanta of the seventh century is a natural progression. The richly adorned walls of the Buddhist caves with images of the Buddha, his devotees and the Jataka stories, not only add beauty to the habitat of the monks but were also an aid in meditation. More than temple sculptures and scrolls, murals have a living presence in the lives of people, be they monks or monarchs. No wonder *havelis* and palaces continued the practice of creating murals which would bring Puranic stories of our gods and goddesses alive, and this would no doubt imprint their minds with the beauty and divinity expressed in these murals. It is as if they were listening to stories and listening to music even as they lived their daily lives. Murals have a living presence and a reminder of the hoary days of meditation and majesty.

Itinerant singers are prevalent in all parts of the country. In their simple but heart warming words, they tell stories of Puranic gods and goddesses or of folk heroes. Going on foot from village to village, they establish themselves under a tree in the village square, and as people gather and the evening proceeds, they continue till the wee hours of the night under the light of a kerosene lamp. In Birbhum district of West Bengal they are called *patuas*.

They travel through small towns and villages of Bengal with their *patas* or scrolls where they entertain rapt audiences with their audio-visual show. A *patua*'s main accessories are his assortment of scrolls which he carries around in his cloth *jhola*. Once painted on cloth, today they are done on paper and pasted together to form a scroll. The *Patua*'s stories vary from traditional mythological stories to stories of folk deities like Manasa Devi, Behula and Satya Pir. Occasionally the *Patua* relates local stories, accounts of politicians, and even scandals. The *Patua* begins his performance with a song that narrates the incidents depicted on the scroll. The story unfolds as he gradually unwinds the scroll, and as it gets dark he would light a lantern. *Patua*s are also referred to as *Jadu Patua*s because it is believed that they perform *jadu* or magic using their painted scrolls as a medium. If on his travels in tribal areas a *jadu Patua* hears of any death in a Santhal family, he visits the bereaved family and then shows them a scroll in which he has painted figures resembling the Santhals, complete in all details but with one important omission, that of the eyes. He offers to paint the eye for an appropriate price. The Santhals buy the scroll since they are convinced that the painted figure is an image of their dead relative. *Jadu Patua*s are an important part of the itinerant story tellers of India.

If the *shilpin* who creates icons for the temple creates majestic icons in keeping with the *shastras*, and which are patronised by the royalty and the nobility, the folk artist is equally capable of venerating icons *albeit* in the folk idiom. The folk painter is an artist of the earth, a *gramin*, or the person who lives in the village and who is involved in the many activities of working with the earth, who lives and functions in harmony with the world around her, the world of the trees and fruits, birds and blossoms, the waters and the wind, the sun and the sky, all of which are not just inert matter but deeply meaningful to him or her and have a living presence in their life and world view. This world of nature is alive for them, the juice that enlivens it resonates with the sap that flows through them, their own growth is tied to the fertility and fecundity of the world around them, and even more this world that they inhabit has not only a form but feeling as well. This is sometimes called a pagan world view. The underlying *gramin drishti* is that of celebrating growth and fertility, of venerating and worshipping the world around them, and ensuring that their material growth is robust and sustained in harmony with the world around them. Beauty is important for the *gramin* artist and they adorn their homes with motifs and patterns, like the sun, the tree, the *kalasha*, all of which have a magico-religious significance for them and confer protection to the home and the household. They express the joy of life and living through song and dance, the celebration of the here and now, an affirmation of the *shakshat* or the immediate, rather than a hidden or distant reality. India is a tropical country and the Indian psyche is touched by the universe in all its abundance and multiplicity of life and form that goes from the earth to the sky. The world for the *gramin* multi-centric artist is inhabited by plants

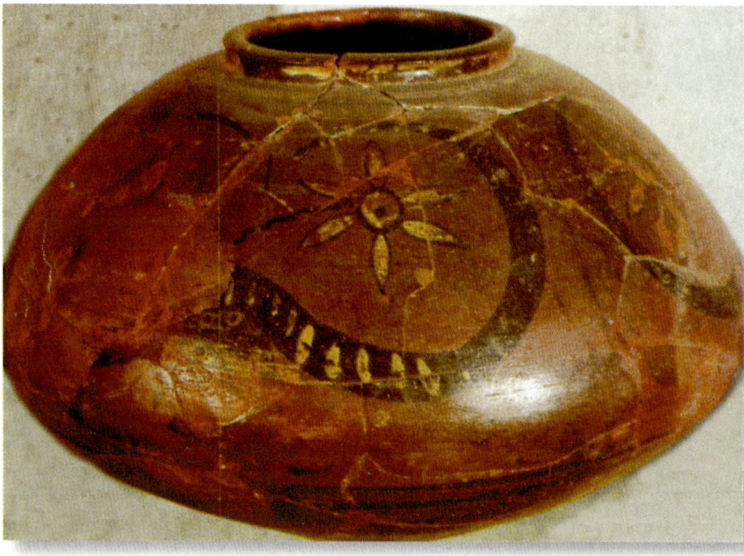

Kalasha, Indus Valley, National Museum, Delhi

and creepers, birds and blossoms, the stars and the planets, mountains and rivers, and all these are an integral part of their life and vision for them in India. The Hindu consciousness and the awareness of the universe around it are interrelated and interdependent, and always transmutable. It is this awareness of natural forms that inspires a great variety of motifs in folk art and craft. These are naturalistic, beautiful and spontaneous on one level and imbued with great symbolic and archetypal significance on another. Hence the various forms and attributes in nature lead to a certain *drishti* or world view. The two move concurrently, as the *akritis* or forms of the folk artist are not just symbols but living visual metaphors. It is this that distinguishes this approach from pantheism and paganism and confers upon folk *akritis* a reality and a bonafide of its own, and makes their *gramin drishti* not just sight but insight and thus it qualifies to be a source of visual knowledge. The various forms and textures, colours and sounds, cosmic objects and phenomena, the movement and the changes of the natural worlds, are not just observed and enjoyed but must be seen as visual metaphors, and this can then becomes their *drishti* and inform their world view and their lived lives. Folk or everyday artists incorporate these motifs in their art, whether it is women's embroidery like *Kantha* of Bengal, *rumal* of Chamba, saris in various parts, or paintings on mud walls, or *dhuli chitra* or *rangoli* in most parts of India, in a variety of fabric, in pottery and a variety of terracotta arts. *Gramin drishti* is that of the *krishi* or the farmer for whom growth, fertility and fecundity are important, and this translates into images like the wish-fulfilling tree, leaf and foliage, two birds on a branch and folk deities. Their art is earthy, for it venerates the earth as mother, ideas that resonate in the Prithvi Sukta of the Atharva Veda. Woman as creator is prominent in the *gramin drishti*, so is the *kalasha* which contains life-sustaining water and is also the womb. Images and motifs interlock in their art but underneath them is the mystery and wonder of growth, of the transformation of a seed into a tree and then into flower and fruit, and then eventual decay and regrowth. The changing seasons are woven into the tapestry of life in their painting, although it sometimes feels as if it is spring all the time, particularly when one sees the *shringara* of Radha and Krishna. There is in the *gramin drishti* and the art that comes out of it, the affirmation and joyousness of life, the celebration of festivals and the various *samskaras* of life. The *gramin drishti* in short, is a celebration of Prakriti, and in it we find a meaning of the life of the people of India.

With a history of 1000 years written in its temples and the footfalls of dynasties of rulers still heard in the soil, Tanjore or Thanjavur is the cultural capital of Tamil Nadu. Thanjavur flourished during the reign of Raja Raja Chola who built the magnificent Brihadisvara Temple. Rising to 65 metres, the 14 tiered pyramidal structure is topped by a cupola. The Brihadisvara temple reflects the glory of Shiva through its sculptures, and standing guard is the huge monolithic Nandi. Tanjore also has the Saraswati Mahal library which is home to several rare manuscripts. The noted Carnatic musician Thyagaraja was born in Tanjore district.

The Tanjore style of paintings was popular during the 17th–19th centuries under the patronage of Maratha rulers Sarbhoji and Shivaji, and in Mysore under Mummadi Krishnaraya Wodiyar. Glass painting was popular in 17th century Europe and spread from there to China, and then to India. Tanjore art was the product of a people who turned to the gods and goddesses for solace and assertion of their identity when the native rulers of Thanjavur and Mysore came under British rule. It was under these circumstances that the Tanjore

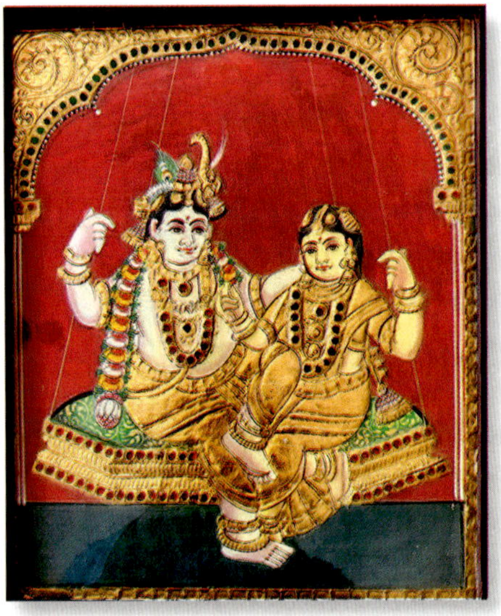

Radha Krishna, Tanjore, 19th century

artists turned to glass painting. The most striking feature of these paintings is the use of gold leaf and gems. The paintings are made on jackwood pasted with unbleached cloth to which a mixture of limestone, chalk powder, gum and honey are applied in layers. After the icons are drawn certain parts of the figures are raised with this paste. Once dry, the gems and the beads are set and gold leaf pressed on to the painting. The Tanjore figures are robust and plump, and are more iconic than narrative. The Western impact on these paintings is seen in the drapery, lamps, furniture and certain architectural features, but they retain a distinct indigenous richness of colour and design.

The Thanjavur artists had shown their flair for adopting new techniques and imparting to them their own stamp. Navneeta Krishna is one of the popular figures for the Tanjore artists although they show a variety of Puranic gods and goddesses and also royalty and nobility. Tanjore paintings are decorative and pleasing, and were popular with people who wanted them for worship or decoration and also for the British who wanted to take home souvenirs. Thanjavur glass paintings became popular with the middle class in the Tamil country who acquired them for decoration and even for worship. The Tanjore paintings are one of the last vestiges of traditional art in India before modern Indian art took over.

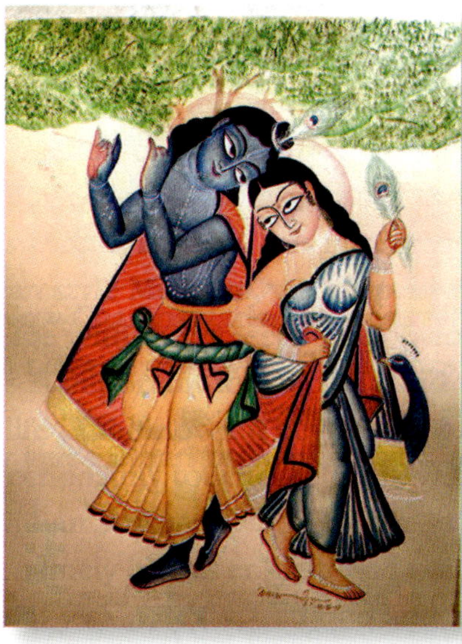

Radha Krishna. Kalighat. 20th century

If the paintings of Madhuban bring to life the rustic presence of Krishna, that of Kalighat in Bengal are reminiscent of the *patas* of Bengal. Tracing their lineage to the *Patuas* or *pata* painters and eventually to Vishwakarma, 19th century saw the emergence of painters, who were displaced from the courts, and who settled themselves in the vicinity of the Kali temple in Calcutta, and produced iconic images in a characteristic style mainly for pilgrims. Featuring robust colours and bold lines with iconic figures against a blank background the Kalighat figures had an aura of simplicity and modernity about them. While painting mythic figures, which included Krishna, the Kalighat painters also expressed themselves through satirical images of the *bhadralok* of Bengal, the dandy and the *babu*, as well as the prevalent scandals like the Elokeshi episode; it is in this context that the Kalighat paintings of Krishna must be understood. 19th century Calcutta was at the vanguard of modernity, with both nationalism and artistic renaissance stirring the people into action, and it is out of these forces that Kalighat paintings emerged. The Kalighat painters painted courtesans with as much ease as they painted Radha, suggesting a cross-over between the two, and it is well to remember that it was here in Bengal that Radha was regarded as a *kalankini* or a defiled woman. One cannot but help in making this connection of the ambivalence of Radha when one sees Kalighat representations of Krishna. Here was a modern Krishna born in the courtyard of the dark and mystical Kali, seated on a chair and under a stylised Kadamba tree, but not in the idyllic Vrindavana, freed from the ethos of the *pata* or the scroll and therefore without a story to go with it, but never lacking in layers of ancient myth, looking wistfully at Radha, but without his flute. Simple, modern and yet not totally divorced from tradition, making his presence felt in the city which was a crucible of Indian modernity, the Kalighat Krishna is unique in the artistic expression of modern India, reminding its patrons that despite modernity the ancient was never too far off. It is here that the noted Jamini Roy found his inspiration and created his inimitable figures, and made us realise that it was possible to be modern and Indian at the same time.

Among painters of the 20th century Jamini Roy occupies a special place. He was one of the first artists to realise the strength of folk art and used it to vitalise his own work. He was born in 1887 in Belatore, a village in the Bankura district of Bengal, and died in Calcutta at the age of 85. His was a time when the grand tradition of miniature painting had come to an end and the British were trying to influence Indian artistic sensibilities. Indian nationalism was stirring the elite and the masses, and this was particularly felt in Bengal, and Indian artists like Abanindranath Tagore were trying to revive a certain Indianness. It was in this epoch that Jamini Roy's career began to unfold. He joined the Calcutta School of Art and his early influences were from Western art. His early work shows his versatility and that he was an artist in search of a style, and it was his discontent with the prevailing styles of painting that led him to search for a new and distinctive style. He felt that a revivial of the elitist Indian style of either Ajanta or the Rajput miniatures could not express the real India. He was to find this in the Kalighat *patua* style of painting, the painted dolls and the terracotta horses. Jamini Roy's early experiments at simplification and stylisation combined the lyricism of the Bengal school with the sweeping brush lines of the Kalighat *pat* and the bold colouration of popular art and craft. The single figures of women like the *gopini* or the mother and child continued to be his motif, and this motif filled the entire area of the picture. He liked to think of himself as an artist craftsman in the tradition of the *patua* painters. The true contribution

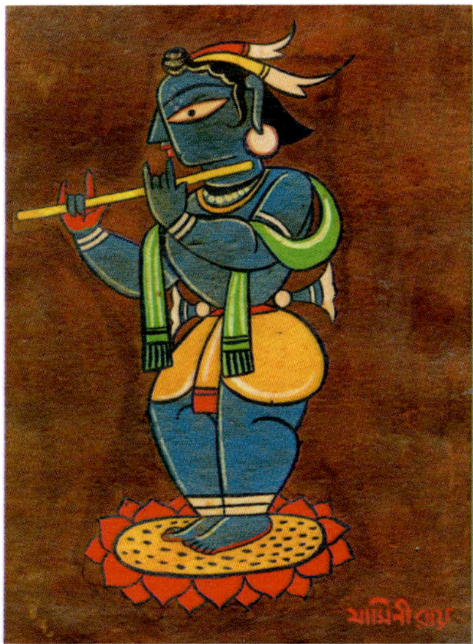

Krishna by Jamini Roy, 20th century

of Jamini Roy lies in directing our attention to the innocence, strength and beauty of the folk and the living arts of India, at a time when Indians were being lured by westernisation in their art and thought.

The women of Madhubani create unique paintings that recall both myth and history, Even when Madhubani art is created on paper rather than on walls, as it is these days, it retains its look of a mural, where the painted Krishna has a living presence in their lived lives and is not merely an aesthetic statement, and where the women express their deepest feelings not by erudite words but

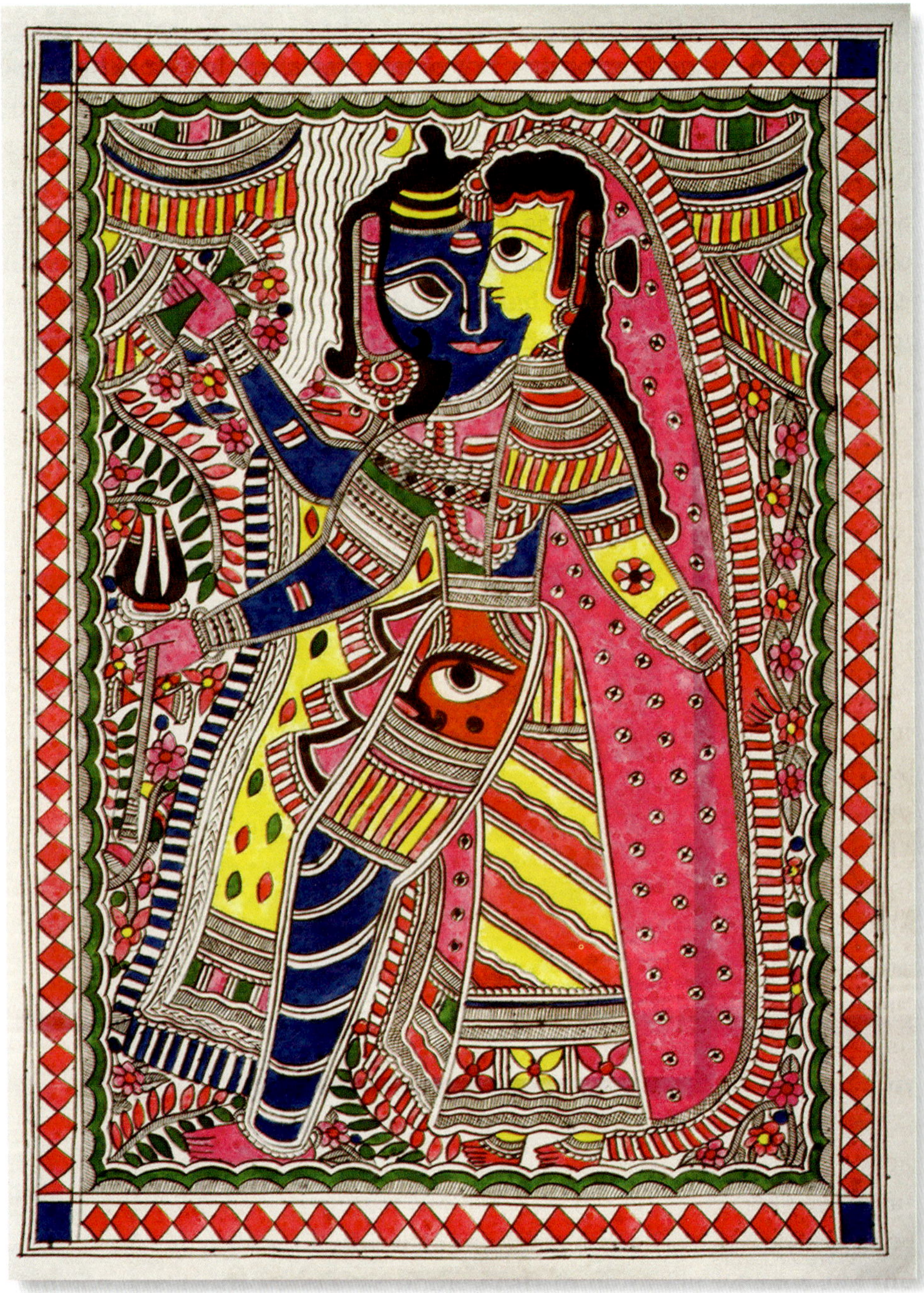

Ardhanari, Madhubani, 20th century

through the expressive eyes of Krishna and the expectant looks of the *gopis*. It is as if the words and songs of the Mithila poet Vidyapati are heard in these rustic but evocative paintings of Madhuban, and the women of Madhuban express their latent and often suppressed romantic feelings. Another ritual painting in Madhuban is the *aripan* or the floor diagram. This is done with the same bright colours and incorporates Tantric motifs and depictions of deities, and is a part of every ritual and ceremony. The women of Mithila believe that if an *aripan* is properly done the deity will come and reside in it and bless their household. The world of gods and goddesses is never far from the day to day world of commerce and daily existence, and this makes these creations of the women of Mithila not art but objects of beauty.

Using the human body our poets and *shilpis*, in a bold step of creative imagination, came up with the androgyn concept of the *ardhanarishvara*, bringing the bodies of Shiva and Parvati together, where the two are in a state of dynamic harmony, biune unity, two as in one. Not only is this a feat of artistic creativity but, even more importantly, it is a spectacular visual illustration of the coming together of Purusha and Prakriti, spirit and matter, man and woman, where each maintains their identity but blends seamlessly into the other. It is an image where dichotomies and binaries dissolve and suggest beautifully the oneness of the human mind which can hold two opposites together, where there is no fragmentation but only the serenity of holistic oneness, where there is no hierarchy but two threads blending together into a seamless fabric. If the *ardhanarishvara* is a coming together of Shiva and Parvati, the image of Harihara is an assurance that Shiva and Vishnu are not two separate identities, the two *sampradayas* are not in opposition but can easily blend into one another into *brahman*. On the surface Shiva and Parvati, Shiva and Vishnu are distinct and separate but on contemplation they are two facets of a higher reality which cannot be separated.

Let us listen to a village potter who has come to the Museum. "I am deeply impressed by the beautiful images in your Sculpture Gallery but it does not reflect the joyous abandon of making images in rural India. We do not follow any canons of image-making but create a variety of images spontaneously from mud and then bake them. We make images for fairs and festivals, for ancestor worship, for home shrines, for children and what these images lack in artistic finesse they more than make up in their earthy splendour. We the potters are the primal *shilpis*, and do you not think that these classical temple image makers learnt something from us? Did they not assimilate some of our motifs and metaphors into their art?" There was a stunned silence in the Gallery, and we wondered why there was none of these rural terracotta images here.

It has been a very pleasant time that we have spent in the Sculpture Gallery, where we have been touched by the beauty and grandeur of the hierarchal scuptures, even though they have been removed from their original home, we have remembered the *shilpis* who crafted the images even though we do not know their names, and the patron who remains anonymous to us who made all this happen. Even as we prepare to leave one cannot help but bring to mind the countless other images that have stood silently inspiring *rasikas* and *bhaktas* alike for centuries, images such as the *Surasundari*s of the Ran ki Vav at Patan, the erotic images at Khajuraho, the *dikpalas* at many temples, the magnificent recumbent Vishnu as Ranganathan, the fluting Krishna at Halebid, the imposing Shiva Linga as Brihadisvara in Thanjavur, the bedecked Radha at the Govind Devji temple in Jaipur and countless other images that have timeless beauty and which will whisper that there is a civilisation that makes ancient stones come alive, that invite and beckon us and stand in mute testimony to the genius of the Indian mind.

As the first part of the journey of our icons ends another should begin. So far we have engaged with various objects and are now aquainted with its surface features, its *shaksat artha*. But these beautiful objects of beauty have another level of experience, a *paroksha artha*, a deeper more contemplative meaning waiting to be had. At this second, later and more contemplative moment, we go inwards, decode metaphors and enjoy the suggested meanings, deconstruct the object into its geommetrical components and let it work on our psyche, be touched by the movements inherent in the object and even more rest in moments of serenity within the object, listen to the voices of the colours and textures, and when we do this we become one with the creator of the object. We are transformed into a *sahradaya*. The objectivity of the various objects disappears and we are in a serene, inward, subjective aesthetic experience. It is this step that transforms the *rupa* to *arupa*, form to formlessness. The *rupa* or the icon is endowed with an inner reality of rhythmic vitality and movement or *prana*. This could be called an aesthetic or inner adoration of the icon, in distinction to ritual worship that is performed with rites and rituals. The words of Tagore come to mind: "Art awakens a sense of the real by establishing an intimate relationship between our inner being and the iniverse at large bringing us a consciousness of deep joy."[12]

The Museum objects reside in the allotted space with academic curatorial notes attached to them. But when we seek their *paroksha artha* through aesthetic contemplation, the objects are released from their bondage in the Museum, and enter our mind and send waves of *ananda* as we are touched by human creativity. Human creativity is all about the joyousness of creation, of giving form to formless abstract sensations. We, who have engaged with the object must partake of the primal *ananda* of the artist and when we do that we are not far from the cosmic creator. It is this that lifts the enjoyment of our journey to a more transcendent level, and even as we return to our quotidian life these beautiful objects will whisper and sing, dance and speak to us.

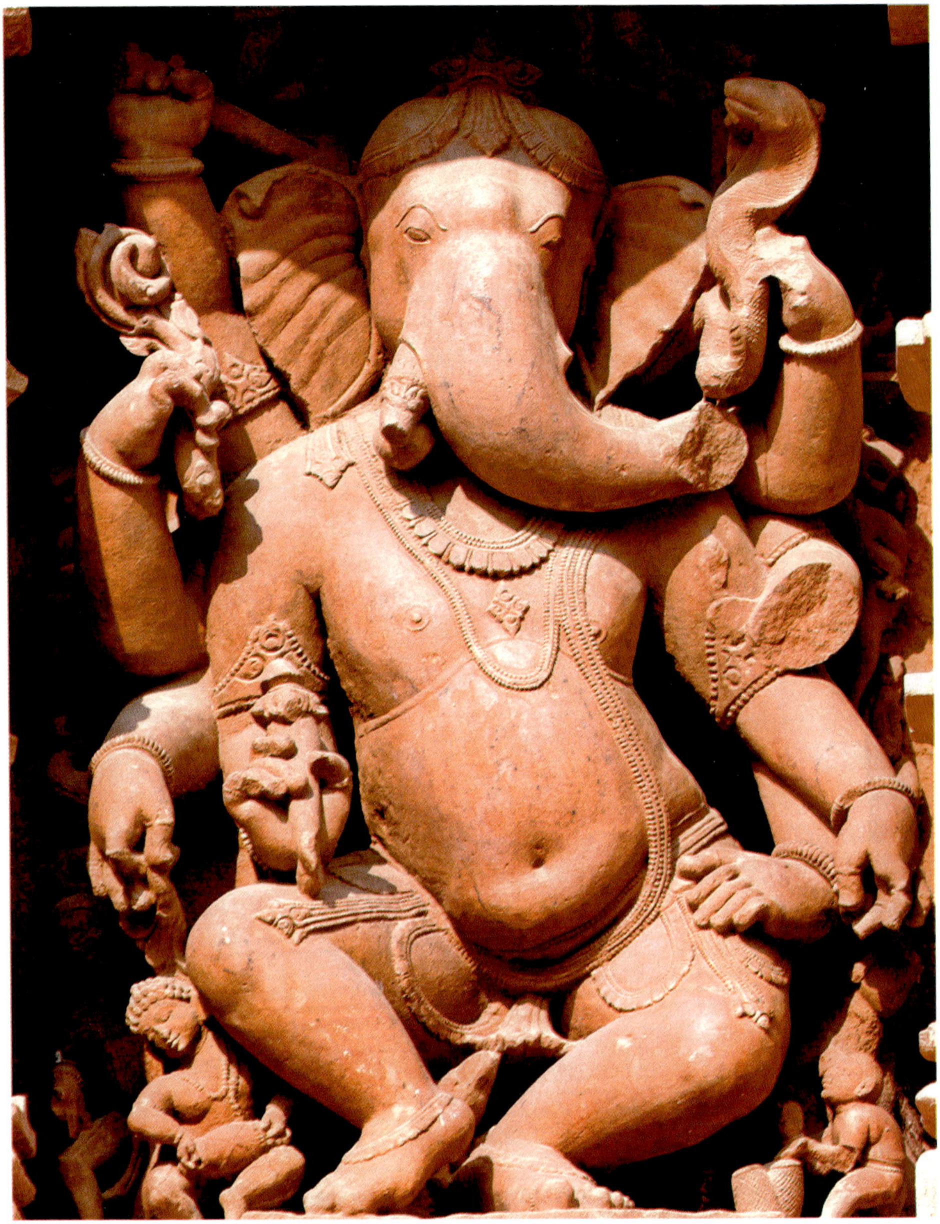

Ganapati as Scribe, Khajuraho, 11th century.
Photograph courtesy: Devangana Desai

Beautiful is the Word

The Word is Beautiful

In a civilisation that lays great store in orality it is interesting that the art of the written word in many different forms is also an important aesthetic consideration. The written word was part of manuscripts, but also of scrolls, paintings, edicts, *farmans*, letters, invitations and much more. Just as the spoken word does not stand alone but is to be sung or chanted, the written word also is adorned in different ways, which takes us back to the difference between *bhasha* and *vani* or ordinary speech and inspired speech. In adorning and beautifying words, both spoken and written, we are ensuring a certain sacrality and beauty to those words. Despite that, the written word has a secondary position in our tradition.

The book, as we know it today, was certainly chronologically late for us in India, both in content and format, and ancient books are best called manuscripts, as they could be in the form of a bunch of palm leaves or even earlier on cloth. For several centuries books for us were *pothis* or a collection of unbound palm leaves held together by a string and protected by a wooden cover. The shape and the size of the palm leaf and the way in which it was read was so firmly impressed on the Indian mind that even today it is the preferred way of creating a sacred book.

Although the Indus Valley civilisation had a hieroglyphic script, our understanding of it is that they were marks on a trading seal, and while interesting in many different ways, they cannot be considered in our survey of Indian words. Similarly pictographs in pre-historic murals in caves must also be excluded in our survey for even though they may have embodied some sort of language they were not words in our current understanding.

The written word for us has a chequered history. While Sanskrit as a language and Devnagari as a script is so dear to us, both of them were later creations

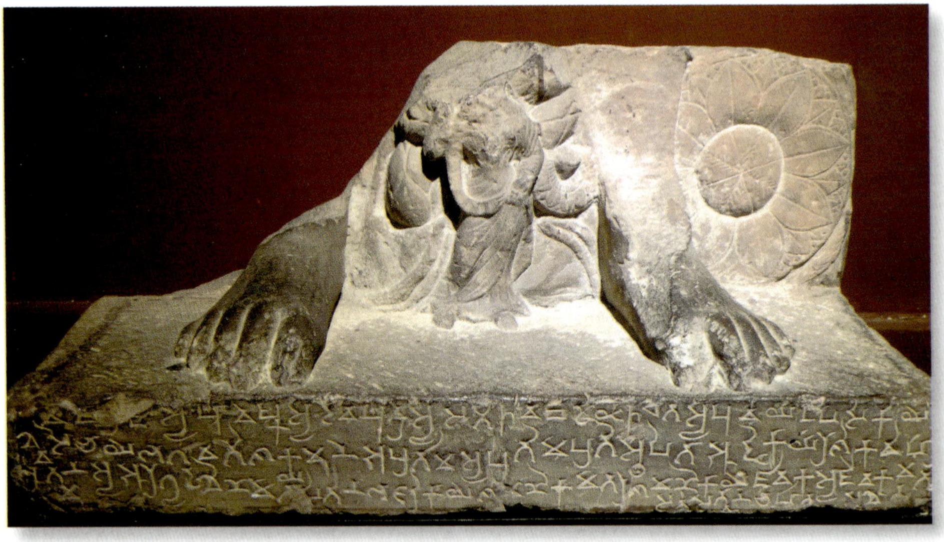

Inscription of the reign of the Kushana King Huvishka on the pedestal of Buddha image in the Brahmi script. Mathura, Uttar Pradesh, 123 BCE

when it came to the written word. As a script, Brahmi was the first to create the written word, and it was Prakrit that was the language that was used and this is what is used in the Ashokan edicts. The Ashokan edicts on pillars or rocks remain the oldest written records for us. These edicts are to be found scattered in more than 30 places in the subcontinent. Generally placed on major trade routes, the edicts proclaimed the emperor's personal beliefs as well as advice to his officers and people. The language of these edicts is Magadhi and it is written in conversational rather than didactics style. Mixed with sincerity there is a puritanical streak in Ashoka's character. He refers to

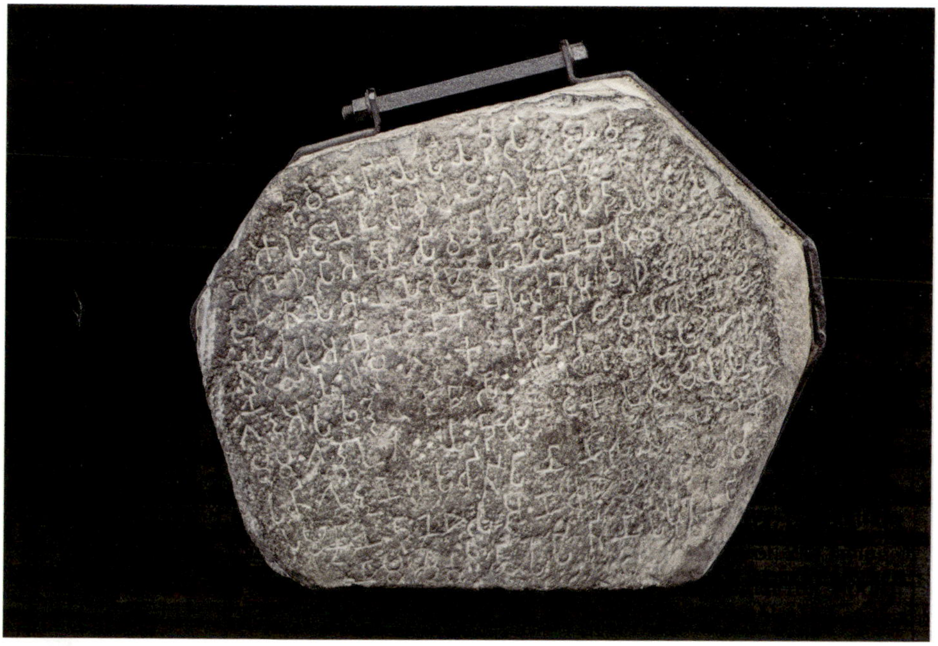

This fragment of the Ashoka edict comes from the ancient port town of Sopara in Thane. In the mid-3rd century Ashoka sent one of his missionaries, Dhammarakshita to Sopara. The edict states: King Devanampriya Priyadars speaks. Men perform various ceremonies during illness, at a marriage of a son or daughter, at the birth of a child and when setting out on a journey. On these and other such occasions men perform many useless ceremonies. Ceremonies should certainly be performed. But these ceremonies bear little fruit. The following bears much fruit namely the practice of morality which includes courtesy to slaves and servants, reverence to elders, gentleness to animals, liberality to *brahmana*s and *shramana*s, these and other such virtues are called the practice of morality.

himself as beloved of the gods, king Piyadasi. The purpose of these edicts was not only to instruct the people in *dhamma,* but commitment to peace through Buddhist principles. Soon after Ashoka's death these edicts were forgotten but despite that they remain a historic record of the written word in ancient India. Whie some have argued that the Brahmi script was derived from the Aramaic script, the consensus is that it was developed in the Gangetic region, and very soon it became pan-Indian. According to epigraphers all Indian scripts are derived from Brahmi. Another ancient script was Kharoshti which interestingly was written from right to left while in Kashmir it was the Sharada script that was used. The Devnagari script emerged around the 7th century. The further development of scripts in India depended on the material on which it was written. While in the South scripts became more rounded as a result of writing on palm leaves, in the North it was more

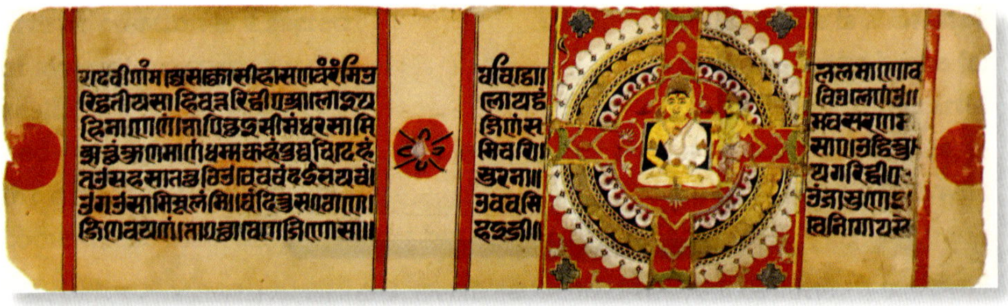

Kalpasutra and Kalakacharya Katha, Patan, c. 1375

angular as the material was cloth and birch bark. However one needs to raise the question as to the extent of literacy in ancient, India and if this was not that widespread the average person may have become privy to the Ashokan edicts by someone reading it out to them.

Questions of antiquity are always hard to answer in the Indian tradition but since the Hindu mind is so comfortable with myths, the story of Vyasamuni dictating the *Mahabharata* to Ganesha should be considered as the beginning of the written word for us. Equally interesting is the story of Shiva who was performing an *ananda tandava* and Ganesha was sitting by his side trying to copy every movement of his father by strokes and dashes, dots and curves, and this was the beginning of the written word. Both mythic stories point to the sacred origins of the written word.

Every now and again pre-historic manuscripts are discovered in ancient trade routes or in the attics of homes which keeps on pushing back the date of the oldest manuscript. The case of the Gilgit and the Afghanistan manuscripts takes the date back to the 1st century CE. It would be safe to say that hundred of thousands of manuscripts must lie buried or hidden in unknown places in India, and the extant material is only a minuscule part of the total manuscript production in the Indian civilisation. This inquiry can hardly do justice to the entire manuscript tradition of India and the history of the written word.

The Hindu penchant was for the spoken word, and it seems certain that the first impulse to write and create a book came from the Buddhists and the Jains, rather than the Hindus, where in the heterodox traditions there was a desire by the devotees to record the master's words before they were forgotten or misunderstood. Added to this were the divisions that took place, especially in the Jain community, and divergent interpretations that were likely to emerge from opposing factions. While the Buddhist manuscripts like the Prajnaparamita were created for the monks and stored in the monastery, in the Jain tradition it was common for the Jain nobility or a rich merchant to commission a manuscript and then endow it to the Jain *bhandara* for religious merit. While the early Buddhist manuscripts were created in eastern India and Nepal, the Jain manuscripts must have been made in Gujarat, probably Patan.

Another part of the Jain culture are the illustrated manuscripts which go seamlessly from the lay devotee to the ordained monk, from homes to temples, from scribes to painters and from aesthetics to theology. In a predominantly oral culture, the sacred word was preserved by the select few and remained engraved in the collective memory, as this was basic to the Indian way of thinking and living. The supremacy of the oral tradition continued until about the 4th century BCE, and at that time there was a need and a desire to relegate the sacred teachings of Jain masters to writing although there is no historical evidence of this. It was the time when a severe famine struck the

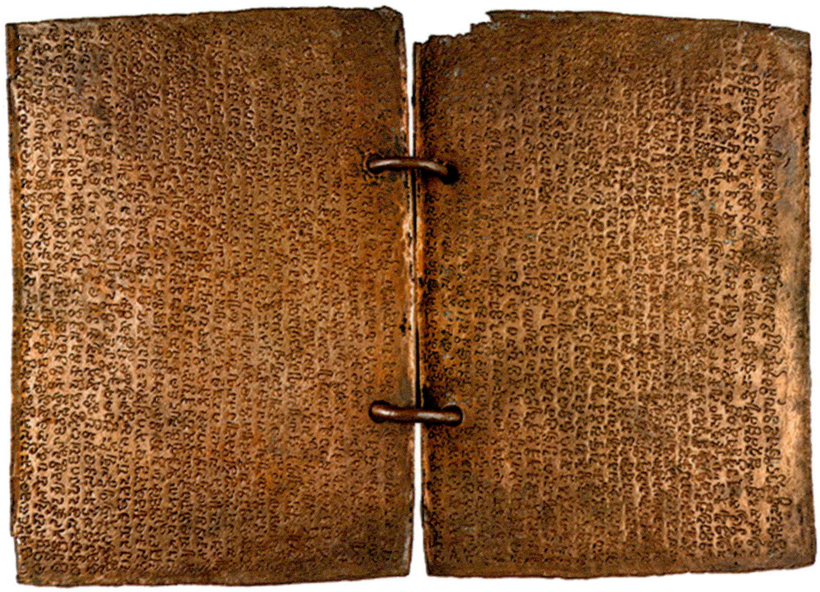

Copper plates or *tamra patras*, also called *raja sasanas*, were a common form of documentation which had both regal authority and permanence and were used especially for land grants by a king to an individual or a temple.The practice started in the early years of the Christian era and continued well into the 17th century when paper replaced it. It was common for these copper plates to begin with a panegyric salutation to the king suggesting that the contents of the plate were read out by the town crier so that the whole village or community could hear it. The permanency of the decree was further strengthened by phrases such as “as long as the sun and the moon shine.”As legal documents, copper-plate grants are distinct from other early metal inscriptions, which are dedicatory, votive or performative. Among the treasures of the Tirupati temple are 2691 plates for approximately 1300 poems by the famous Annamaya from the 17th century. This is described as possibly the most expensive publishing project.

region of Magadha and a large body of monks migrated to the south. Of the monks who remained in Magadha many died of starvation, and those who remained suffered memory lapses. Unlike the Hindus, the Jains had not inherited a monolithic tradition of divine origin and felt the need to record the word of the master.

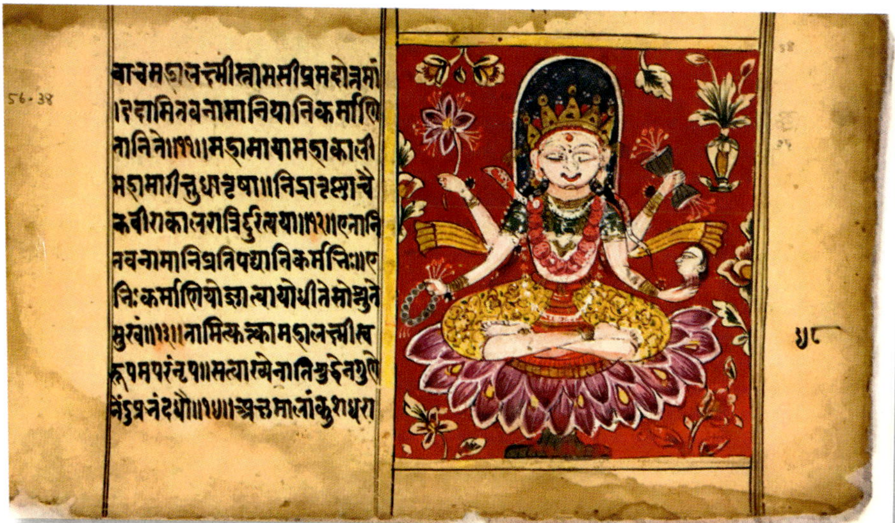

Devi Mahatmya, Surat, 1719 CE

To recover and preserve the teachings a council of monks was convened at Patliputra where the learned assembly compiled the extant sections of their canonical teaching. However, there was a split in the community between the Southern, who were the Digambaras and the Northern, who became the Shvetambara, as to the authenticity of the recorded wisdom and even more of their behaviour. The Shvetambara Jains summoned a council of monks at Mathura in the 4th century CE and thereafter convened two at Vallabhi in Saurashtra. It was the Vallabhi conclave in the 6th century CE that was the most constructive. It was there that the Jain scripture was finally redacted, and therefore, this date can be considered as the date that the Jain scripture was written down. There is a 2nd century CE stone figure of Saraswati holding a Jain mansucript in the Patna Museum which indicates that the practice of creating such manuscripts must have been quite ancient.

However due to a variety of reasons, it was not until the 8th century with the appointment of Bhattaraka or the head of a Jain religious establishment that sacred manuscripts began to be created. The Bhattarakas encouraged the creation and donation of sacred Jain manuscripts to the *bhandaras* of Jain temples, and thus a large number of manuscripts were produced. The Bhattarakas were zealous collectors of manuscripts, and the *bhandaras* of Jain temples soon acquired a number of manuscripts on a variety of subjects. It is a matter of great regret that none of the manuscripts from that time has survived, either because of ravages of nature or of invaders. During the 11th and 12th centuries, a number of manuscripts were transcribed in eastern India, at Buddhist centres in Bengal and Bihar. The Prajnaparamita was the most common manuscript to be created on palm leaf with small miniature paintings of the Buddha. This Eastern Indian style of painting came to an abrupt end in the 13th century when the iconoclastic Islamic armies swept across the plains.

One of the most popular Jain manuscripts to have been created and donated was the Kalpasutra attributed to Acharya Bhadrabahu, and the earliest extant manuscript is from the 14th century like the folio in our Museum. The first illustration is of Mahavira, and comes from the beginning of the text, which introduces the story of Mahavira and the structure of the five *kalyanakas* or auspicious events that frame the life of every Jina. The Jina is specifically identifiable as Mahavira due to the *lakshana* or identifying mark found in the throne directly beneath the seated Jina. In this case it is a lion, the *lakshana* of Mahavira. The second illustration shows the new-born infant Mahavira in the arms of his mother Trishala and provides the date of birth as Chaitra Shukla Trayodasi.

The Sutradhar reminds us that the next question is the origin and style of paintings that illuminate these Jain manuscripts. We are sure that none of the manuscripts before the 10th century was illustrated. The earliest available palm leaf manuscripts today are from the 11th century, from Jaisalmer where the painting style is similar to the frescoes of Ajanta and Ellora. Over the centuries this evolved, in what is now called the Early Western Indian style, with its taut wiry figures and the further eye. These manuscripts featured iconic representations of the Tirthankaras, monks, lay devotees and even donors. However the paintings bear no connection with the text and are placed only for their magical value which served to augment the mystical truths as well as to protect them. These miniatures played an esoteric, rather than an aesthetic role. This is not to deny its beauty through robust colours and ornamentation reminiscent of Gujarat textiles. Some of the ornamentation is suggestive of the Patola sari, which therefore makes it very likely that our Kalpasutra was created in Patan, the ancient capital of Gujarat. The Kalpasutra, among the many Jain manuscripts, had a strong ritual function. It was during the four rainy months, the *chaturmasa*, that Jain monks rest in temples and undergo spiritual cleansing and the Jain laity aspire to spiritual upliftment. An important part of this is the reading of the Kalpasutra. This practice started around the 5th century CE and has continued until today. This ritual required the ready availability of the Kalpasutra, and that is why it is the most reproduced sacred text of the Jains. These manuscripts were lavishly illustrated and had beautiful miniature paintings. Not only was the Kalpasutra able to keep the lives of Tirthankaras alive but equally preserve their teachings, and in the tradition of illustrated manuscripts the Kalpasutra has a pride of place. In being ritually potent the Kalpasutra, at least for the lay devotee, was an object of veneration more than of knowledge. While Gujarat was the main centre for the creation of the Kalpasutra, Mandu and Jaunpur also had important ateliers. When one sees the evolution of the Kalpasutra from the 14th into the 16th century, one sees the transformation of the Western Indian style of painting into the Chaurapanchashika style. Combining aesthetic finesse along with ritual function, the Kalpasutra is a delight for the eyes and a source of spiritual *sadhana*.

One of the earliest Buddhist manuscripts was that of the *Prajnaparamita*, a sacred text of the Buddhists. Done on palm leaf, the manuscript was represented mainly, the text illuminated with small paintings usually of the eight miracles of Buddha's life. These paintings were unconnected with the text and had a magical and protective function. The manuscript was decorated with geometrical designs in the margins, and very often had decorations around the hole through which was passed the string to hold the leaves together.

When one thinks of sacred words it is Vasant Panchami, the fifth day of the bright half of *Maghashirsha*, that comes to mind. On this day, and in Bengal in particular, women dress in yellow, and goddess Saraswati who holds a book in one hand is worshipped along with sacred books and writing implements. Very often the child's first lesson is performed on this day and the sacred word as the source of knowledge is recognised and venerated. Most Hindus hold any book, whether or not it is sacred, in reverence, for they feel that Saraswati resides in every book.

While writing in ancient India may have taken place on copper, stone or cloth, manuscripts were produced either on birch bark or palm leaves. Bhurja *patra* or birch bark was used in ancient India, particularly for Buddhist manuscripts as the tree grew in the Himalayas. Another tree was the Sanchi or the Aloe which grew in the valley of the Brahmaputra and was used in that region for writing. However, the most popular writing material were leaves of the Talipot, exclusively in South India, and the Palmyra palm which became the universal medium for creating manuscripts until it was replaced by paper. The association of sacred manuscripts or *pothis* with palm leaf was so strong in the Indian mind that even after paper was available certain regions like Odisha continued to make manuscripts on palm leaf, and even more, artists would use paper in the shape of the leaf. Anything sacred or important, in Indian view, must be in the *pothi* format.

Indian scribes developed an expertise in working with palm leaves. The palm leaf was harvested even when it was green, boiled, dried, pressed and polished. An iron stylus was used to write on the prepared leaves, charcoal black was smeared and then cleaned with sand. Leaves of the *pothi* were not bound, not because the method was not known, but when each leaf was loose it could be held in the hand and passed on to others who were present so that the text could be shared. However, the leaves were held together by a cord going through a single hole on the left side. Later, two holes were made, although it was the left hole that was functional. The leaves were then protected with a wooden cover or *patli*, which would be decorated or painted with an appropriate image. Sometimes cloth purse-like covers with embroidery were used to keep the loose leaves together.

In the entire genre of illustrated manuscripts the Jain tradition of the *Kalpasutra* is perhaps the most evocative and remains the gold standard in the many splendoured world of manuscripts. There is some evidence, going by the Gilgit manuscripts, that paper may have been available in India as early as the first millennium. However, the late 13th century is when paper was freely available in India and replaced palm leaf, though not totally, as the preferred writing material.

The second millennium saw a sustained activity in the area of manuscripts, and the presence of Islam in the country was one of the driving factors. Mughals, and Akbar in particular, was a bibliophile and his atelier teemed with scribes and artists; some of the finest manuscripts like the *Hamzanama* and *Tutinama* were made at that time. What the Islamic book culture also did was to encourage the royalty and the nobility to patronise the creation of manuscripts in their atelier, not for religious but for aesthetic reasons.

The Hindu penchant for the *pothi* was not totally lost as paper was cut in the shape of the palm leaf and horizontal manuscripts were created. The Islamic courts however, preferred the vertical codex format and Hindu courts followed suit, and this started the transformation from *pothi* to *chitravali* where a number of painted pages in the vertical codex format were kept together.

Before that however, it is interesting to note the many different ways in which manuscripts were made. *A Kurma Purana* manuscript was made in the shape of a tortoise, a *Gita Govinda* manuscript was made on beads of palm leaf and strung together like a necklace, some palm leaves were cut like the shape of a bird. In Odisha, where palm leaf manuscripts are still created, they are sometimes made in the shape of a fan or a concertina. And then there are scrolls where pictures tell a story. The many scrolls of Andhra come to mind. Land grants and imperial *farmans* are also beautifully created either on stone or paper. Astrological charts and astronomical positions are also made. Afflictions of horses and elephants are documented, mathematical puzzles are illustrated and made in the form of books. Of special interest are *gutkas* or prayer and chap books made for the devotee which are easily portable and read even when away from home or temple. While patrons who

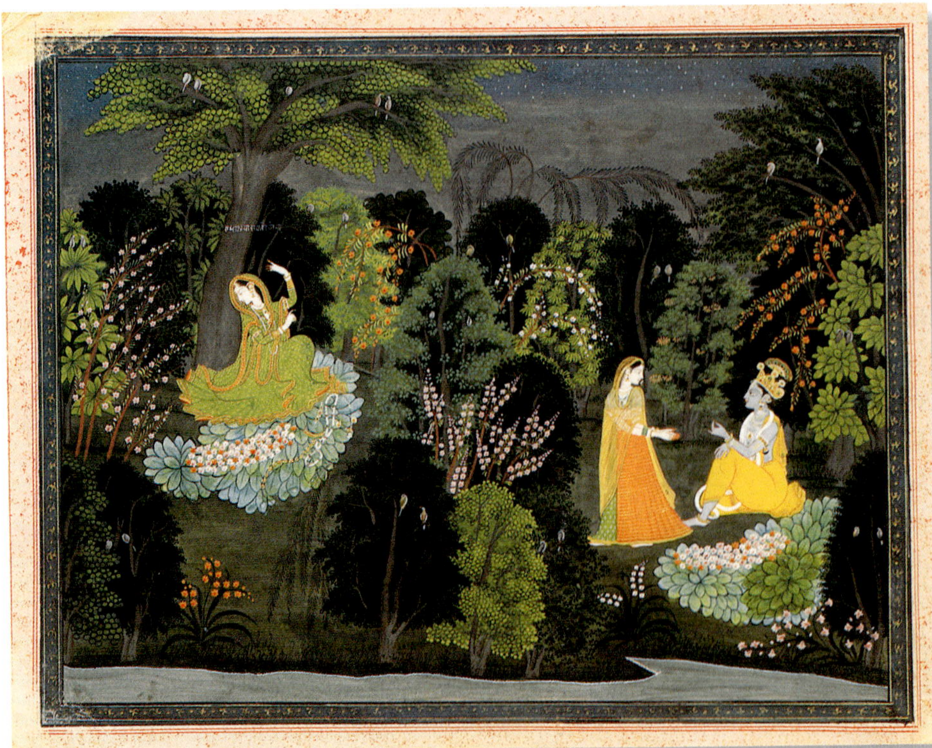

This lavishly-painted *Gita Govinda* comes from the late 18th/early 19th century Guler in the Pahari region. What is noteworthy is that the written text has totally disappeared. The artist was confident that the images that he created were able to stand and speak for themselves without the written word.

commissioned the creation of manuscripts must be remembered, the scribes and the artists are the real creators of manuscripts and scrolls.

The scribes valued their creations as scribal notes like this attest:

> This manuscript needs to be adored like a beloved child; to be guarded from others' hands like a virtuous wife; to be treated tenderly like an injured limb of one's body; to be looked up every day like a good friend; to be kept tied securely with strong cords like a prisoner; and to be seen as a reminder of the Lord's name.

The scribes were a profession to themselves, and it is known that they would go from town to town offering their services. In particular, peripatetic Kashmiri scribes were well known. While the tasks of the scribes was laborious and the act of creating a manuscript was considered sacred, what is disappointing is that the quality of calligraphy in Hindu manuscripts, as compared with Islamic manuscripts, was poor. The obvious reason is that while the Hindus lay great store in the spoken word, for the Muslims the written word was a reflection of divinity.

To write about the written word in a single essay is an impossible task. Miniature paintings afford us another opportunity to study how words are used along with the text. The relation between text and image is brought out when we see the evolution of miniature paintings. One of the earliest Hindu manuscripts were of the *Bhagavata Purana* in Gujarat of the 15th/16th centuries. These paintings were done in the *pothi* format, and almost half the space was reserved for the text. As paintings evolved from the horizontal *pothi* to the vertical codex style, and this was to happen first in Malwa, the text was reduced to a band at the top of the painting but there was correspondence between the text and the image. In the Rajput period this practice was continued, but when we enter the Pahari period of miniature painting the text disappeared and, only sometimes, would be written at the back of the paintings. Pahari artists were so confident of their creations that they felt that the paintiings could stand on their and the text was unnecessary. Most miniature paintings arise from a bedrock of *sahitya*, and both text and image should be read and seen concurrently. It behooves both the scholar of Hindi and Braj literature and the connoisseur of miniature paintings to heed this suggestion.

Just as an aniconic tradition burst into a thousand images, a tradition that staunchly preferred to remain oral, blossomed into countless manuscripts covering a wide variety of subjects, from Purana to *kavya*, astronomy to medicine, folk tales to moralising stories, texts on the care of elephants and horses and mathematical puzzles. The world of Hindu manuscripts is one of magic and erudition, of the world of patrons and scribes, of artists and librarians, of merit-seeking nobility to knowledge-seeking devotees, of

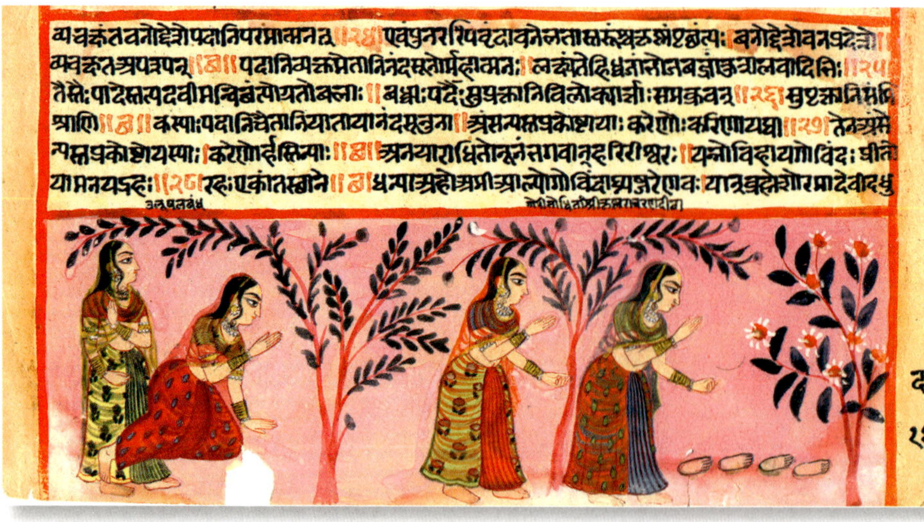

One of the first texts to be transformed into a miniature painting was the *Bhagavata Purana* in Gujarat in the 16th century. Gujarat prides itself in Krishna *bhakti* and it already had a talent of scribes and painters who had created Jain manuscripts, and it was not difficult for them to work on Hindu themes. What is interesting is that the written word and the painted space are almost equal.

bhandaras and libraries, of marriage alliances and dowries, but above all the universe of manuscripts is a testament of the Hindu mind that venerated the word and celebrated the manuscript, adorning it and ensuring that the word in which it was kept was beautiful. While the calligraphy *per se* would not be exceptional the entire document, whether on palm leaf, paper, stone or metal would be exquisite. The Hindu veneration of the spoken word as *vak* is well known, so is the association of *vak* with Saraswati the goddess of learning. It is interesting that the Hindus accord the same veneration to manuscripts and books. Not just religious books, but all books are considered a repository of knowledge and are respected. Sacred books are especially venerated, given a *vastra* and covered with a fabric, put on a pedestal, adorned as if it were an icon. In the Sattras of Assam where Shankardeva ushered in Vaishnavism in the 16th century, the *Bhagavata Purana* assumes an iconic position as there were no other icons, and the book is wrapped in the Vrindavani *vastra* and venerated. The Guru Granth Sahib in Gurudwaras and the home shrine also comes to mind. The worship of ledger books, a day before Diwali is also another instance where the book, rather than an icon is worshipped.

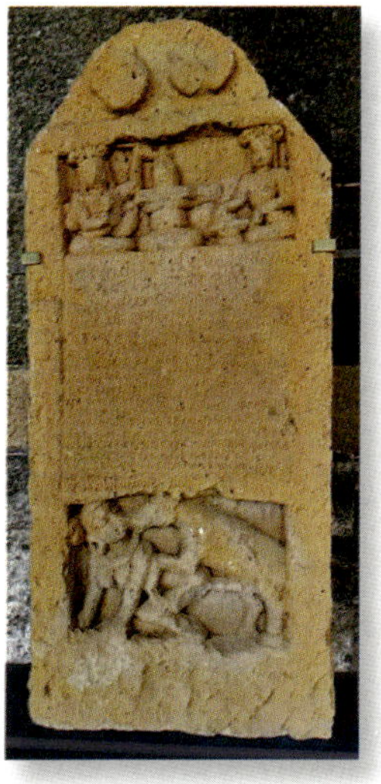

Gadhegal shila, Maharashtra, 11th century

An unusual edict are what are called "ass-curse-stones" or more crudely *gadhegal shila*. These are stone edicts generally pertaining to land grants. What is unusual about them is the punishment that is spelt out. "If anyone violates this order, a donkey will have congress with your mother". These stone slabs are found scattered in Maharashtra and Goa, and even in Mumbai. The vertical stone slabs typically feature three panels: the top panel depicts a round sun and crescent moon, the middle contains an inscription in the

Devnagari script (or, in some rare cases, Arabic) and the panel at the bottom shows the striking image of the donkey-woman intercourse. According to some archaeologists the woman featured on the stones is symbolic of mother earth, or fertility. The donkey is the *vahana* (vehicle) of Sitala Devi, the goddess of pestilence and plague, whose cult was very strong during the 11th century Shilahara period. At that time, there was also a widely-held belief that if a person's farm were ploughed by donkeys, they would become fallow and barren. The donkey and its protruding phallus, then, become symbolic of such ploughing.

In fact, there is a well-known Shivaji legend in Maharashtra that invokes this idea. In the 1630s, the Adilshahi ruler Rayarao had sacked Pune and it is said to have had the land there ploughed by donkeys. Around that time, a young Shivaji came to live in Pune with his mother Jijabai, and when they saw the ruins that Pune was is, he had the lands re-ploughed with a golden blade. The gold was symbolic of the light of the sun, and after that Pune is said to have flourished again. The study of the ass-curse stones reveals that such a tradition of land grants and sexual threats was popular for nearly 250 years during the Shilahara rule, and the location of the stones reveals the extent of the dynasty's reign. In South Mumbai, for instance, there is an 800-year-old *gadhegal* at Pimpalwadi in Girgaum that is now worshipped as a local deity by devotees visiting the a nearby Shiva temple.

A survey of the written word cannot be complete without looking briefly at letters or epistolary art. Even though they may not be in verse they are nonetheless very beautiful. *Patracarca* or epistolary art has an ancient history and could be traced back to the enigmatic hieroglyphics of the Indus Valley seals. One encounters a variety of letters in Sanskrit and Prakrit, and this includes letters such as *vijnanapatras* or letters by Jain devotees on certain auspicious occasions, *rajapatra* or epistles by kings, *dutakavyas* or an entire poem like Kalidasa's Meghadutam in the form of a message, *patrakavyas* or long letters in verse like the Suhrilekha written by Nagarjuna to king Udayana extolling the virtues of Buddhism. Romantic letters are associated with Kama and therefore are called *anangalekha, madanalekha* or *manmathalekha*. They were written on leaves, such as those of lotus and *tamala*, petals of flowers or *bhurja* bark.

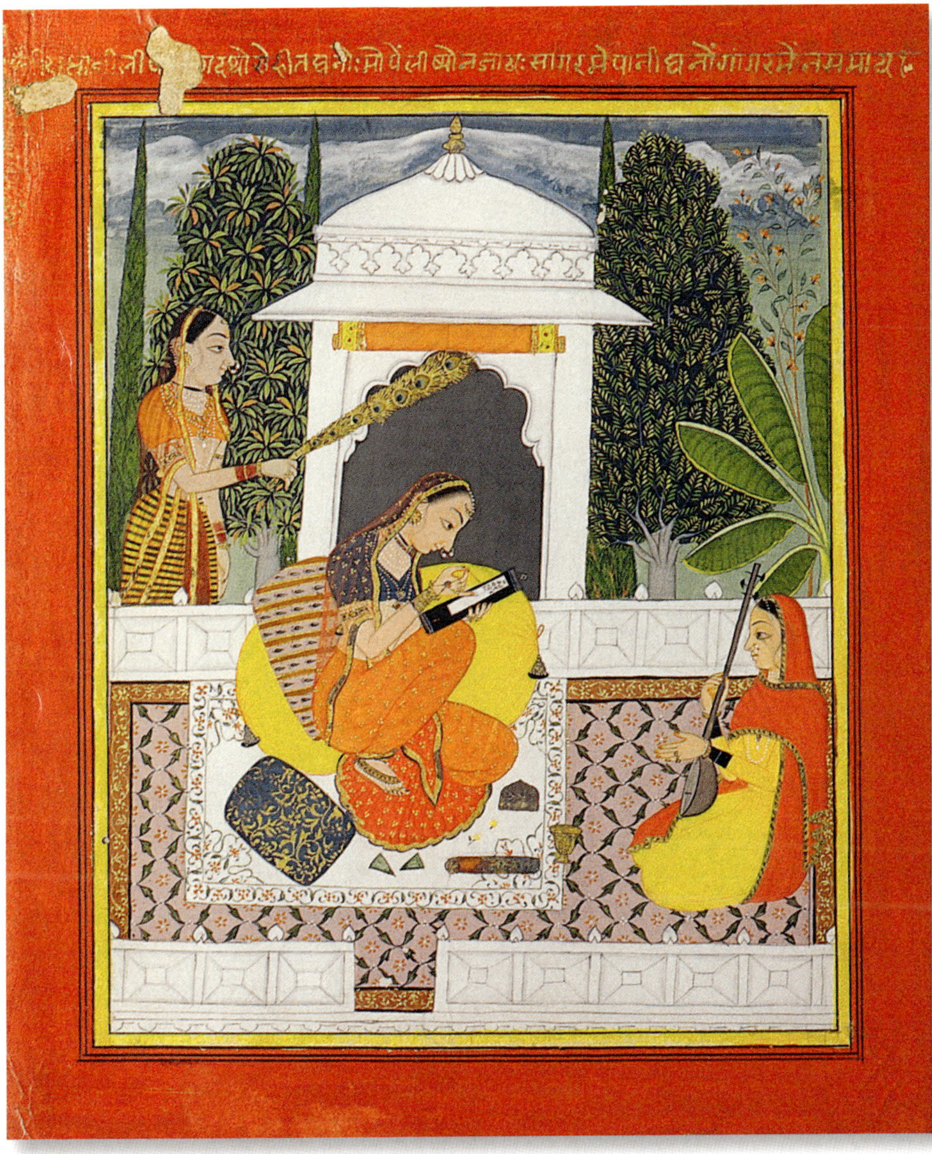

Love Letter. Pahari. 1820–40

Both Bharata in the *Natyashastra* and Vatsyayana in the *Kamasutra* refer to *patrahariduti* or love messengers, and in Sanskrit and Prakrit literature, messengers can be friends, servants, traders, birds and even clouds. As early as the *Bhagavata Purana* we encounter a long and moving love letter written by Rukmini to Krishna, asking him to come and rescue her before she is married off to Shisupala. In his *Lalitamadhava*, Rupa Gosvamin, the 16th century Bengal Vaishnavite recreates this episode, and Rukmini writes a letter that is taken to Krishna by a brahmin:

> O cloud of dark colour, let your sonorous sound deceive the opponent and deceive the peahen with a downpour of nectar. I am your expectant, do quench my thirst.

In the *Padmapurana* we come across this love letter written by Madhava on *mala* flowers to Sulochana whom he wished to marry:

> O damsel I have crossed the sea on my horse
> Please accept me as your life partner
> No other person other than me can fathom your excellence,
> as the beauty of a lotus is only appreciated by a bee but not by frogs.
> The planet Gemini and the cloud appear in the sky but the lily admires only the moon.[13]

Kalidasa celebrates love letters in his own unique way, when he writes in *Kumarasambhavam* that Vidyadhara maidens are seen to have incised throbbing of their hearts on the bark of *bhurja* trees. In another Kalidasa play Priyamvada asks Shakuntala to engrave a message with her nails on a lotus leaf, charming as a parrot's breast, which she will then carry concealed under flowers to Dushyanta. Not only do nails serve as a stylus but are a suggestion of Shakuntala's longing for her much cherished embrace by her beloved. In that letter she wrote:

> O ruthless one, I know not your heart, but day and night Kama exceedingly heats my limbs with my yearning for you.

In Banabhatta's *Kadambari* is found this delightful description of how a love letter is written. Pundarika plucks twigs from a Tamala tree and pounds these leaves on a stone to extracts their juice. He then writes with this juice on his *angavastra* and deputes Taralika to take it to his beloved Mahashveta. In the genre of epistolary creations romantic letters occupy a special place, and as Rabindranath once said, "Letters like tiny Jasmine flowers appear to be very small in shape but the environment wherein they flourish is as expansive as the creeper of Jasmine." For this, environment is not only the preparation of the materials on which the letter will be written and the tenderness with which it is inscribed, but equally its imaginative delivery

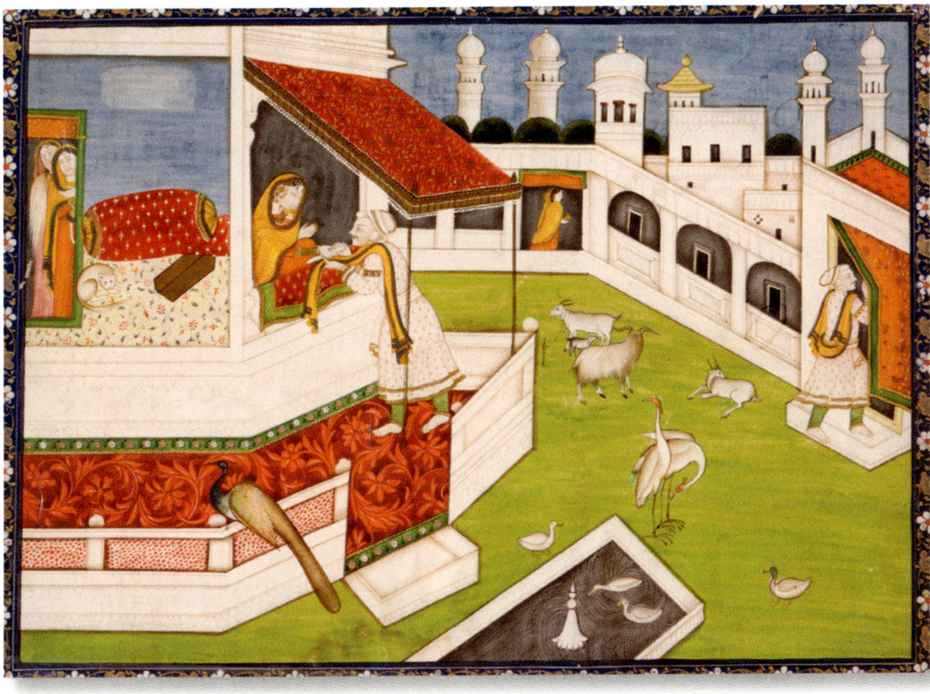

Rukmini sending a love letter, Pahari, 1820–40. Private Collection

and the thrill of its recipient. Within the few words of that romantic letter is hidden a whole gamut of emotions, an entire universe of excitement and anticipation, a complete alphabet of romance. More than poetry and not in so many words, and even more than what words and gestures can convey, a romantic letter is able to convey a certain urgency and immediacy, sincerity and intimacy of love, and therefore forms an important part of the corpus of romantic literature.

Fabric is another ancient material upon which we wrote. Here again the Buddhists were a step ahead of other communities, for they wrote *mantras* on fabric which they displayed as flags, which ensured that not only were spoken words written but also that the wind carried these words in all the eight directions. It is said that Chinese pilgrims returning home via the Silk Route carried Buddhist wisdom texts written on fabric.

So great was our desire to create manuscripts that we created treatises for the care of animals and birds which were also illustrated.

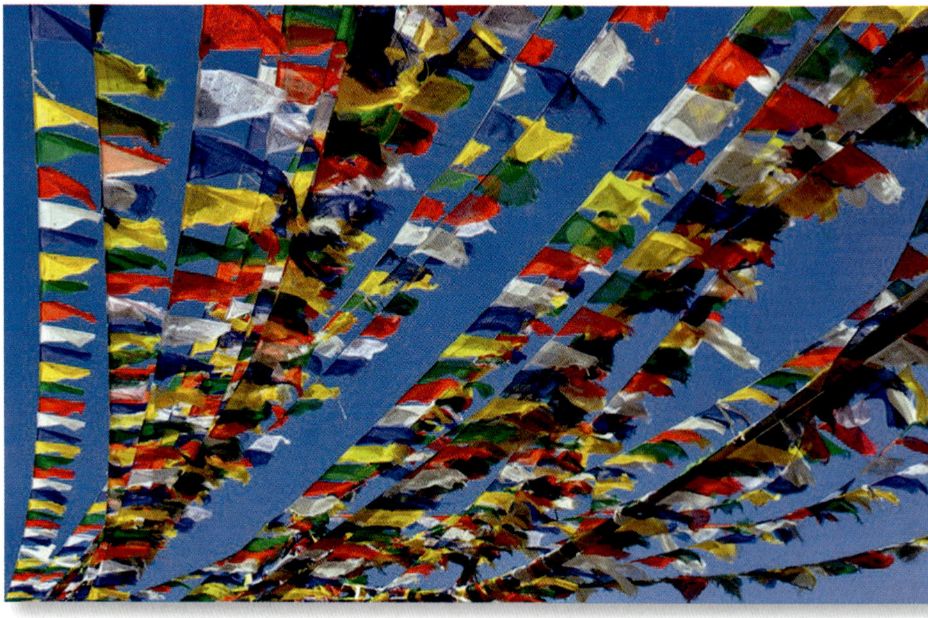

Buddhist Flags outside a Monastery in Sikkim

In passing, let us remember what are *chitra kavya* or word pictures. One of many examples, when a line is read from left to right it is about Rama, and when the same line is read from right to left it is about Krishna.

Here is one such example

तं भूसुतामुक्तमिुदारहासं वन्दे यतो भव्यभवम् दयाश्रीः ।

Taan bhoosuta mukti mudaarahaasan vande yato bhavan dayaashree ||

"I pay my homage to Him who rescued Sita, whose laughter is captivating, whose incarnation is grand, and from whom mercy and splendour arise everywhere."

श्रीयादवं भव्यभतोयदेवं संहारदामुक्तमितासुभूतम् ॥
Shree yaadavan bhavy latoy devan sanhaaradaamukti muta subhootaan ||

"I bow before that Sri Krishna, the descendant of Yadava family; who is a divinity of the sun as well as the moon; who destroyed Putana who only gave destruction; and who is the soul of this entire universe."[14]

In a country like ours where there is significant Islamic art and culture, a comparison between the Hindu and Islamic calligraphy is not out of place. While the Islamic civilisation has developed calligraphy to a very high level so that it can by itself suggest divinity, Hindu calligraphy mixes word with image. This is so because we do not have a proscription against depicting the sacred and the divine through images. One sees this coming together of word and image throughout the centuries. Manuscripts of most sacred texts are illustrated with paintings of varying sizes. Even a sacred text like *Jnaneshvari* is created combining words and appropriate images. Word and image for us are synaesthetic, one complementing the other. The written word in our hierarchy of the wisdom traditions occupies a lower place compared to the spoken word. As our journey of the written word comes to an end it is reasonable to ask why the written word is called *akshara* or that which is not destructible. One obvious reason is that once the word is written on stone or copper it outlasts the spoken word.

Even as our journey of *shabda* or the word ends, let us celebrate the creativity of both the scribe and the artist who ensure that the written word is beautiful.

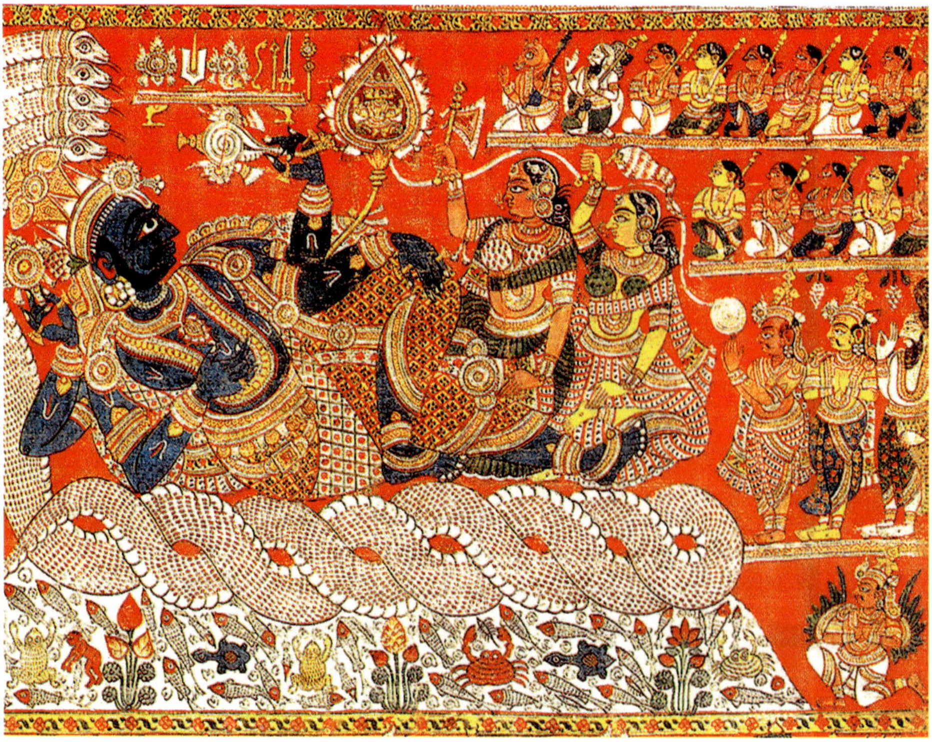

Telangana Scroll. 20th century. Jagdish & Kamala Mittal Museum of Art

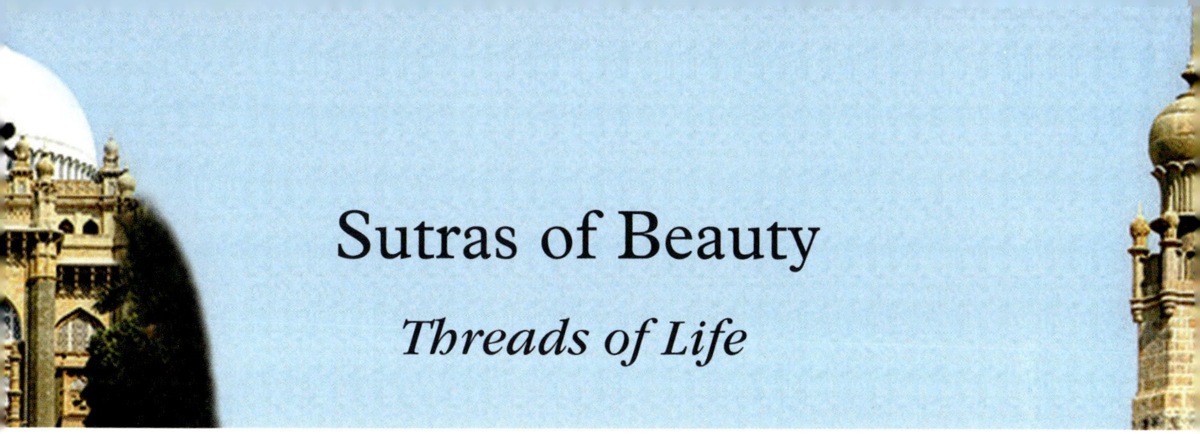

Sutras of Beauty

Threads of Life

As we enter the Textile Gallery we hear whispers of the sound of the loom, the hushed conversation of embroiderers and the dance of the *tulika*. It has been said that the history of India could be written with a thread. Equally, it can be said that it is with a vibrant and colourful thread that stitches together the joints and seams of the subcontinent's history. An important part of the Indian tradition are clothes and fabric. for they beautifully articulate emotions and feelings, narrate a story, and in many ways they are the most personal expressions of our mind. Clothes, both sacred and secular, have a protective function, they ornament the body, state the social and economic status of the person, store memories, express the wearer's persona and are markers of a tradition. We are concerned here about the fabrics and clothes of India, and how they express our view of life, and even more human creativity.

Fabric, and woven fabric in particular, have a pre-historic pedigree, and evidence of weaving has been discovered in the artefacts of the Indus Valley Civilisation. A number of temple fabric are known such as the Pichhwais of Nathadwara, the Matani Pachedi and Chandarvo of Gujarat and the Gita Govinda shawl of Orissa. However, at the ordinary level threads and fabric play an important part in the lives of the people. Threads connote continuity, a joining, a bond, an attachment, a union and can convey some of the deepest sentiments. It is said that it was Indrani who tied a thread to Indra in the *sangrama* of the *devas* and the *asuras*, and the thread became an amulet. Red and yellow-coloured threads are especially important in marriages and are used to sanctify ritual objects. Tying a thread around a tree, as is commonly done by women, is not only an act of worship but is to be identified with the fertility and fecundity of the tree. Rags or *odhnis* from an old sari or *odhni* play an important part for it is in these rags that wish or a prayer is tied and then entrusted to the tree, secure in the belief that not only does the tree understand the problem and the predicament but that the petition would be favourably considered. The *chindi* is not just a piece of fabric but a messenger who has been a part of the woman's body; it has wiped her tears and felt her heart throb, felt her pangs and has sheltered and protected her and knows only too well her pain. There could be no other trusted messenger to carry her prayer and petition. While trees are recipients of these petitions, there are icons called *chindi devis* where the only offerings to her are of *chindis* and where these petitions are favourably heard and answered

Fabrics are an important part of the Indian tradition be it cultural, personal, religious or aesthetic, and they have an ancient and mythic pedigree. The story is told of how the Padmashalis became the first weavers. When Vishnu was resting on the cosmic serpent Adishesha, Bhavana *rishi* plucked a fibre from the lotus that emerged from the navel of Vishnu and gave it to the Padmashalis and told them to weave fabrics for the gods. Weaving thus acquires a sacrality and legitimacy, and has a mythic presence.

Fabric can be both personal and private, as well as public and prized at the same time. They convey the warmth and intimacy of a beloved, and at the same time express loudly and majestically what it wishes to convey to the world at large. Fabrics can be private or public, for one's personal use or for the benefit of the community, whether it is courtly or the common. They can be created in the privacy of *chowks* of homes by housewives and her *sakhis*, or be commissioned by patrons and created by artists and weavers in ateliers and studios. Whether they are art fabric or everyday fabric they have a story to tell, and in its warp and woof is the human hand.

From times ancient we have used fabric to express some of our most cherished sentiments, whether it is to adorn or to decorate, to worship or to celebrate, to protect or to sanctify, to tell stories or to carry messages, as flags or as backdrops in our temples, as wall coverings in temples or homes, as scrolls or wraps and also to clothe our bodies. Both the creation and the wearing of fabric is considered sacred. Fabrics are central to the Indian world of art and adornment, rites and rituals, and also personal protection, privacy and dignity. A fragment of madder dyed cotton has been found at Indus Valley sites and it speaks of a highly sophisticated process of dyeing cotton even 5000 years ago. Also, Indigo vats have been discovered in artefacts of the Indus Valley, and this attests to the presence of the dyeing technology of Indigo in times pre-historic. Fabrics were one of the earliest items that were traded, and ancient Indian fabric have been found in many parts of the world; India was known the world over in times ancient and also modern for its beautiful and colourful fabrics. At Fostar in Egypt, and in Nigeria in Africa Indian fabrics going back to the 10th century BC have been found.

Rajeev Sethi is right in saying:

> Central to the aesthetic celebration of fabric is *pehchaan*. *Pehchaan* is the direct encounter with the fabric, its count, weight, structure and feel. It is the telling detail, the restraint and understatement, the abandonment in modulations of colour, luster, sheen…it indicates an understanding of when and how the fabric surpasses its kind; where exactly it falls short and why. It signifies a sense of context, proportion and of purpose. It implies the ability to visualise the fabric lavished, draped, accented; at its most subtle, to foresee the grace with which it will yield itself like a woman to the softening and maturing of the ageing process.[15]

It has been said that India's cultural history can be written with a thread, so pervasive is textile to our culture. There is archaeological evidence of a cotton textile industry at Mohenjo-Daro in the Indus Valley around 3000 B.C. Spindles and Indigo vats survive from this period and speak of a flourishing textile culture. Due to ravages of climate no specimens survive from this period and, the earliest surviving swath in our Museum is from the 12th century from Gujarat and was excavated in Fustat near Egypt. There is evidence of maritime trade as far back as the 11th century from ports in Gujarat, like Cambay to Egypt and Indonesia. Trade at this time across the Indian ocean was dominated by Indians and Arabs. There is some suggestion that Gujarati tradesmen were Muslims and that would possibly account for the robust trade. The remnant of the fabric shows not only the typical Gujarat *bandhani* pattern that we see in Jain Kalpasutra manuscripts but equally the use of red and blue dye. India's natural dyes, especially those for blue and red, have been renowned for millennia. Blue dye was so closely associated with India that the ancient Greeks took its western name, *indikos* (indigo), from the country itself. Red dyeing with fixing agents or mordants was known to the Indus Valley Civilisation by about 2500 BC. Fixing the colour is a challenge of dyeing cloth. Indian dyers' use of mordants was key to their mastery, which was unrivalled until the invention of western chemical dyes in the 19th century.

A handbook of administration, the *Arthashastra*, tentatively dated to the third century BCE, dealt with methods for distributing materials to spinners and weavers. India's textiles were so central to its identity abroad that in ancient Greece and Babylon the very name 'India' was shorthand for 'cotton'. The ancient Romans called India's finest cottons 'woven winds' because of their airy lightness. The country's cotton fabrics range from the sheerest muslin to robust pieces for everyday use, though fine cottons in particular, were much sought after and are a key element of India's supremacy in textiles.

Even before the advent of copper plates or palm leaf, fabric was important to us in expressing our religious ideas and sentiments. There is evidence that the text of the *Prajnaparamita* was written on fabric and carried along the Silk Route by Buddhist monks. Buddhist prayer flags on fabric are an important

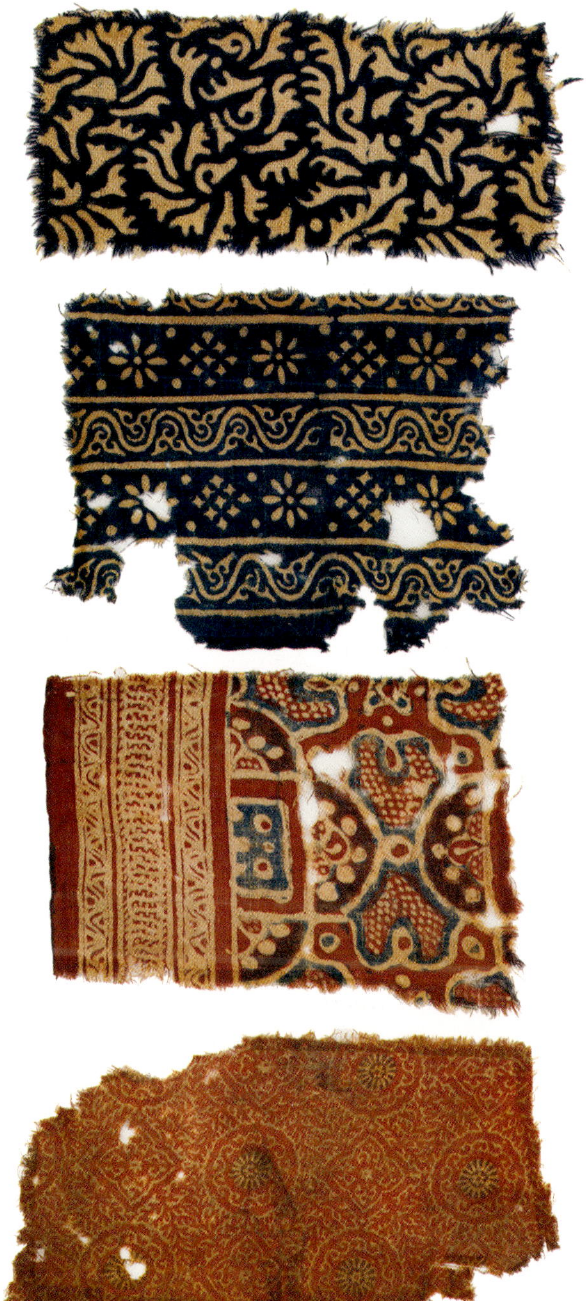

Swaths of fabric From Gujarat, 12th century

part of stupas in times ancient, and even today. The Buddha's body, it is said was wrapped in fine cotton from Kashi. The Jains were equally prolific in using fabric for their sacred images in their *patas*. None of these ancient fabric before the 15th century has survived for obvious reasons of climate in a tropical country.

At the very core of Indian textile design was religious tradition. The finest weavers in ancient India settled around temples, and *shrenis* (associations)

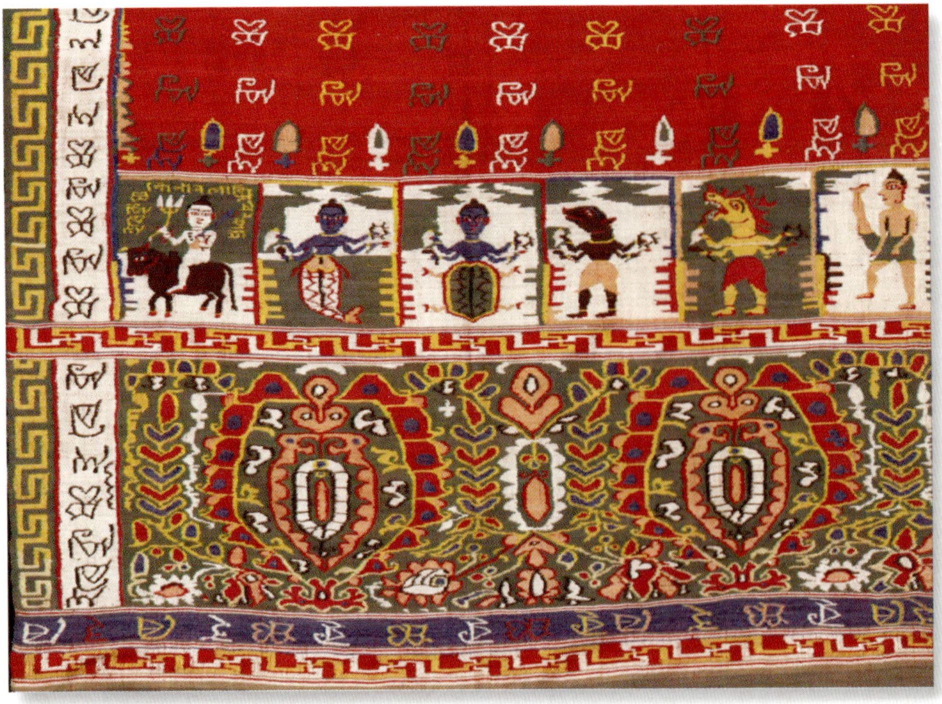

Sambalpur, Odisha Sari

of craftsmen flourished in temple towns to cater to the needs of temple rituals of devotees and pilgrims alike. Temple cloths were not only created to narrate a story but also to decorate the walls, serve as a backdrop or adorn the chariot for *utsava murtis*. If the temple was the centre of the town, the home shrine was the life of the family where fabric also played an important part. No garment for the Hindu was totally secular. The dress worn by the young girl, the sari by the bride and then by the pregnant mother, that worn by the woman in mourning, the *dhoti* worn by the man when he sat down for his *puja*, were all prescribed and dictated by ritual, and considered sacred.

Weaving is a very ancient tradition in India, and weaving and philosophy share many common words, such as *sutra*, *yantra*, *grantha* and *tantra*. *Sutra* is a thread and it is also a condensed thought in verse; *yantra* is the loom and it is also a diagram for meditation, *grantha* means to tie or string together as also a compilation of ideas in a book. *Tantra* is not only the warp but also a system of philosophy. In the Rg Veda the concept of time is understood as the warp and the weft. It was in the growing, spinning, weaving, dyeing, printing and embroidering of cotton that the Indian craftspeople found their richest expression. Threads or *sutra* are an important part of Indian tradition, both religious and secular. There is a sense of wonder in creating a thread from a cotton pod and then weaving a fabric from it. And it is from threads that fabric of all kinds are woven. Weaving has often been described to music, both are fine arts and done with a dedication and *latifa* or pleasure. To fully understand a certain piece of textile, its colour and texture, design and motifs, one must bring to it not only one's sight but touch as well. Just as music begins with a single note, textile begins with a single thread. And like the many notes of the musical scale there are many types of threads and they can be combined in many different ways to produce a fabric. The loom is the weaver's instrument, and like the musician, he adjusts and sets it like a musician tunes his instrument. When the weaver fills his *bani* or weft and throws his shuttle it is as if the musician has started the *alap*, and like a *raga* weaving has a certain rhythm of *laya*. And just as a raga has a certain *rasa* or *rang* the weaver infuses a certain feeling in what he weaves, and each fabric, like each *raga*, requires a different technique. The environment in which the weaver lives filled him with wonder: green leaves, the bark of a tree, roots of a date palm, fruits like the mango, birds and blossoms, the feather of a peacock and the fine thread of a spider web filled him with wonder, and he incorporated that in his fabric. And then there are colours which the weaver derived from the world around. Truly has it been said that weaving is like music.

Even before the cloth is woven, the *sutra* or thread is laden with many associations for the Hindu. It is significant that verses of sacred texts are called *sutra* and a philosophic system is called *Tantra*, tying religion and philosophy to threads and the act of weaving. Tying threads around a tree is a common practice seen particularly on Vata Savitri day where wives worship the banyan tree asking for a long life for their husbands. *Raksha bandhan*, where a sister ties a thread to a brother and he in turn offers her protection, tying a yellow-red thread after completing a puja while repeating the names of the seven *chriranjivis*, tying *chindis* or rags to a tree by women looking for an off spring, are some of the common ways in which the thread becomes important to the Hindus. The *yajnopavit* or the sacred thread of the Brahmins is another example of the importance of the thread. The mangalsutra of the bride confers upon her the sanctity of marriage. It is not just the thread in all these instances but the tying of it that is equally important, for to be tied or bound is an expression of oneness, and equally of love or solidarity. In a ceremony dedicated to Gauri a less well-known ceremony associated with the goddess, long threads are placed in a clay pot before the goddess's shrine to absorb her holiness. The threads are then removed and tied around women's necks or wrists in order to absorb this transmitted power.

One of the first thing that arrests us is the Hindu penchant for the unstitched fabric. Whether it is the *pheta* or the *odhni*, *angavastra* or the *dhoti* and the sari, Hindus traditionally drape themselves in the unstitched fabric. The thinking is that stitching defiles the fabric by creating holes in them because of the needle, and this admits malicious forces and energies from the outer world, and in draping the body without any violations the fabric preserves the positive energy of the body. Associated with this is the belief that fabrics hold memories and the spirit of the person that wears it and it is important to preserve and nourish them. It is for this reason that a new born baby is always received in a fabric that has been used by someone in the family and never in new and unused fabric for such a fabric is used as a shroud. Women take pieces of old and soft saris and embroider them to make them into receiving blankets for the new born.

Of all the fabric the sari is perhaps the most elegant, expressive and evocative. It incorporates many aesthetic traits: colour, design, motifs and then when it is draped, it acquires movement and shape. Whether it is a simple cotton handloom sari or an exquisite silk brocade, the beauty of the sari is both in the way it is draped as well as the texture and patterns that are created on it. The sari accentuates the woman's body, it gives it grace as she moves, protects it from lustful eyes, falls beautifully even as she walks, hides as well reveals and becomes nine or six yards of sheer delight. Every part of India creates its own distinctive sari combining in it workmanship and artistry, highlighting the colours and material of the region, and the sari does not remain merely a decorative fabric but an art object. The draping of the sari has changed from times ancient to the present and not only does it vary from one region to another, but sometimes even from one caste to another.

An interesting legend about the origin of the sari comes from the ancient city of Kashi where a weaver sat at his loom and he dreamt of a woman. As he began to work on his loom he reflected and captured the shimmer of her tears, the drape of her beautiful hair, the colours of her many moods and the exquisite grace and softness of her touch. He wove all these together in one continuous fabric, and when he finished he felt that this was the perfect fabric for a woman, and thus the sari was created.

Our information about the history of the sari comes best from examining ancient sculptures and murals. Starting with the Didarganj *yakshi* which is perhaps the oldest surviving sculpture and the through the Maurya, Kushana and Gupta periods, the murals of Ajanta and Lepakshi, female figures were draped in a sari or *antariya* that covered the lower part of the body, going between the legs and held together with a clasp at the waist. The upper part of the body was covered by a second fabric or *uttariya*. One is not sure when the sari was draped as a single fabric, but there is some suggestion that this happened during the 8th century Pallava period in South India, and hence the term *pallu* which is the end of the sari and its most decorative part. There is historical evidence that in times historic the sari was nine yards long and worn by taking it between the legs, and it is interesting that when Raja Ravi Verma toured the country to decide how he was going to drape the goddesses that he was to paint, he chose the nine yard sari.

Endless are the varieties, manifold the colours, many the patterns and the sari remains one of the most artistic and beautiful fabric of India. It is a delight both to the wearer, the weaver and the viewer, bringing together design and colours, patterns and textures, *akritis* and *rachana*, it is a product of the imagination of the weaver brought to life by a sensitive and sensuous woman. It is the most distinguished statement of feminine beauty and one cannot imagine a festival or *samskara* for a Hindu where the appropriate sari is not an important part of the celebration. Within its folds are heard the hushed voice of a romantic *nayika*, the whispers of a bashful bride, the regal resonance of a queen, the simple joys of a housewife, the noise and clamour of the labourer. But wherever the sari is seen there is the assurance of a sensibility, in its shimmer is the pride and sophistication of a woman, and when the *pallu* moves and dances the woman becomes a *gajagamini*, when she covers her head and lights a *diya* at the home shrine is she not a *devi*? By its presence the sari is a testament that our values and ideals of Indian womanhood will always survive and reassert that the sensuality of a woman is the doorway to spirituality.

Soha Parekh sums it aptly when she says:

> The diversity of styles and motifs and the intricate relationship between ritual, lifestyle and saris reflect the diversity of Indian cultural life and a complex web of inter-related social relationships. The sari has evolved as a cultural fabric which has gathered in itself over 5000 years the symbols, flora, fauna, festivals and manifold communities. In its designs and variations are encompassed the motifs and rituals of birth, puberty, betrothal, marriage and death. In other words, the sari serves as a living compendium of folklore, technique, economics and art.[16]

In traditional India the weaver was also the designer, and thus there was a unified approach between design and development. The weaver was part of the community, it is the same tree and its leaves that he saw that provided shade and protection to the people and it is this tree, its leaves and creepers that became a part of the design of the sari. He drew his colours from the world around him, *gerua* from the earth, red from *kumkum*, yellow from *haldi*, pink from *gulal*, blue from indigo. The sari, therefore, was a part of our world and did not emerge from the design of a remote computer. And when this sari was worn it was our living connection to the world around.

The *pallu* is the most decorated part of the sari and falls either in front or at the back, depending on how the sari is draped, and functions in many ways similar to the *odhni*. The *pallu* and the *odhni* is the most expressive past of a woman's attire, it hides as well as reveals, it invites as well as denies, it wipes tears as well as shares in the laughter, it saves memories and protects dreams and wishes and through its colour signals states of her mind. As a young girl she chooses many different colours, and when she comes of age her mother gives her an *odhni* with a large red *bindu*, when she is getting married a more festive *odhni* suggests her happiness, and if she were to become a widow the colours fade and are replaced by black or white. The colour and the textures, the motifs and the patterns on the sari are in keeping with the general trend of ornamentation and adornment in the Indian tradition. Thus vegetative motifs like the *lata* and the *aam butta* (*keri*), the lotus and *vriksha*, are used by weavers and printers with great abandon and tie the woman with the lush world of nature around her. Religious symbols like the Vishnupada and *shankha* are also seen. Geometrical patterns are seen particularly in southern saris and are reminiscent of the *vedi* of *yajnas*, while *shikahar* designs remind us of temples. Ceremonial saris are special to events like wedding or festivals. Thus the *Patola* and *Bandhani* are a specialty of Gujarat, the rich *Paithani* and the large-bordered *Narayana Peth* of Maharashtra, the iconic *Baluchari* and the white Shantiniketan of Bengal, the opulent *Jamdani* of Varanasi, the gossamer thin *Chanderi* of Madhya Pradesh, the temple sari of Kanchipuram in Tamil Nadu, the bright *Telia* of Andhra Pradesh, the brilliant *ikkat* of Odisha are some of the examples that come to mind of regional fabric creations.

A sari that captures the culture and the architecture of Bengal is the *Baluchari* sari. Medieval Bengal from about the 16th to the 19th centuries saw a lot of weaving traditions. It was in 1504 that Mohammad Quli Khan moved his capital to Murshidabad, and this attracted a lot of artists and weavers to this city. It is said that weavers from Patan in Gujarat and Assam also came there, and brought with them both the technique and technology of weaving. The Bankura district as well as the beautiful brick temples of Bishnupur were rich with weavers. A half forgotten town which played a very important in the culture of Bengal is Bishnupur, once the capital of Mallabhum, an old princely state. Adimalla was the first king of the dynasty that ruled Mallabhum and he ascended the throne in 694 CE. Adimalla and his successors enlarged their empire over much of Bengal, the core of which was the Bankura district. The Malla kings were either Shaktas or followers of the Tantric Buddhist cult but converted to Vaishnavism in the 17th century, and it was a major centre of the Chaitanya brand of Gaudiaya Vaishnavism expressing its ethos in art and architecture, music and literature. Bishnupur has temples and palaces, gateways and gardens. The Malla dynasty came to an end early in the 19th

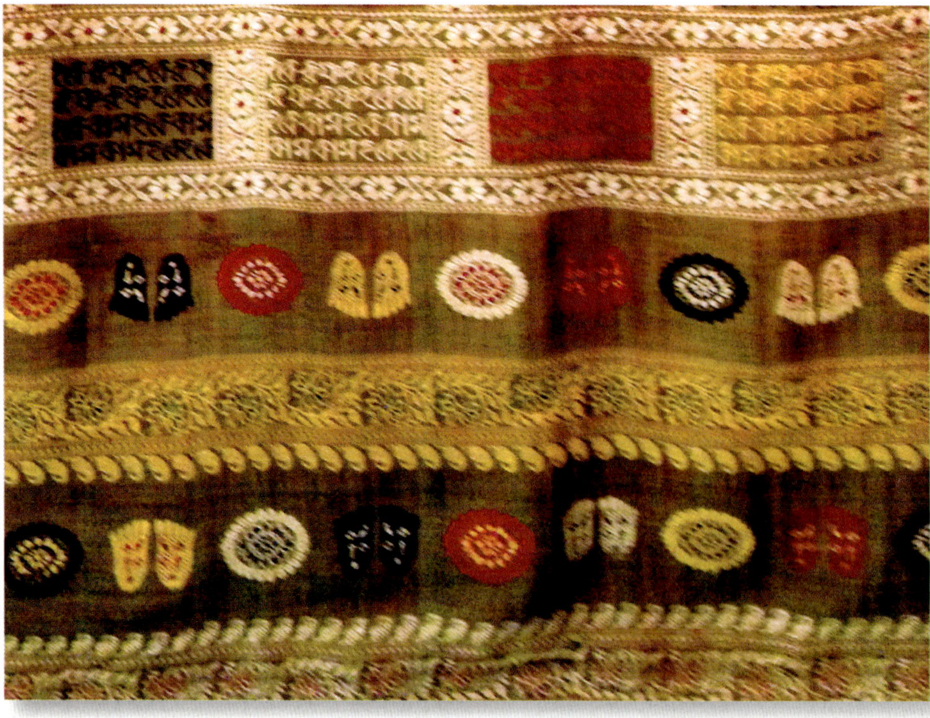

Baluchari Sari, late 19th century. Tapi Collection

century. Bishnupur boasts of a number of temples. But in the thatched hut style the temples were made of brick rather than stone and had a number of Vaishnava images, especially those of Krishna in terracotta on the wall. No less attractive in Bishnupur are its palaces and gateways. Bishnupur also produced illustrated manuscripts on Vaishnava themes. Another important contribution of Bishnupur is the *Baluchari* sari and conch shell bangles, favourite of Bengali women. Bankura is known best for its stylised horse which has come to be called the Bankura horse. Bishnupur was also a centre of music. Diverse folk styles such as *yatra*, *panchali*, *jhumur* and Ramayan *gan* were some of the genres of music. Classical music reached Bishnupur through contact with the Mughals. Debendranath Tagore employed successive musicians from Bishnupur for his newly-founded Brahmo Samaj and the Tagore family home in Jorasanko became the seat of the Bishnupur Gharana. The glory of Bishnupur has faded, the kings are half forgotten but its brick and terracota temples still stand majestically reminding us of its days of glory.

A product of Bishnupur is the *Baluchari* sari. *Baluchari* weaving incorporated both the Rajput and Mughal motifs from these temples and wove them in the *pallu* of the sari. Weaving of the *Baluchari* sari was a complex process and it took several months for a sari to be woven. Banana plant stems, bamboo trees and natural products like flower dye, fruits dye, neem leaves, turmeric leaves and dried twigs are used in the weaving process which used silk from the mulberry silk yarn. This sari had an unusually long *pallu*, and it has been suggested that the sari was not meant to be draped by a woman but was probably a fabric used for wrapping treasured gifts. The motifs in the *pallu* were architectonic and placed in separate squares. Episodes from the *Ramayana* and the *Mahabharata* were the most popular, and in many ways the *Baluchari* sari was a woven narrative. Other motifs were animals, Europeans sitting in a train, *nawab*s smoking a *huqqa*. The *aam butta* was another popular motif in this sari and there is some resemblance of this to the similar motif in Kashmir shawls of that period. Sometimes words like Hari Krishna would also be woven. Bengal at this time had a common artistic pool and motifs seen in *Baluchari* saris were also seen in Kalighat paintings, so that the weaver of Baluchar did not have to look beyond Bengal for his inspiration. The *Baluchari* sari was a treasured fabric and only the Nawabs of Bengal could afford to buy it for their personal use or for gifts. This sari was also shown at international exhibitions, and soon became a collector's item. The fabric of the sari was tussar silk and it features bright colours. In the 19th century the art of creating *Baluchari* sari died but it was revived once again but this time in Benaras, rather than Bengal.

Weaving, embroidering and painting on fabric is also visual and handcrafted poetry. When it comes to fabrics of Krishna most of them take their inspiration from the *dashama skanda* of the Bhagvata and the 500 years of romantic Krishna poetry that followed it. The words of the *Bhagavata*, *Gita Govinda*, *Asthchhaap kavis*, Vidyapati and the *Ritikal* poets not only inspire but inform the creations of the weavers.

We in India bring Krishna into our lives in many different ways, through songs and stories, literature and painting, sculpture and murals, ornaments and fabrics. Among the many representations of Krishna those on fabric are particularly evocative, they take many different forms and vary from the classical to the folk and from one region to another. These fabric are created either by painting or printing, weaving or embroidery, and through artist and artisan, painter and housewife, each region of India has created its own unique tradition of Krishna fabrics. While some fabrics have become extinct others flourish even today, and are a part of our living cultural traditions and speak of our abiding endearment of Krishna.

Some of these fabric may not have a religious imperative and in the hands of interior designers may even be used to enliven and decorate homes and other spaces in our lives. However, for those of us who are chastened by the poetry of Krishna and who have ben touched by centuries of Krishna painting, sculpture, dance and music, every image of Krishna, ancient or modern, brings to us the whisper of his *madhurya*, a hint of his mellifluous flute, resonances of the *rasa lila* under the full moon of *sharada* and take us to the enchanted Vrindavan where we wait under the Kadamba tree for his *darshan*.

During the mid 16th century Prince Chilarai, brother of the king of Cooch Behar asked the Vaishnavite theologian Shankardeva to commission a great silk scroll depicting the life of Krishna. Shankardeva, who was responsible for bringing Vaishnavism to Assam, was not only a reformer but an artist as well. He asked the weavers of Barpeta in Assam to make a fabric depicting scenes of Krishna's life from the *Bhagavata Purana*, which was the central text for Shankardeva. This fabric was called Vrindavani *vastra*. It is said that it took 12 weavers more than a year to complete this task, and this was presented to the prince in 1569 just before Shankardeva's death. Soon after its installation in the Sattra in Assam the fabric disappeared and, it is believed that it found its way into Nepal and Tibet, probably travelling along trade routes. Nepal was not only a trading partner with Assam but also a safe haven for many Hindu artefacts. What is interesting is that this *vastra* was used in Nepal and Tibet as linings for Buddhist *tankas* and also for ornamental clothes. It is important to note that the term *vastra* means both fabric and clothing.

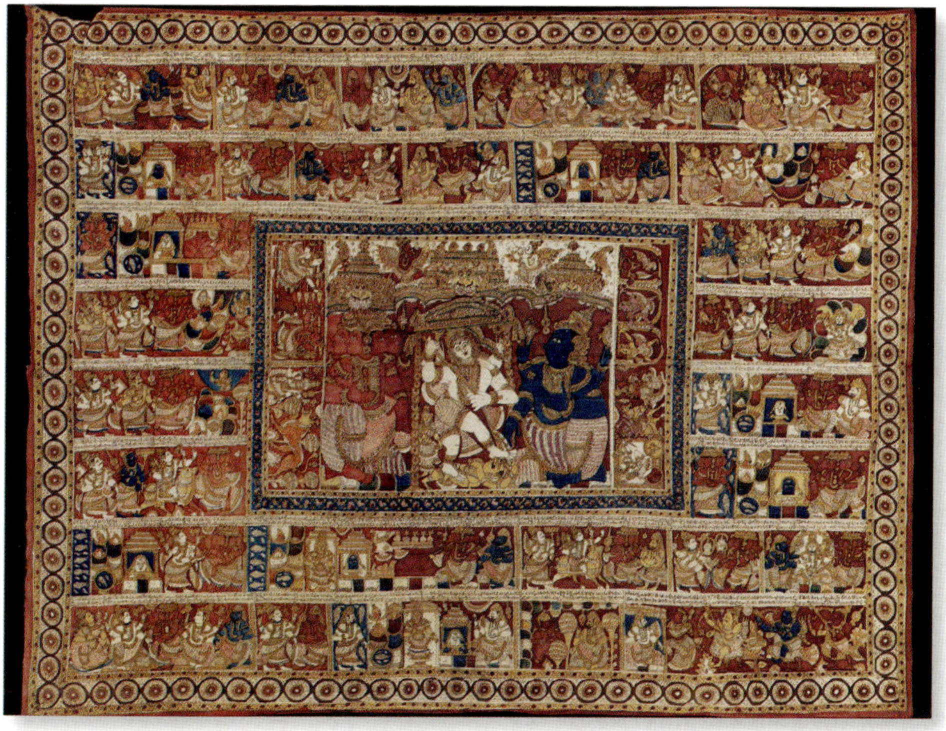

The Holy Trinity, Kalamkari, Andhra Pradesh, 19th century.
Private Collection

Shankardeva undertook a 12-year pilgrimage mainly in the Braj country of Krishna and later championed the teachings of the *Bhagavata Purana* in Assam, and it was this text and not an icon that was the central object of worship in the Sattras. Shankardeva was a zealous Vaishnava and this did distance him from the pundits at the royal court of Assam. He established Sattras or monasteries and *namghar* or prayer halls. The Sattra housed monks but was also the centre of Krishna devotional songs, dances and plays. The Vrindavani *vastra* was used to cover the altar on which the *Srimad*

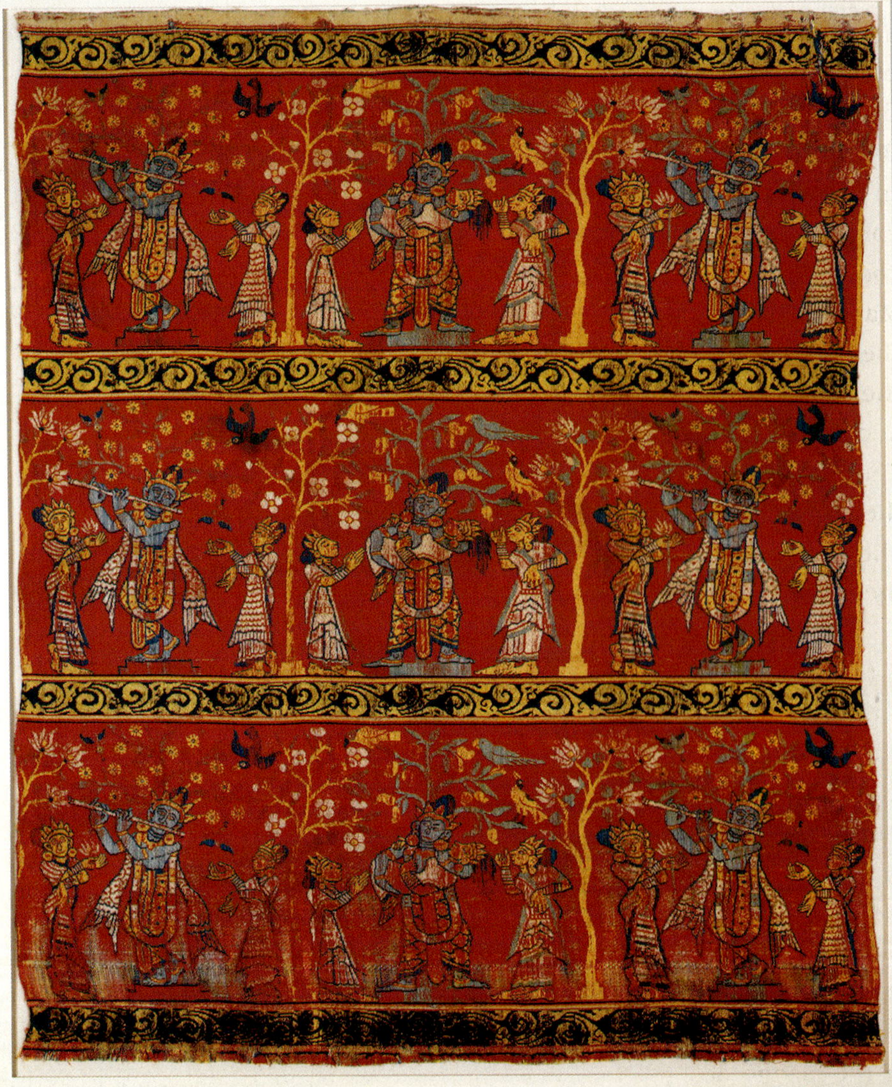

Vrindavani Vastra, Assam. 19th century
Victoria & Albert Museum

Bhagavatam was placed, and also to cover the text and to drape the walls and ceilings of the Sattra. The *vastra* was also called *gosair kapoor* or a drape for priests, similar to the present day *gamusha*. The fabric which was aesthetically pleasing thus acquired a sacred status. In the 16th and 17th centuries the iconography on the fabric was complex, with a number of finely-woven figures of the life of Krishna from the *dashama skanda* of the *Bhagavata* along with some text, but with the passage of time and decline in the standards of weaving the figures became coarser and bigger. The commonest motifs were *kaliyamardan* and *bakasura mardan* and also the *cheer harana* episode. The various *avataras* of Vishnu were also woven. Many of the woven figures in the *vastra* are similar to the figures drawn on the murals of the Sattras suggesting that the artist for both may have been the same. In addition to the figures words were also woven into the fabric, and it is believed that these were from the songs composed by Shankardeva. The iconography of the Sattras, both in the murals and the *vastra*, drew from the Pala traditions of Bengal and the western Indian traditions of Gujarat. The Vrindavani *vastra* is an important fabric of the Vaishnavas and remains the oldest surviving fabric of this tradition.

If there is one fabric which is both an essential body covering as well as a fashion statement, which was admired by the Mughals and wanted by Europeans, which adorns the wardrobe of the *raja* and the *praja*, it must be the Kashmir shawl. In the Mughal period it was worn mainly by men, but when it reached Europe in the 18th century it becamed a fashion accessory of the royalty and the nobility.While the origin of the shawl is ancient, going back probably to the 10th century, the Kashmir shawl as we know it now has a number of Persian features in it. It is said that the Persian motif of the Cypress tree or the Saru was brought to India in the Mughal ateliers, and when it reached Kashmir embroiderers they converted in into the *aam butta* or the mango design. This design became so popular that it soon became pan-Indian and was exported to England and adopted by the weavers in Paisley from which it got its name. The gifting of shawls was a common practice with the Mughals, and the ceremony was called *khil'at*. Akbar was fond of fabrics and he asked that the Shatoosh shawl be made long enough for a *jama*, from which comes the term *jamawar*. It was Jehangir, who was particularly fond of the flowers in Kashmir, who encouraged the use of the *aam butta* and other floral patterns in the shawl and *patkas*. The Shahtoosh wool, which came from the underbelly of the Tibetan antelope and which was much admired for its softness was sought after, although it is currently banned. Today it is Pashmina that is the popular wool. So popular was the Kashmir shawl that it led to the word 'cashmere' for a type of soft woven fabric.

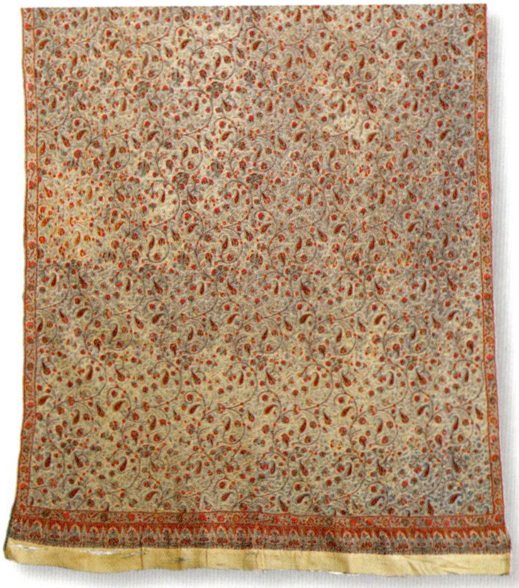

Kashmir Shawl, 19th century

Fabrics play an important part in the rites and practices of the 12th century Jagannatha temple in Puri, which is one of the seven *mokshapuris*, or sacred places in India. The fabric is known as *kenduli pata* or *kenduli khandua*, the title referring to Kenduli the village, where legend has it that the fabric was first woven. The first historical document referring to *ikkat* weaving in Orissa dates to Ramchandradev II, who ruled over Puri in 1719. This document forms part of Madala Panji or the daily diary of activities in the temple of Jagannatha. Legend has it that Jayadeva wanted to offer his poem to the icons of Jagannatha, and could not think of any other way except having it woven in fabric which would therefore be closest to the deities. He, therefore, asked weavers in his birthplace of Kenduli to produce such a fabric with all the verses from the *Gita Govinda* woven in it. The weavers agreed, only on one condition that Jayadeva sing the poem while they were weaving. Jayadeva agreed but when he came to the seventh song he was overcome by emotion and fainted. The weavers stopped working, but just then a *sadhu* came along and said that he was Jayadeva's brother and that he would sing. The weavers continued weaving but when Jayadeva recovered he told the weavers that he had no brother. He realised then that Jagannatha himself had come and it was he who sang the first verse from the third canto. Thus it is that this verse is the most popular verse that is woven.

kansariapi samsara basanabandh srunkhalam
Radhamadhaya hrydaye tatyaja braja sundarah.
Krishna, the enemy of Kamsa, finding Radha bind his heart
with chains of memories of other worldly lives
abandoned the beautiful cowherd girls. III.1

Another popular verse is I.16

vedan uddharte jagan nivahate bhugolam udbhirate
daityam darayate balim chalayate ksatra ksayam kurvate
paulastyam jayate halam kalayate karunyam atanvate
mlecchan murchhayate dasakriti krte krsnaya tubhyam namah
For upholding the Vedas, supporting the earth, raising the world,
tearing the demon asunder cheating Bali, destroying the warrior class,
conquering Ravana, wielding the plow, spreading compassion,
routing the barbarians homage to you Krishna in all your ten forms. I.16[17]

Other such apocryphal stories relate the opposition to this from priests, and it was the Raja of Puri who asked Jayadeva to throw the fabric into the Markandeya tank, and if it did not sink it would then be accepted for the temple rituals.

There is no confirmation of this apocryphal story and the only documentation of the weaving of the Gita Govinda fabric comes from Nuapatna where the art still continues. It has been suggested that the earliest method of producing the Gita Govinda fabric was block printing with freely drawn resists, and that *ikkat* weaving was a later introduction into the making of this fabric. The earliest surviving Gita Govinda fabric is only about a hundred years old.

The Gita Govinda fabric performs multiple functions. It is used mainly to wrap the deities in the temple and this is how it acquires a certain sacredness, for by being in contact with the icons the energy of the icons is rubbed on them and then transferred to the one who wears the fabric. It is also used by the hereditary *sevakas* or servants of the temple, where the fabric not only confers a legitimacy to the wearer but gives a status as well to the *sevakas*. And finally the fabric is a prized possession of the many devotees of this temple. In particular, the fabric is an indispensable part of the *ratha yatra* where throngs of devotees wait patiently to catch a glimpse of Jagannatha and carry home a fabric for their home shrine.

While hereditary priests preside over the daily rituals of the temple the *daitas* perform the seasonal rites. One of the first rituals called *sadhi bandha* is the draping of the fabric over the icons after a ceremonial bath. The unstitched fabric is six yards long woven by *ikkat* resist dye technique and resembles a sari with a *pallu* and borders in three colours, green for Balabhadra, red for Subhadra and yellow for Jagannatha. The main field of the fabric features a verse from the *Gita Govinda* woven generally in Sanskrit but also sometimes in Oriya.

Of the sixteen daily *upacharas*, or temple rituals, *bhoga* or the offering of the meal, is an important part, and during this the three deities are covered with the silk *ikkat* cloth. Cloth and food are both indispensable in this ritual, and are distributed after the ritual as *prasada* to the devotees. At the end of the day is the *shayana* ritual where the performance of the *Gita Govinda*, with song and dance, is an integral part of the evening liturgy of the Jagannatha temple; from inscriptions on the Jayvijaya gateway within the temple complex there are records that this was sanctioned as early as 1499. During the *shayana* the three main deities are dressed in the Gita Govinda cloth, lamps are slowly extinguished and the gods are put to sleep.

The distribution of the ritual Gita Govinda fabric is not only an important part of the *prasada* of Jagannatha for the devotees, a *prasada* which is highly sought after and prized, but it also played an important part in the concept of kingship associated with the Jagannatha temple. Ever since the founding of the temple in 1135 by Anantavarman Chodaganga (r.1078-1147) kingship and divinity of the Jagannatha temple has been a layered connection, and in this the Gita Govinda fabric has played an important part. Distribution of this ritual fabric was not only a part of the daily liturgy, but also of the political contract. The supply of various material for the temple by the kings of Orissa was rewarded by the temple through the gifting of this ritual fabric. Equally, when the kings in their palaces gave gifts to visiting dignitaries, the Gita Govinda fabric was always a part of it. The presentation of the fabric

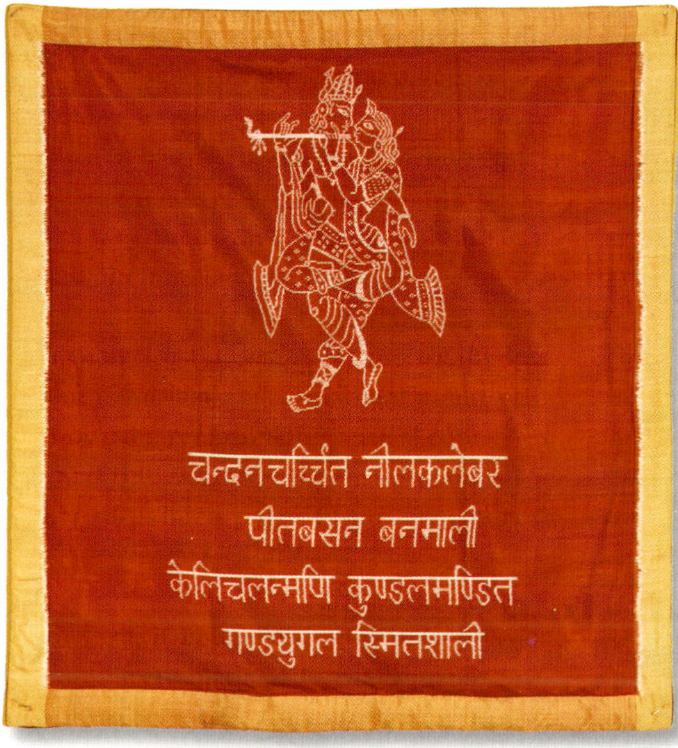

Gita Govinda Fabric, 20th century

was considered an honour and the type of cloth, silk or cotton, simple or elaborate, small or large, were all a sign of the importance of the visitor. When Jagannatha temples were constructed in other parts of Orissa the same rituals around the offering of the fabric were continued. The practice continues even today and is seen particularly during the *ratha yatra* when the king ceremonially arrives, covered with the Gita Govinda fabric, and inaugurates the festival by sweeping the street on which the *ratha* will pass. The images are ritually bathed, painted and dressed in the fabric before the *yatra* begins. When new images are to be made every 12 years or so, a tree is first selected, circumambulated and sprinkled with holy water, and then wrapped with a new Gita Govinda fabric.

At present the Gita Govinda fabric is woven in Nuapatna, a village along the Mahanadi river near Cuttack. The majority of the 4000 people in this village are hereditary weavers. The temple purchases a set of twelve pieces, each piece having a separate name, of the Gita Govinda fabric for the seven images inside the temple. Besides the three main iconic images of Jagannatha, Balabhadra and Subhadra there are smaller images of Sudarshana, Lakshmi, Sarasvati and Madhaba. The fabrics are called *bara hata* (shawl), *paharana* (upper garment), *khandua* (lower garment).The verse from the *Gita Govinda* was originally woven in *devanagari* but this has been replaced by the Oriya script. The fabric is always made of silk and red is the prescribed colour.

Weavers in Nuapatna weave fabric for pilgrims and devotees alike. These are smaller in size, red in colour and have verses from the *Gita Govinda* or the *Chaitanya Caritamaritam* woven in *devanagari*. These fabrics are worn by pilgrims as scarves or shoulder coverings to resemble that worn by *daitas*. The male-dominated family of weavers follow strict rules and maintain ritual purity in the making of the fabric. Like other temple rituals there is a sense of fear as well, as even committing a small mistake in the making of the fabric can have bad consequences for the weaver.

Hacker writes:

> ...cloth at Jagannatha temple serves as a visual reminder of the covenant between individual and temple in the all important sari binding ceremony, where cloth previously worn by the divinity is tied around the head of the new *sevaka*. This is one of the cloths many meanings -garment, blessing and honour, status and prestige, rebirth, relic and commodity- whose sphere of influence increasingly radiates out from its locus at the Jagannatha temple.[18]

The Gita Govinda fabric has been a part of the rites and rituals of the Jagannatha temple for the last 300 years and more, and carries with it not only the lyrics of the celebrated poem by Jayadeva but more importantly, the grace and blessings of Jagannatha to the person who wears it.

Chamba, in present day Himachal Pradesh boasts of a rich cultural heritage dating back to at least the 8th century, and this is present in the form of temples, sculpture, bronzes and wood carving. Chamba has a long tradition

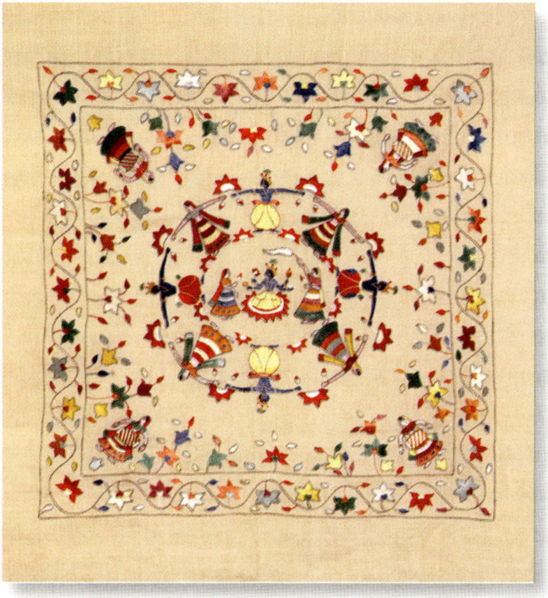

Chamba Rumal, 20th century

of embroidered garments, and in a stone slab preserved in the Bhuri Singh Museum dating back to the 12th century embroidered garments are to be seen. A unique embroidery of Chamba is the Chamba *Rumal* which can be dated back to the 17th century. Raja Prithvi Singh who ruled Chamba from 1641–1664 and who was a patron of miniature painting brought back Muslim artists from the Mughal ateliers and encouraged them to create painting on fabric, and this was the beginning of the Chamba *Rumal*. Used as a coverlet for offerings to the deity the *rumal* found many other uses such as a scarf or sash, a covering for precious documents such as horoscopes or land records, as protection for jewellery and also as a dowry during a wedding. Created on handspun cloth with coloured untwisted silk floss, the women of Chamba use the *do rukha* stitch, which creates the same pattern on both sides of the fabric, and create human figures along with animal and plant motifs. The figures were drawn on the fabric by miniature artists and it was then left to the women to embroider them, who started the process by doing the outline in black thread and later embroidered them with colourful silk threads. The figures of the Chamba *rumal* bear a striking resemblance to those of Pahari miniature paintings and the themes are also similar. One of the commonest themes is that of the Rasamandala of Krishna, the ashta *nayika*s and *dashavatara* of Vishnu. Plant motifs are drawn from the landscape of Chamba and add to the beauty of the *Rumal*. Some *rumals* also have inscriptions which further establishes their connection with the tradition of miniature painting. It has rightly been said that the Chamba *rumal* is a painting that is done with needle and thread.

Among the various fabrics of Krishna, the Pichhwai is the most evocative, and like the Gita Govinda fabric, it has had a continuous presence with both deity and devotees for the last several centuries. It was in the late 15th. century that Vallabhacharya (1479-1531) founded the Pushtimarg sect of Vaishnavism. The foundation of this school emphasises the celebration of Krishna through the arts, and especially through painting. Krishna in the Picchwais has both an aesthetic and an ontologic presence, for the Pushtimargis believe that the painted image of Krishna is a *svarupa* of Krishna himself and not just an icon. Vallabhacharya was greatly influenced by the murals in Rajasthan *havelis*. However it was his son Vitthalnath (1516-1586), who was an artist and played a big part in the development of Pichhwais and other artistic traditions of the *haveli* of Shrinathji. The icon in the Pichhwais is Krishna as Govardhana Giridhari, the cowherd lifting the mountain to protect Vrindavana. Hung behind the main deity the Pichhwai expresses the mood or a *lila* of the deity, the spirit of the season or the theme of a festival. The portion of the Pichhwai which falls behind the icon is left blank or cut out, but in *haveli*s where the image is small, a large figure of the *svarupa* is painted in the central portion of the Pichhwai. It is the latter type of Pichhwai that is the most popular. The Pushtimargis lay great store in *shringar bhakti*, also called *madhurya bhakti*, where Krishna is adored with loving devotion and emotional exultation. Madhur *bhakti* includes *seva* through music, singing and dancing, *bhoga* or offerings of food and *shringara* or adornments with painting, decorative textiles, flowers and jewellery

There is anecdotal evidence that Pichhwais were made as early as the period of Akbar. It is said that Raja Mansingh visited the Gaudiya temple at Vrindavana at which time the icon of Shrinathji was dressed in a *zari jama* and a *zari* Pichhwai was placed behind the icon, and that the Raja disapproved of this. While the authenticity of this story may be in doubt it is fairly certain

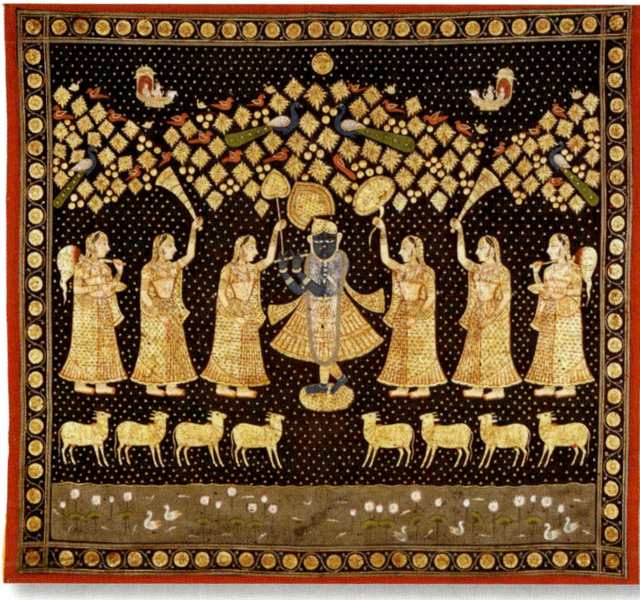

Deccani Pichhwai, early 20th century

that during the time of Vallabhacharya the rituals in the *haveli* were simple and consisted of only using a *morchnadrika*, *gunjmala* and *pitambar*. The practice of placing an elaborate Pichhwai behind the icon of Shrinathji was essentially a Gaudiya practice, later taken over by the Pushitimargis, and that too by Vitthalnath. The earliest definite evidence of the use of Pichhwai appears in the Vitthalnath period. It was he who was artistically inclined and who organised the various rituals in the *haveli* and also assembled the *asthachhap kavis*, and the word 'Pichhwai' appears in one of the compositions of Govind Swami. Vitthalnath was in, good books of Akbar and it was Akbar who conferred on him the title of Gosain and the two met quite often. We know that Pichhwais of this period were either embroidered, brocaded or printed, but not painted.

Vitthalnathji besides adding an aesthetic touch to the rituals in the *haveli* of Shrinathji also brought together the celebrated *ashtachhap kavis* or the group of eight poets, the chief of whom was Surdas, entrusting them with the task of composing and singing various *padas* in honour of Shrinathji.

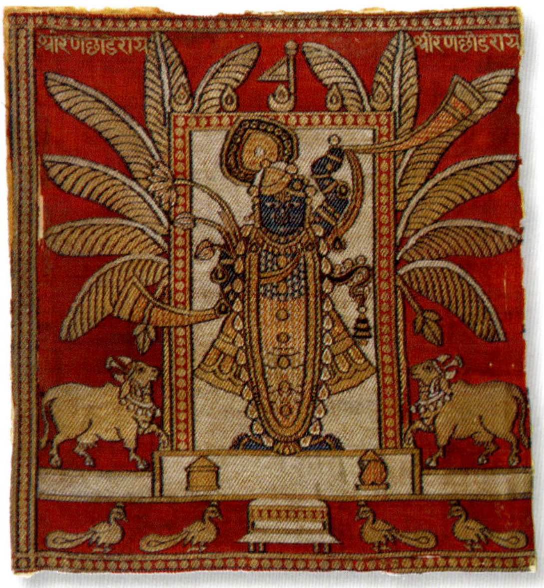

Shrinathji in Brocade, early 20th century

The *goswamis* or priests who looked after Krishna in his *haveli* and tended to his every need, consider themselves as gopis or *nayikas*. Each of the eight poets assumed a *gopi's* name and identified himself with a particular *sakhi* of Krishna in their *bhava* or emotional state. Surdas was called Champaklata, Parmanandadasa called himself Chandrabhaga, Nandadasa went by the name Chitralekha, Govindswami was Bhamasakhi, Kumbhandas was Vishakha, Chaturbhujdas was Sushila, Chhitswami became Padma and Krishnadas was called Lalita. The precedence for this was set by Vallabha himself who was considered Swaminiji or Radha herself, and his son Vitthalnathji took on the name Chandravali.

Early Pichhwais were non-iconic and showed mainly trees and blossoms, and they took their inspiration from Mughal tents and wall hangings and murals of Rajasthani forts and *havelis*. The main function of these Pichhwais was to recreate the mood and the ambience of Vrindavana in the *haveli*, and it is in Vrindavana that devotees were to participate in a *darshan* or insight of Krishna, and this was not to be a *puja* or a ritual in a temple. Painted Pichhwais probably started in the 18th century when the *haveli* had shifted to its present location in Nathadwara, and the earliest dated Pichhwai is from 1739, the earlier Pichhwais, if any, have been lost or destroyed.

The function of the Pichhwais is not only to provide a backdrop in the *haveli* of Shrinathji but to bring to mind of the devotee the ethos of Vrindavana as described in the *Bhagavata* and in the poems of the *ashtachhap kavis*. The two forms of expression, the poetic and the visual, work together in their emotional and aesthetic effect. Some of the common themes of the Pichhwais are: Snana Yatra, Dolotsava, Nandmahotsava, Gopashtami, Annakuta, Dana Lila, Govardhan Puja, Hindola.

At Nathadwara, and especially in the Pichhwais, we see the rare coming together of *shringara rasa* and *shringara bhakti*, where Krishna is venerated in his divine form as well as celebrated in his human form. The essence of Pushtimarga is in Vallabha's own words, "He dwells not in wood, in clay or in stone; in *bhava* He dwells, which holds the first place of all" emphasising the emotionally ecstatic and richly adorned, rather than the contemplative worship of Krishna. Whether in the image of Shrinathji or the various rituals that are performed, the place of the love of Radha is never forgotten. The mirror held in front of Shrinathji as He dresses for the *shringara darshan* is compared to Radha in whose heart Shrinathji is ever present. The metal box on a stand contains twelve folded *bidas* of *pan* which represent *dvadasha nikunja lila*, the twelve bowers where Krishna and the *gopis* held their *lilas*, the lotus garland around his neck is Radha's heart which Shrinathji keeps close to himself, the U-shaped *tilak* mark on his forehead is supposed to be the impression of Radha's foot left there when Krishna bowed to her, the *jhari* or the tiny pitcher wrapped in a red cloth contains water from the Yamuna and represents Radha's *madhurya bhava*.

We are not sure whether or not artists from the Mathura region accompanied the icon when it moved from Mathura to Nathadwara during the Aurangzeb period, however, the major artistic influence on the Pichhwai painters was from the ateliers of Mewar of the late 17th and 18 centuries. The influence of other centres of Krishna painting in Rajasthan like Bundi, Kota and Kishangarh on the Pichhwai painters of the 18th, 19th and 20th centuries cannot be discounted. One feature of the Pichhwai that is often cited by historians is the position of the feet of Shrinathji. In the 19th century the feet were splayed but at the suggestion of Bharatendu Harishchandra the feet were straightened. The large and bewitching eyes of Shrinathji are enamelled, and while some say they are taken from the Kishangarh *kalam*, others say that Gosainji is said to have instructed the enameller to use the eyes of his third son Balakrishna as a model. Another variation is the Deccani Pichhwai with a dark background and gold work. We know that Gujarati merchants belonging to the Pushtimarg sect lived in Hyderabad and may have patronised this type of Pichhwai.

The art of painting Pichhwais is alive even today, and even though present day Pichhwais are used for decorating walls of homes and even hotels, a true aesthete or devotee of Shrinathji cannot but be touched by its evocative colours, the richness of its expressions, the texture and colour of the paints and even more by the textual resonances from Krishna poetry that they bring to it, that even a commercial Pichhwai draws us towards Krishna and excites in us a *gopi bhava* in His adoration.

Sujuni is a term Bihari women use for straight running stitch embroidery on layered cotton. Traditionally made by Hindu women in their homes, old worn-out saris were layered and held together by fine coloured threads pulled from the sari's edges. Religious and secular narrative themes were illustrated as well as geometric patterns, flowers and local life. Patna and Busara in northern Bihar are two centres where Sujuni flourishes. The art of Sujuni takes its inspiration from the figures of Madhubani and the poetry of Vidyapati, and thus it is that the women of Bihar are able to transform the love of Radha and Krishna into stitched drawings. While this is the foundation of Sujuni, the women are influenced also by their own lives and what they see and hear on television and cinema. They translate this into their own pictorial idiom making their works at once products of their own contemporary existence. A Sujuni should not be seen as a work of a single woman but rather the collective expression of a group of women, for when Bihari women gather to embroider, they exchange stories, sing songs, recall lines of poetry that they had heard as children, and bring the ethos of Vrindavan alive in their own homes. Stitch by stitch, they recreate their own interpretation of Krishna's romance with the *gopis* and bring into it their

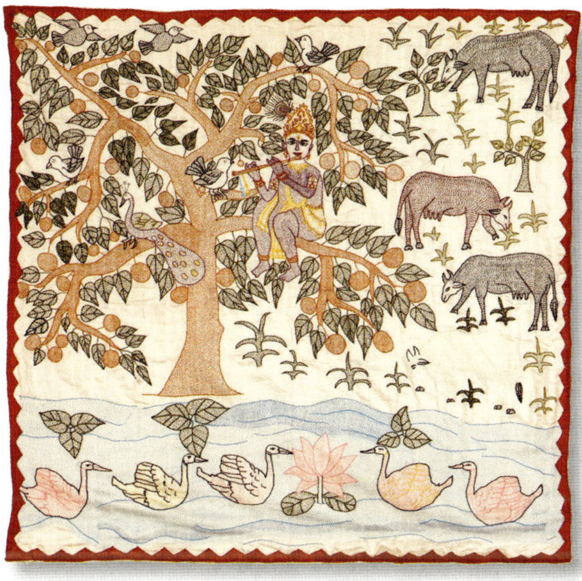

Sujuni, Bihar, 20th century

unexpressed and personal romantic thoughts. Sujuni is not a decoration, it is a narratage. The woman drawing the story on the plain cloth is the story teller; the women stitching, piecing, chatting and changing that drawing into an embroidered Sujuni are participants, in an activity that is kept alive as it passes from hand to hand, through observation and conversation. As the Sujuni takes shape the lives of these ordinary women are being reshaped, as ancient memories and repressed feelings take a beautiful form without

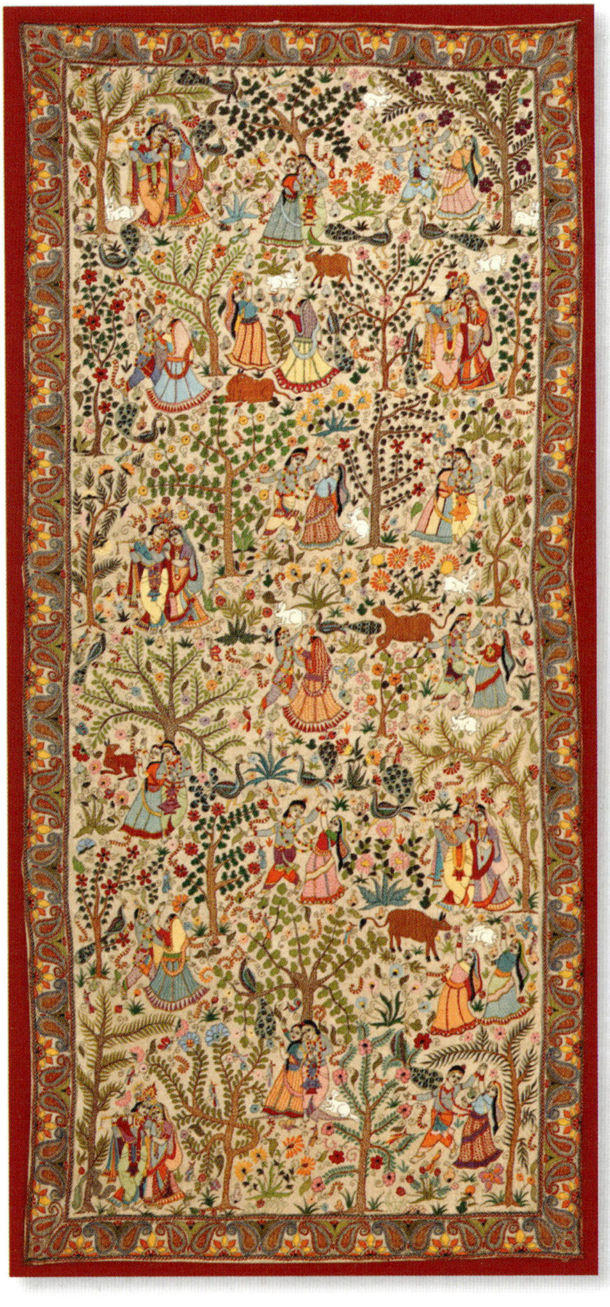

Krishna Leela, Kantha. 20th century

words, but through a needle and a thread. This is the true meaning of Sujuni, *suchi* and *jani*, the needle and the woman, joined by a thread to feelings. It is important to remember this when viewing a Sujuni.

A leisure time activity of the women of Bengal is an embroidery called Kantha. Kantha means rags, and traditionally a number of worn-out saris are layered and sewn together with threads drawn out of borders of old saris, and the entire field is then quilted into small blocks of different shapes using simple running darning stitches. The piece is then embroidered using a variety of plant, animal and geometric motifs. Traditionally, seven different kinds of Kanthas are known. The *lep* is a thickly-quilted warm wrap for the winter, the *Sujni* is used as a bed cover or as a blanket for small children, the *bayton* is a wrapper for books and valuable articles, the *arsilata* is a wrap for combs and mirror, the *durjani thalia* holds the wallet and the *rumal* is a handkerchief. The colours of Kantha were red and blue in the 19th century, and in the later half of the century yellows and greens were also included.

Kantha takes its inspiration from both the *alpona* and Tantric imagery of Bengal. Flowers and trees, animals and fishes, geometrical and curvilinear patterns and the ever present pan Indian motif of the mango are very much a part of the floor diagrams of Bengal which are a part of the vocabulary of every women, and these are then translated into the Kantha. Wedding scenes, procession of musicians, local and Puranic legends, parrots and fishes, *shankh* and *kalash*, are some common motifs. The motif of the central lotus radiating in every direction and along with fertility symbols like the fish and bamboo is a carry-over from the Tanric yantras. Trees of life or *kalkas* are often placed in the four corners. Vaishnava families place Krishna and Radha in the centre. Motifs from the world around, such as cars and trains and everyday people, also find their place in Kanthas.

The art of Kantha is a rural art of the Kayastha and Muslim women of east Bengal and present day Bangladesh. While it is imbued with Hindu myths, it is also a perceptive of the life of the ordinary Indian, and in its many layers integrates many aspects of daily life. The Kantha is a work which gives wholeness to things that were of no use, to fragments that were without significance, and in doing this, it not only creates something beautiful from what would have been discarded, but creates a fabric that gives warmth and comfort and brings with it the personality of the person who creates it also of the woman who wore that sari when it was whole. A Kantha is not just embroidery but carries voices of the women who make it.

Bengal is known for its handloom cotton fabrics with the plain white undyed fabric and a coloured border being the most commonly worn sari by Bengali women. Bengal was also home to *jamdani* as well as the European (Dresden) embroidery techniques in the 18th century. Out of this fertile context the Kantha continued to evolve in the 19th and 20th centuries, with mill-made fabrics replacing handloom cloth, and in present-day India it has become one of the commercially made prized ornamental fabric.

Kantha carries with it a message of wholeness, of making something whole from fragments and therefore, brings with it a socio-economic as well as metaphysical symbolism. In not discarding worn-out fabrics but making something new and beautiful out of it, Bengali women show their sense of thrift and frugality. In joining rags Kantha resonates with the robe of the Buddha which is a patchwork of rags and therefore, represents the restoration of wholeness from the tatters of rags or fullness or unification from momentariness.

The Kantha is an object of love, its symbols have universal validity, it is given as a gift and brings with it the wishes and experiences of the person who made it, and is an assurance of protection and security. It is an expression and carries the voice of ancient memories, treasured ideals, family history and worldly aspirations of the ordinary woman of Bengal. Kanthas are an important part of the traditional embroidery of Bengal, and when Krishna appears in their creations it carries with it the sweet love of Radha and the *gopis*.

Kalamkari or pen work refers to textiles that are printed or painted using a particular technique. Modern Kalamkari can be traced to the 17th century Andhra Pradesh. Kalamkari, like most other Indian arts, owes its birth to temple rituals. Kalamkari textiles were used as aids to story telling in temple precinets. While the motifs of Kalamkari are drawn from Hindu mythology, Kalamkari owes a lot to Persian influences which came into this area when trade links were established between Safavid Persia and Qutub Shahi dynasty in Golconda. The two centres of Kalamkari are Masulipatnam and Shrikalahasti. Kalamkari textiles were used to decorate temples and palaces as well for narrative scrolls, but over the years they have been used for household purposes, like furnishings and even clothing. In British India

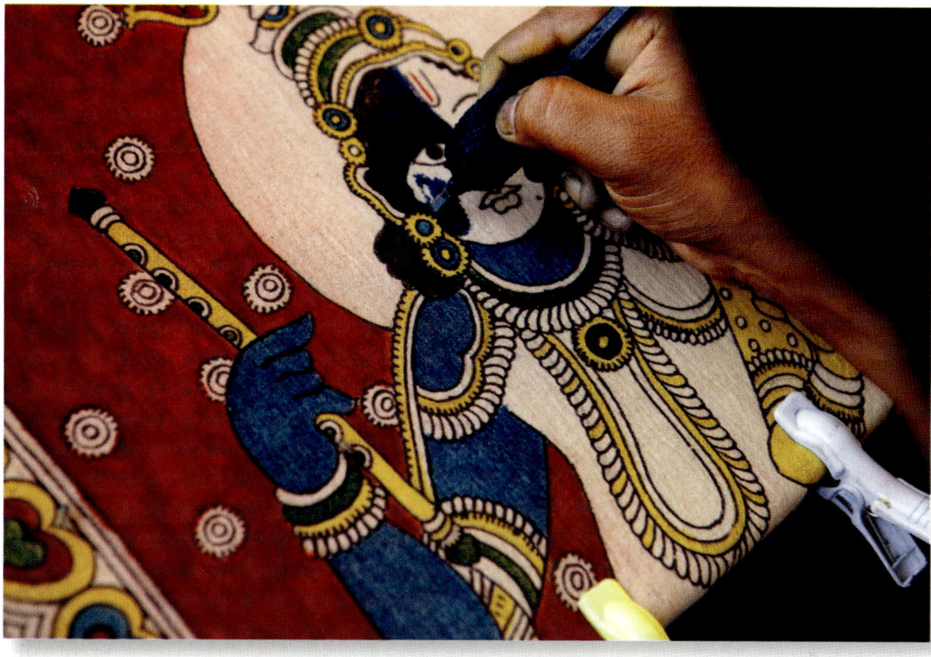

Kalamkari, Andhra, 20th century

Kalamkari fabrics were particularly popular as bed covers and came to be called *palangposh* or *palampore*. The procedure for producing a Kalamkari starts with preparing the cloth, which is first bleached, then soaked in myrobalan solution mixed with fresh buffalo milk. The outlines are then drawn in red and black. The cloth is then washed in running water before sunrise, then starched and waxed.

The pen or *kalam* is made of a bamboo stick at the end of which a thick pad of human hair is attached, and figures are drawn with this pen or a wooden block. Red, blue, yellow and green are the main colours, and the Kalamkari

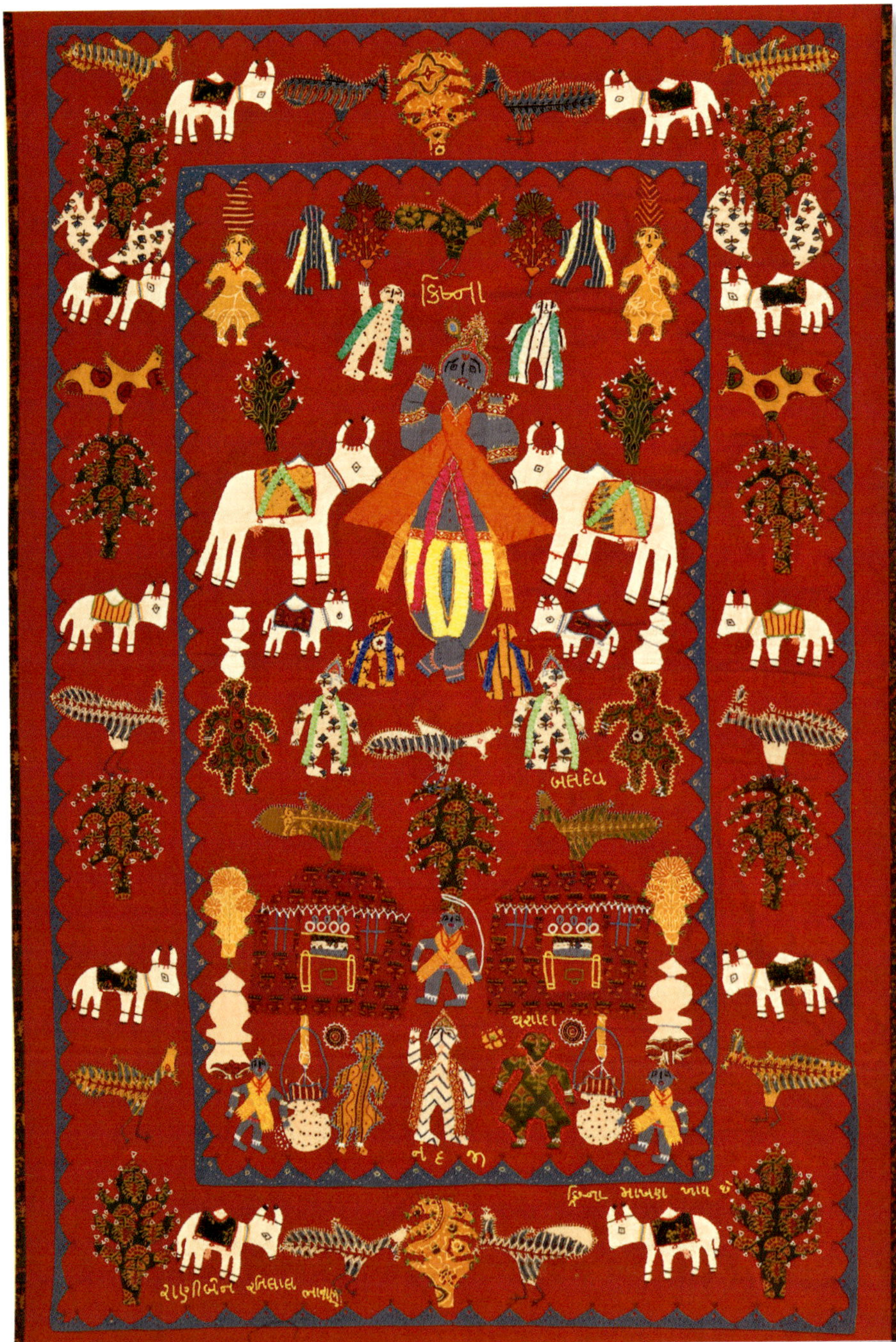

Krishna Fabric from Kutchh, 20th century

artists worked with the techniques of a mural painter and the usual themes were taken from the Puranas as well as from the Mahabharata and the Ramayana. The Kalamkars were able to produce two-dimensional figures that equalled temple sculptures and murals. Kalamkari textiles thrived on Muslim court patronage, Persian trade and the markets of Europe, and remain even today an important part of the artistic repository of India.

If there is recompense in the arid desert, the gnarled Babul and the fierce noon sun of Kutchh, it is the use of colour in their fabric. Kutchh is the home of nomads and migrants.The Rabaris are a nomadic people who despite their peripatetic life, create beautiful embroidery. They are basically camel herders, and while the men move from place to place, the women, who live in a house called *bhungo*, look after the household. The Rabari women are skilled with their hands and create embroidered fabrics like *kothlo* and *kanjiri* for themselves. More importantly, a young girl and her mother work towards creating a trousseau which will be given as a dowry at the time of the girl's marriage. Fabrics in Kutchh are a tangible marker of rites of passage, group identity, marital status and the skill of the maker. Other important group are migrants from Sindh who create quilts with applique work with fragments of fabric and incorporate narratives in their creations. These people easily resonate with the flute-playing pastoral Krishna and create fabric of Krishna with disarming spontaneity and abandon, where colour rather than design dominates the composition, as in this Vrindavana narrative applique fabric by Raniben.

The Mughal emperors who came to India from arid Central Asia expressed their love for flowers by creating artificial gardens around them in the form of beautiful tents, awnings and screens. Cloth tents called Qanats, erected for ceremonies or as encampments, were part of their nomadic tradition and also a means of displaying their wealth and stature. It was common practice for monarchs and kings, royalty and nobility to hold *durbars* both routinely and on special occasions. Timur in th 14th century built elaborate tents in his garden. Although the Mughals built imperial cities they were on the move all the time and tents were an important part of their lives. Humayun built a tent of exquisite fabric consisting of twelve partitions corresponding to the signs of the zodiac. Abul Fazl writes in the Akbar Nama that Akbar once had a two-storeyed tent called Gulal-bar where beautiful carpets were hung. The concept of creating an artificial garden of flowers on fabric arises from the Islamic idea of paradise. Akbar's most valuable textiles were kept in the Farrashkhana and used in the construction of tents. Due to climatic conditions very few of these *Qanats* have survived but we learn a lot about them from miniature paintings of that period. During Jahangir's reign Qanats were richly decorated with flowers. Many of these beautiful fabrics, which included brocades and sheer gold thread were made in Ahmedabad. According to the French traveller Francois Bernier who was at Aurangzeb's court in the 17th century the royal encampment featured many tents lined with hand printed chintz made at Masuliptanam. In the 18th century hand painted fabrics from

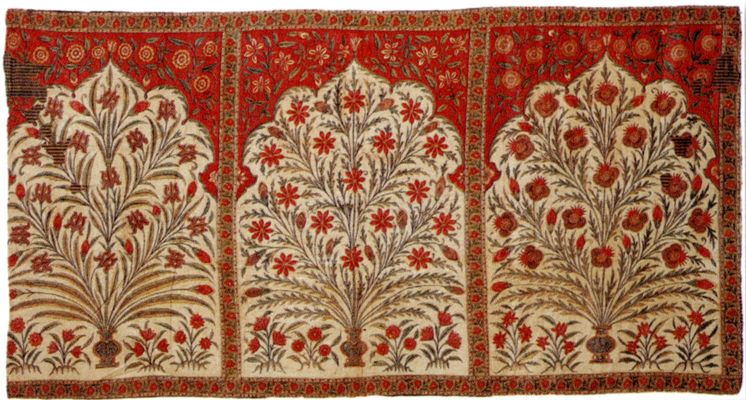

Qanat. Mughal, Probably Burhanpur, Khandesh, Maharashtra.
Early 18th century.

Rajasthan and Khandesh were used in the tents of the Indian royalty. *Qanats* and hangings played an important part in the decorative art of the Mughals. Not only did they bring a certain freshness in the middle of arid landscape, they also were a public display of the emperor's wealth, but above all they created a paradise on earth.

A fabric very special to Gujarat is the Chandarvo. For Gujaratis the Chandarvo, a richly embroidered fabric is the Mother Goddess herself, and the real purpose of the Chandarvo was an offering at a shrine of the goddess. The Gujarati weaver, when he finished making the Chandarvo, danced and sang and went into a trance. At the moment of his trance, the weaver draped the Chandarvo around himself to establish identity with the goddess. Anyone, it is said, can make a Chandarvo, but only a *bhakta* of the mother, can breathe life into it. Another fabric of religious significance to the Gujaratis is the *mata ne pachedi* which is a fabric on which images of the goddess is painted or printed and used to make a sacred enclosure for the celebration of the goddess. *Mata ni Pachedi* is also called the Kalamkari of Gujarat, thanks to its resemblance to the art of Kalamkari from South India and the same method of painting, namely using a pen (*kalam*) made out of bamboo.

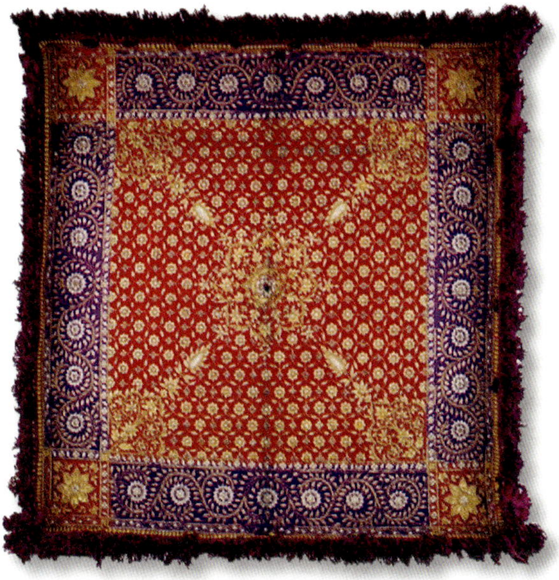

Chandarvo, Gujarat, late 19th century

Mata ni pachedi means 'behind the mother goddess' and is a cloth that constitutes a temple of the goddess. The story goes that when the nomadic Vaghari community from Gujarat who worship Mata, were not allowed to enter temples, they instead created their own places of worship with illustrations of the mother goddess (Mata) on pieces of cloth. While the floor and the walls of these *mandaps* were important, what was most significant was the ceiling for it recreated the sky and provided a protective canopy above our heads. The concept of a canopy is deep in the Indian tradition. The ceiling of the Rangamandapa is ornately decorated with musicians and dancers, *surasundaris* and *madanikas*. The shrine of a mother goddess, especially in Gujarat, is adorned with the chandarvo. The king's throne is never without a parasol, and even when he travelled on a horse or an elephant there was an umbrella over him. The Buddha sat under the Pipal tree which became a protective canopy while he meditated. While providing protection from the wind and the rain, sun and dust are some of the obvious reasons for a canopy, a canopy in the ultimate analysis is the human recreation of the sky, a

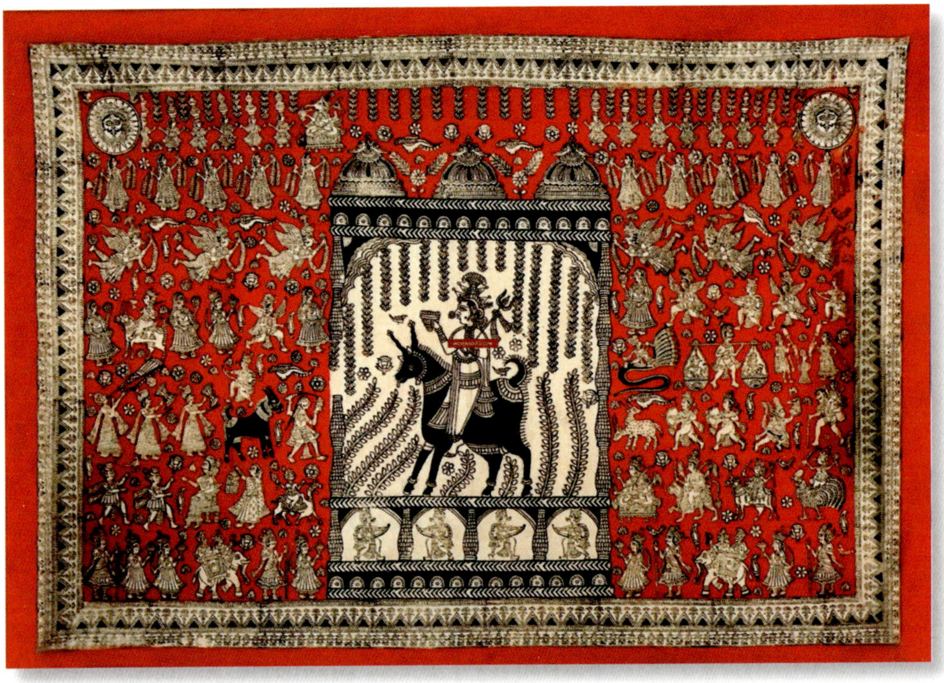

Mata ni Pachedi, Gujarat, 20th century

representation in finite terms of what is infinite, it brings what is celestial and distant close and reachable to us, for to feel complete we need to create an axis mundi which connects the earth to the sky, our earthbound and limited life to the vastness and freedom of the sky. A canopy is that recreation of the sky which would otherwise remain abstract and distant.

As we end our journey of *sutras* and threads, we realise how important they are in creating beautiful fabric, designs and patterns, all of which reflect our vision of what is beautiful. So distinct are our traditional fabrics that whenever and wherever we see them we recognise them, it gladdens our heart and we whisper, "That is an Indian fabric." In royal ateliers and village markets, in *chowks* and *havelis*, when people get together to create an Indian fabric, not only are they creating a beautiful object but at the same crafting a community. That is the genius of human creativity in India where a *sutra* creates, binds and beautifies.

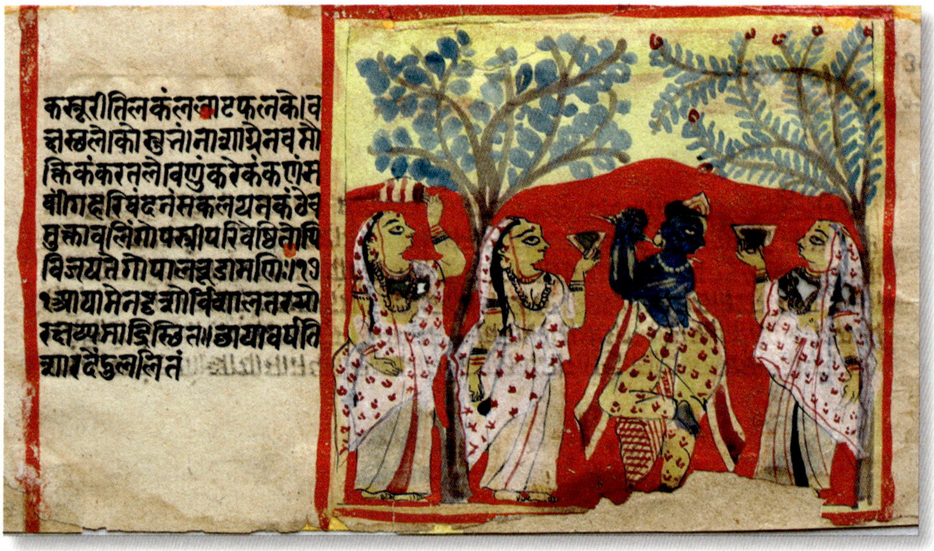

Krishnakaranamrutam. Gujarat. c. 1600

The Journey of Kavya to Kalam

From Pothi to Chitravali

When we celebrate miniature paintings we need to traverse a journey of *kavya* to *kalam* to truly appreciate Indian artistic creativity. As we have noted previously our sacred and secular narratives were in the form of *shravya kavya* or aural poetry, and this was the preferred expression of our story tellers and balladeers. However, what was heard was evanescent and a need was felt to transform *shravya* into *drashya*, or the oral into the visual, and this was to happen through dance, sculpture and painting, and among the visual arts it was painting that was to embark on that beautiful journey that would do justice not only to the narrative, but even more to the many nuances and textures of human emotion.

The Indian artist was not only adept in sculpting images on temple walls, but was equally well versed in the task of painting murals in caves and temples as well as iconic and religious images in sacred Buddhist and Jain texts. However, when the rich poetic lore of ancient India in the post-*Bhagavata* period became the life throb of North India, whether it was in temples or *havelis*, royal courts and or village *chowks*, that artist undertook the challenge of portraying the many and delicate realities of the heart, for that reality needed not only the *kalam* or the brush but *kalpana* or artistic imagination; it required a certain aesthetic sensitivity and not just the technique of the brush, it was necessary for the artist to understand the sensuality of poetry and develop a visual language of line and colour robust enough to represent the beautiful visual imagery. This called for both aesthetic sensitivity and artistic finesse, for the poetry knows no rationality and follows no rules, and has a language of its own. And above all, it needed the self confidence to absorb various foreign trends and strands of painting that were simultaneously flourishing in the country such as Persian, Turkish and even European, but despite that to remain resolutely Indian, for after all our gods and goddesses were, on and of, the Indian earth. The artists had to evolve a visual language that could transcend intellectuality, shun rational order, treat the pictorial space not with rules of artistic perspective so important to non-Hindu patrons and their painters, but as spaces of the mind, to use colours not merely to decorate but to evoke emotions, and employ lines not just to create forms but to give these forms a lyrical movement, to create faces that not only reflected pomp and power, but that were alive with feeling of love and longing, and with eyes that speak not the language of lust but of tender love and set them in a landscape that resonated with the rich echoes of love, a landscape in which the sap that flowed through the *nayaka* and the *nayika* was no different from that which animated the birds and the blossoms or the opulence of a *haveli* or a court where courtly love could shine. This is what created a living painting and it is that journey of the miniature artist which we will trace. Of the many journeys of our painting tradition we shall walk on the path of paintings of *shringara rasa*.

The painter was called upon not to just to create a pretty picture, or merely to titilate his audience and draw them out of their jaded sensitivities but to become a visual poet and present a vision and a story, by transforming the well-sculpted words of poetry to create resonances of sound and music, form and feeling, motifs and metaphors, colours and texture, from his brush and palette.

A historical survey of Indian painting has been done well by art historians and we shall not tread that beaten path for it contributes only slightly to our understanding and enjoyment of the creativity of the Indian artist. Our intention is to see how the Indian painter was able to translate the rich lore of love poetry into painting, to examine the techniques and methods, the motifs and the metaphors that the artist used in creating a two-dimensional space that was able to scale the many dimensions of the beautiful texts.

It is customary especially with Western, or Western trained, art historians to use Mughal painting as a reference point, as if it were the gold standard of Indian painting. Perhaps it was so with art historians, when it came to a study of historical paintings, such as portraits and the depiction of court and historical scenes. However, when it comes to the representation of our love poetry there was in the innate and indigenous Indian *kalam* enough robustness and passion, and sufficient strength and skill, to beautifully represent the many shades and colours of those texts.

The 14th and 15th centuries were an axial period in the history of Indian art and culture. While temple sculpture had reached its zenith in the previous centuries, the Indian mind found new inspiration in literature, specially *kavya*, and there was an efflorescence of painting mainly in the Rajput courts of Western and Central India, Orissa and the hill states of the Himalayas. The *Amarushataka*, *Bhagavata Purana*, *Gita Govinda*, *Rasamanjari* and *Balagopalastuti*, texts of *shringara bhakti* in the first few centuries of the second millennium, had chastened the Indian mind, and it was ready to celebrate *shringara* through painting, and this was to inaugurate about five hundred glorious years of miniature painting in these regions, and the royal ateliers were humming with activity.

The *Bhagavata* had postulated that Krishna was to be celebrated not through ascetic rites and sacred rituals but through song and dance; however the *rishis* of the *Bhagavata* had little realised that painting would become an equally evocative vehicle of the ecstatic *bhakti* of Krishna and speak eloquently of the love of Krishna.

The end of the 14th century found India in a state of cultural and political exhaustion. Temple building, that had soared to grand heights in the Gupta and the Chandella dynasties, had come to an end. The magnificent sculptures on these temples had raised aesthetic sensibilities to a degree of sophistication not witnessed in India before. Indian sculpture was not only a source of religious sentiment and fervor, adorning as they did the grand and imposing temples, but they were an aesthetic statement of the beauty and strength in its

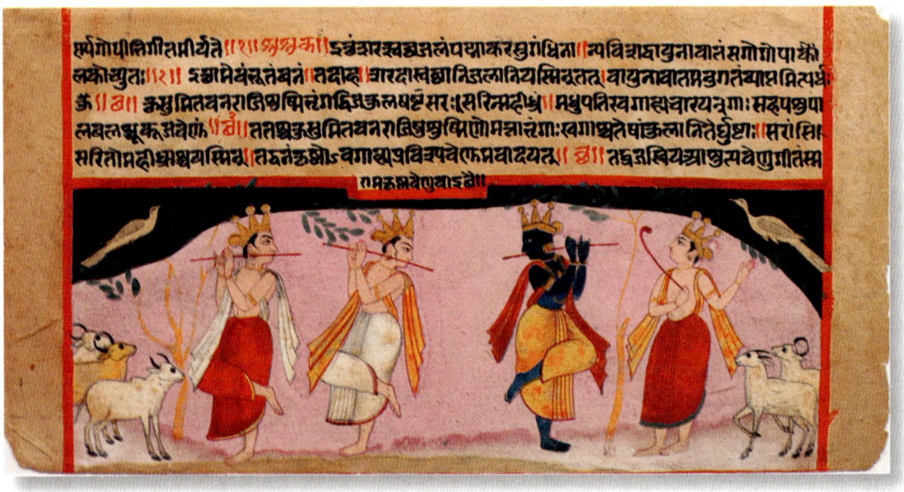

Bhagavata Purana. Gujarat. 16th century

ability to suggest transcendent truths, silently and in stone. Muslim invaders had created both political and cultural disintegration, major dynasties like the Pratiharas and the Palas in north India and the Chalukyas in Western India had fallen, and a large number of small, independent Rajput states had emerged, and it was left to them to defend the country against these Muslim invaders. Hindu nationalism, staunch piety and military prowess were forces that drove the Rajputs. It has been rightly said of the Rajputs that their unparalleled heroism and sacrifice for about eight centuries since the first Muslim conquest in the 8th century, had a critical influence on the course of Indian culture and art. Bhoja of Pratihara, Jayapala of Bhatinda,

Jayachandra of Kanuaj, Prithvi Raj Chauhan of Ajmer, Mulraj Solanki of Gujarat, Chandelas of Bundelkhand and the Palas of Bengal, among the many kings and chieftains, created new traditions of valour and national pride, along with a commitment to Pushtimarg Vaishnavism, and there was a resurgence in the Indian continent of Hindu fervor in the West, and Buddhism in the East, against an alien religion and conqueror. The South was protected from these invaders and marauders but miniature painting had to wait several centuries before it was to make its presence there. These Rajputs took early to the Pushtimarg Vaishnava faith and keenly celebrated this through various artistic representation such as poetry, story telling, song, dance and painting, but did not patronise sculpture to any great extent, for theirs was a not a period conducive to temple building given as it was to a strong Islamic presence. These arts inter-penetrated each other so that painting was visual poetry, and dance was three-dimensional painting, and there was thus a living and vibrant ethos of Krishna in the courts and the *havelis*, the *chowks* and *mohallas* of North-western India from the 15th to the 19th centuries. It is through this coming together of poetry and piety that Krishna came alive in the homes and courts of the Rajputs, and in the persona of Krishna human romantic love was celebrated in all its sensuality, and elevated to transcendent heights, where the individual and the universal met, where human emotions resonated with the landscape around it, where the inner and the outer sensations met in enduring aesthetic experiences, assuring us that sensuality and spirituality were not bipolar states of the human mind, but one beautiful and unbroken continuum to be realised through the love of Krishna. The love of Krishna tied poetry and piety in a seamless whole in the hands of the artists of Rajput ateliers, and this was the main inspiration for the grand tradition of miniature painting for five hundred glorious years.

The *Bhagavata Purana*, that arose from the emotionally-charged *Aham* Tamil poetry and the romantically throbbing *khanda kavya* in Prakrit of Hala Saptasati, had established Krishna as the prototypical romantic hero as early as the 10th century and had ushered in *shringara bhakti* or the ecstatic adoration of Krishna. Jayadeva's *Gita Govinda*, Bilvamangala's *Balagopalastuti* and Bhanudatta's *Rasamanjari*, texts that followed the *Bhagavata Purana*, ensured that Sanskrit *kavya* had richly embraced the romantic relationship of Radha and Krishna. This was followed by the rich treasure of romantic poetry in the *bhashas* which brought Krishna to the people. Pilgrims and priests, merchants and mendicants, traders and temple goers, the royalty and the nobility and people in *chowks* and *havelis* chanted and performed these *kavyas*, and this ensured that *shringara bhakti* of Krishna had a strong aural presence mainly in the Muslim dominated areas of the north and the west. This brought them, not only religious solace but equally an emotional and cultural enrichment in their otherwise parched and arid life. The love of Radha and Krishna filled their militant and peripatetic lives with an emotional meaning and vitality. The arid landscape of North-Western India, under the cloud of a militant Islam, did not allow outdoor religious celebrations or the building of temples, and the time was ripe for a visual and colourful presence of the romantic Krishna in a more intimate and sensual setting within the security and comfort of the court and the *haveli*, and this was to happen through animated groups and courtly soirees, and this was a stimulus to painting in the 16th century, and it was this that was to transform the Krishna of the idyllic Vrindavana of the *Bhagavata* to the painted Krishna of the Rajput courts. This was Hindu artistic and religious sensibility at its evocative best where poetry, painting and piety came together.

In spite of abundant references to painting on walls and on wood and cloth in ancient Indian literature, no definite reference to early painting, apart from stone inscriptions, is available. The spoken word for the early Hindus was paramount and it were the Buddhists and the Jains who saw the value of committing to writing sacred words. It is probable that at the third Jain council at Vallabhi in 454 CE, at a ceremony called *pustaka arohana* that the first Jain manuscript was produced. There is also evidence that Buddhist canons were engraved on sheets of gold in the fifth century. However, very little is known of early Hindu manuscripts in the first millennium as the ravages of climate and the use of perishable materials would have destroyed them, and it is therefore customary to place the origins of miniature paintings in the Buddhist illuminated manuscripts of the 10th and 11th centuries produced in the monasteries of Eastern India at Nalanda and Vikramsila and which disappeared entirely in the late 12th century due to the Muslim invasions, and it is then that they were taken to Nepal and Tibet for safe keeping. Another early manuscript tradition were the scrolls and birch bark painting of Gandhara which was an early Buddhist stronghold, and finally there was the Western Indian style of painting of the Jain sacred texts of the 13th and 14th centuries that were produced in Western India and gifted to the *shastra bhandaras*. The Prajnaparamita of the Buddhists and the Kalpasutra of the Jains were the most commonly-illustrated manuscripts at these centres in Gujarat. Of the two, namely the Buddhist and the Jain manuscripts, the Jain manuscript artists were to exert a strong influence on early Krishna paintings of the 15th century. The tradition of producing illustrated Jain manuscripts was well established in western India, and even within the small space of the manuscript, painters were able to produce figures in the typical Western Indian style of the farther eye and angular forms.

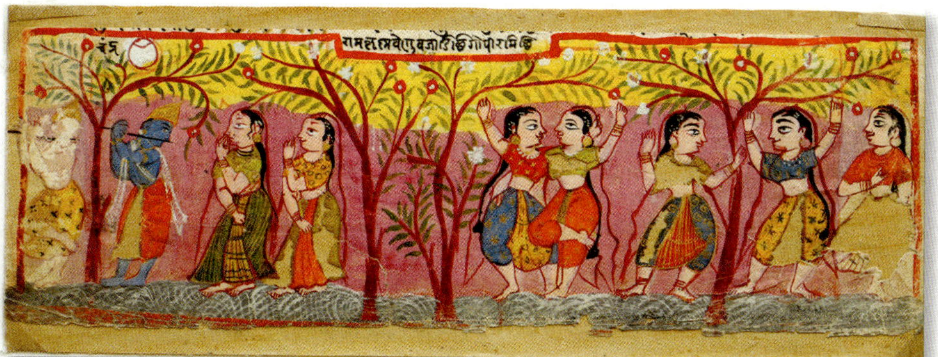

Gita Govinda. Gujarat. c. 1600

However, even before the painted manuscripts one cannot overlook the well established murals of ancient India as seen at Ajanta, Bagh and Badami and at other Himalayan sites such as Ladakh and Lahual Spiti, for it is here that we see some of the earliest paintings of the Indian tradition. Which must have influenced the art of miniature paintings much later. It is safe to assume that the Indian artist of medieval India had inherited this rich treasure of mural panting through accounts of travellers. The art of painting in these murals had reached a high water mark in terms of technique and content. The deep-seated Buddhist concept of *karuna* was translated by the mural artist of Ajanta in the many placid forms of the Bodhisattva, his contemplative inward look, his grace and gentleness reflected in his fluid movements, the wholeness and the unity of life in everything that lives, and above all the joy of that life that pulsates in man and animal, the plants and the birds. The artists of Ajanta brought to life the vision of the Buddha and the *shanta rasa* that he championed, not just as an adornment within the caves but to enable the monks to get a *darshana*, a transfiguring vision, that would inform and chasten their meditation and foster their Buddhist faith. It is important to note that most of the figures in the murals are frontal, iconic and sculpturesque, they look at us as we look at them, in that charged meditative moment. There is a direct interaction between the viewer and the images in the mural. This is the continuation of the Indian sculptural tradition as practised in the centuries of temple art that was brought to the murals. We also see in the murals the three-quarters face with the projecting or farther eye, a feature that was to dominate 14th and 15th century miniature painting. Along with the ability to create iconic images the mural artists knew and showed their versatility

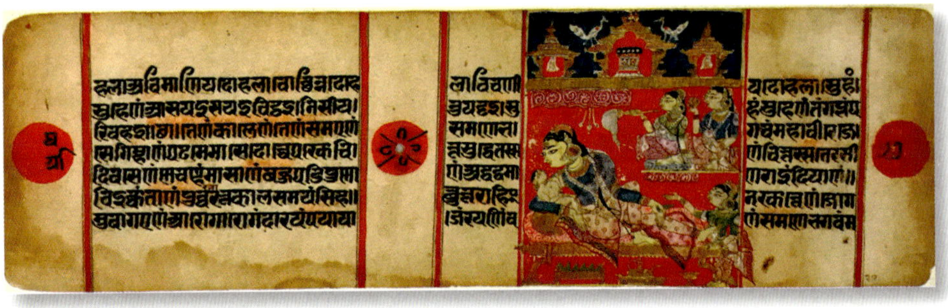

Kalpasutra and Kalakacharya Katha, Patan, c. 1375

with rational perspective, a technique in painting that was to become such a defining feature of later Mughal miniature painting, but which the indigenous artist was to reject later when it came to portraying *shringara rasa*. Rational perspective which was known to the Indian artist was useful in painting the iconic images of murals and of kings and monarchs in later historical miniature paintings, but was an impediment when it came to painting the many nuances of romantic love, for the pulsating and throbbing romantic heart creates realities of its own and defies rationality, and demands not just rational perspective but being able to roam in lyrical and arational spaces of the mind. Those spaces are above and beyond rationality, and the Indian artist recognised this early and excelled in the technique of converting that mood of love within the two-dimensional space of a painting. This was Hindu artistry at its best, as it portrayed the mind and not just the situation, painted an emotion and not history, captured the spirit and not just the form.

Paper was available in India by the 13th or early 14th century and it came probably through China along the silk route, or through Asia along trade routes across the oceans. While the mural tradition was ancient and well mastered, the technique of miniature painting on palm leaf in the Jain and the Buddhist manuscripts was already well established, at least since the 11th century and probably even earlier. The Jain manuscripts like the Kalpasutra and the Kalakacharyakatha, initially done on palm leaves and later on paper made to look like these palm leaves, saw the emergence of the sensuous woman, drawn with a firm but wiry line, tentative but not timid, gazing frontally outward with her three-quarter profile and the large farther eye projecting out, self-assured and free standing in a monochrome background, her sensuality suppressed but not denied, her emotions controlled but not annulled, and the excitement taut and hidden in the sacred and austere ambience of the Jain manuscript surrounded as she was by the Tirthankaras. The woman of these Jain manuscripts, as seen in the 15th century Kalpasutra of the Devasanopado was drawn with a taut and wiry outline, with a three-quarter face and the farther eye projecting into space. However, it was this very same artistic creation of the woman in the tiny space of the Jain manuscript that was to emerge through the artists of the later Rajput courts as a full fledged sensuous and romantic *nayika* that was to be the cynosure of our attention in the depiction of the *shringara rasa* of Krishna. The hesitantly sensuous woman of the Jain manuscripts was the harbinger of some of the most beautiful artistic representations of the woman in love that was to follow, for she had the poetic and pictorial potential, and equally the conditions were right for her to evolve into a sensuous, dallying, heart-throbbing *nayika*, the beloved of Krishna. While *shringar bhakti* found its utterance in poetry, its best visual expression were to be the miniature paintings from the 15th century onwards.

The 15th century *Vasanta Vilasa* scroll on cloth established in no uncertain terms the veracity and the vibrancy of the indigenous Indian *kalam* in expressing *shringara rasa*, a *kalam* that had motifs and metaphors which were born on Indian soil and of the native Hindu mind, and which were sometimes overpowered or tempered later by Persian and Mughal styles, but never totally replaced by any foreign influences. Such was the robustness and sensuality of the Hindu style, whether executed by Hindu or Muslim artists, that even with changing patrons and different artists, that quintessential indigenous stamp of emotional fervour was never lost, for it incorporated the earthiness of romance, the passion of love, the poignancy of longing and the meaning of *viraha*, all set within a two-dimensional space of a painting that could soar to heights of excitement and passion. The question of the indigenous Hindu origin is important, as art historians tend to overlook this in favour of Persian or Mughal creativity. It cannot be denied that Persian cultural influence in Western India in the 15th century was significant, mainly through trade and partly through diplomacy. Persian-illuminated manuscripts came to India and were responsible for moving Indian artists to produce paintings that illustrated the text rather than producing iconic figures in sacred texts that served mainly a magical or protective function, as they did in the Jain and Buddhist manuscripts. Persian figures of the Sahi nobility are to be seen even in many Kalpasutra renderings. The Indian artist was now able to produce even in the limited space of the sacred texts, narrative illustrations of the lives of the Jinas as is seen in the Devasanopado Kalpasutra. The stage was being set for the *chitravalis* that were to follow about a hundred years.

The *Vasanta Vilasa* scroll of 1451 which is an ode to Kama, the god of love, resonates with animated and sensuous though wiry figures, with the three quarter face and the farther eye, set in a luxuriant landscape of lush trees, singing birds, caged parrots and aquatic animals, buzzing bees and dancing peacocks, richly patterned Gujarat textiles, romantic swings in silver moonlight, women applying sandal paste and embracing couples in love pavilions, set against a monochrome evocative background that creates the ambience of love in spring, and signals the artistic talents of the native Gujarat painter of the 15th century in converting the stanzas of a love poem into a two-dimensional space which is alive with feeling, and this is the harbinger of paintings that are to follow. Underneath the not so refined lines and colours lies a whole universe of tender feelings and pulsating passions that are epitomised by the joy of spring and the throb of romance.

One of the earliest *shringara* texts to be painted were the *Bhagavata Purana* and the *Gita Govinda*. Both the texts bring to life a sacred poem about Krishna, which had gained considerable popularity throughout India, through the crude but animated figures set in a monochrome background. There is in them the signature and the stamp of the native Indian *kalam*, where matters of the heart are expressed without inhibition, where love in all its unabashed sensuality is affirmed and celebrated, where the *rasa* of *shringara* flows

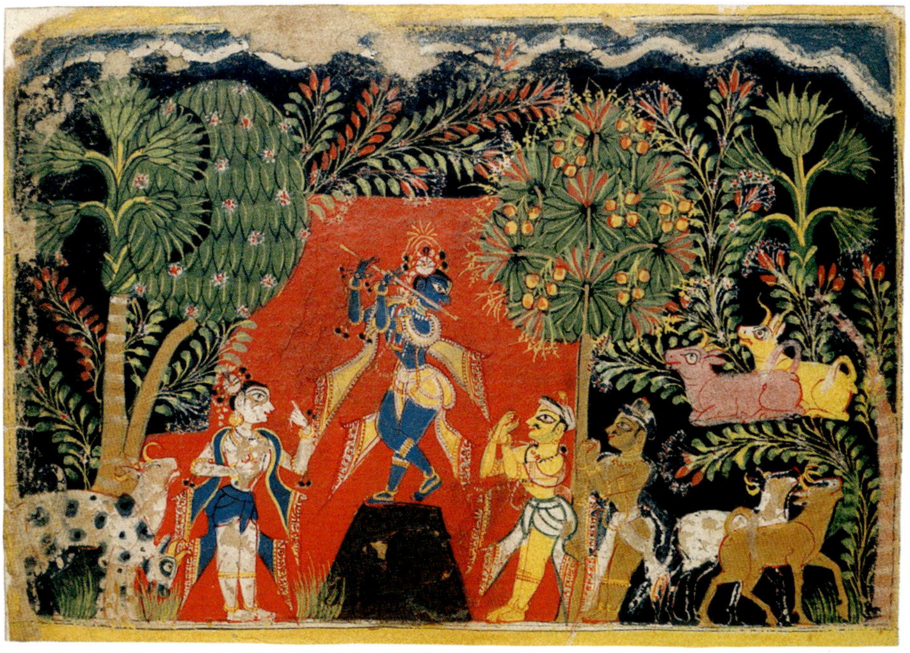

Bhagavata Purana, Delhi-Agra, 1525–40.
Jagdish and Kamla Mittal Museum of Art.

through human beings and equally in everything in the world around them, where there is a holistic feeling of joy and abandon, where to be human is to love, and where painting is visual poetry and poetry, is a language of the deepest longings of the heart and mind that is chastened by love. The human figures in these early illuminated texts are marked by the characteristic protruding eye and angularities and embellished by richly adorned textiles. It was common to refer to this style as Jaina but scholars such as Moti Chandra showed that this style of painting in the 15th century had penetrated Eastern India and even Nepal and therefore a secterian designation such as Jaina was not appropriate, but instead it should be called Western Indian.

With the advent of the 16th century the early Western Indian style of painting had reached a certain maturity and showed that it was capable of entering the heart of *shringara rasa* by depicting the animated interaction of a *nayika* and a *nayaka*, and that the visual figures were as animated or perhaps even

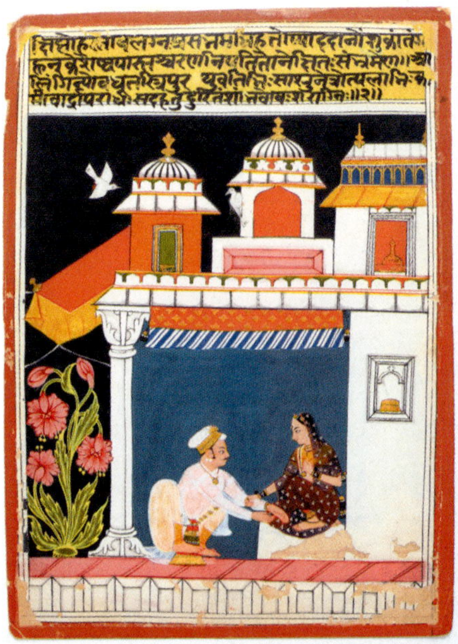

Amarushataka. Malwa. 17th century

more than the text. Early in the century one of the centres of artistic activity was Mandu. Mandu had a strong Persian influence with a combination of artists from Persia and Indian artists trained in the Turkman Shirazi technique. However, the Kalpasutra that emerged from this court in 1439 showed that it had the seeds of sensuality but it was left to the Sultans of Mandu to forge a unique style of painting that continued the passion and the warmth of the *Vasanta Vilasa* and the Western Indian style of painting, and once again asserting that the robust and sensually evocative native Indian ethos could never be eclipsed by foreign influences. If the *Vasanta Vilasa* established the poetic and artistic basis of the effusive and evocative ambience of love, and the Mandu Kalpasutra of 1439 showed that it had the seeds of a sensual line, the *kalam* of the Mandu court ensured that nothing could corrupt the native Indian passion for telling a romantic story, for after all Krishna was very much of the Indian earth and espoused the warm and passionate *shringara rasa*. While it was Mahmud Khilji who took Malwa in 1436, it was his son Ghiyas-ud-din Khilji (1469–1501), followed by his son Nasir-ud-din Khilji (1501–1512) who inaugurated an era of peace and prosperity in Malwa, and made Mandu a city of joy and a centre of the arts. During the reign of the Khiljis there was a strong Persian presence in their courts, as is seen in the paintings of this period such as the *Nimat Nama* which was a book of culinary delicacies, and comprised Ghiyas-ud-din's favourite recipes which were compiled shortly after his death. While the *Nimat Nama* is heavily Persianised and although many women appear as men in Persian dress, others are frankly Indian both in costume and physique. Already the Indian delight in a sumptuous feminine form is evident, a trait that was to develop in the centuries ahead, and while the Persian style was still in the ascendant there was an unmistakable Indian aura in the Mandu *kalam*. Malwa passed from the Khiljis to the Pathans and it was Baz Bahadur who was only tepidly a Muslim (r.1554-1562) and who made Mandu a city of joy that pulsated with his heart throbbing romance with his Hindu courtesan Rupamati, and which was to resonate with song and dance in romantic spaces in opulent palaces directly tied to the Malwa *kalam* of the 16th century. Mandu resonated with love poetry, and of this the 7th century Amaraushataka was especially favoured; even a century later the Malwa artist rendered this with the passion and vigor that we had come to expect from the Indian *kalam* with the floral border at the bottom being the only vestige of the Persian style, while the solid monochrome background, presaging the standard Rajput idiom, was a mirror of the mind.

The Indian artist in the 16th century was trying to break out of the very restricted palette of both the early Western Indian style, seen in the Jain manuscripts, and the Persian style of Nimat Nama, by evolving motifs and metaphors, methods and techniques, to express visually the vitality and warmth of *shringara rasa kavyas*. One of the most important change brought in by the Indian artist of the 16th century was the turning of the head to full profile, the dropping of the further eye while the body remained frontal. This was seen in a seminal form in the Bihar book cover at the end of the last century, but in the 16th century this style was to find full maturity and establish itself as the prototypical indigenous style and the flag bearer of Indian painting capable of expressing the hues and heartbeats of *shringara rasa* in all its manifold richness, and has been called the early Rajput style.

The Sultanate paintings of the 15th and early 16th century, made not for the Sultans but probably for wealthy individuals, still maintain a Persian ambience with figures standing on the baseline and the landscape functioning as a shallow backdrop without any pictorial depth, as is seen in the Mandu c. 1500 painting of the Laur Chanda. The Indian artist in the Sultanate period once again broke away from their Persian exemplars who paid equal importance to the text as well as the image. The Indian artist on the other hand, produced a series of images that almost needed no text, and this was the beginning of the *chitravali* or the picture book tradition, of several paintings in a loose leaf format with the text reduced to the verse or only a few lines at the top. In a *chitravali*, each image could function both individually and collectively and this was particularly important in images of Krishna where every moment had a different story to tell, every image had a romantic message to convey but the very persona of Krishna demanded that the entire *chitravali* be enjoyed and understood in toto. The image rather than the text was gaining importance and the Indian artist in the 16th century, like the sculptor of ancient India ,was interested in creating figures that speak for themselves and that could stand on their own. Just as the ancient Hindus emphasised orality the Indian medieval artist of miniature paintings relied on the visual primacy and efficacy of the human image and the emotion they expressed. This was the beginning of the ethos of courts and *havelis*, where connoisseurs gathered along with an assembly of poets, where Krishna was alive through song and dance, where miniature paintings were not silently or individually enjoyed but were passed from person to person, till the ambience was rich with the presence of Krishna, and it was only then that the painting was covered in a silk cloth and replaced in the *basta* and then another painting would make the rounds of the *rasikas*, and thus it went through the evening. It is patently clear how, in an activity such as this, each painting had to tell its own story individually and therefore an album or book of paintings would not work, but yet at the end of the evening a certain mood of Krishna's love would prevail after all the paintings were considered in their totality and each individual painting would have one underlying ethos, and that was the love of Krishna.

The 16th century thus saw the Indian artist perfecting the human form within the limitations of a two-dimensional pictorial space so that it was capable of expressing the full range of human emotions, and this was particularly important in representing the *shringara rasa* of Krishna. The face had turned to full profile while the chest remained frontal and the background was a backdrop like a curtain on the stage giving primacy to the human figures and the many nuances of the body, its gestures and movements, the eyes and the gaze. It was as if we were in the audience and we were watching a romantic play on stage, where the characters look at each other and not at us, and as Losty says "for the first time in India painting has become divorced from the sculptural tradition and moved into an independent world of its own". Once again to quote Losty:

> The new and vividly expressive stylization of the figures, the full profile confrontations, the balance of the composition, the elegance of the poses and of the hand and eye gestures, all combine to heighten the emotional tension and set up the appropriate aesthetic response in the viewer.[19]

The next step in the evolution from *pothi* to *chitravali* in the 16th century was the emergence of the Chaurapanchashika style of painting. While it is difficult to pinpoint the exact geographical home of the Chaurapanchashika genre of painting, Gwalior or Chottir in Mewar are possibilities. A frieze in the Man Mandir palace at Gwalior is done in the Chaurapanchashika style, and this is one of the most compelling reasons to locate this style in and around Gwalior. Man Singh and his consort Mriganayani were adept musicians, and his court was teeming with a creative synthesis of music and dance. This style of painting most certainly evolved under a Hindu patron and does not owe anything to the strong Mughal style that was emerging almost contemporaneously. Chaurapanchashika refers not only to the style of painting but also to artistic representation of the 12th century poem by Bilhana of the same name.

Some art historians assert that the Chaurapanchashika style of painting was a pan-North-Indian style in the pre-Mughal time and not restricted just to central India. While borrowing from the Western Indian Jain manuscripts and sharing the culture of neighbouring Mewar, the Chaurapanchashika style played a pivotal role in the 16th century in establishing a uniquely Indian palette, and remains the touchstone of the visual representation of *shringara rasa* early in the painting tradition. They are sometimes also referred to as the *kulahdar* group of paintings, from *kulah* or a small conical cap that the men are shown wearing. Drawing its inspiration from the 12th century love poem

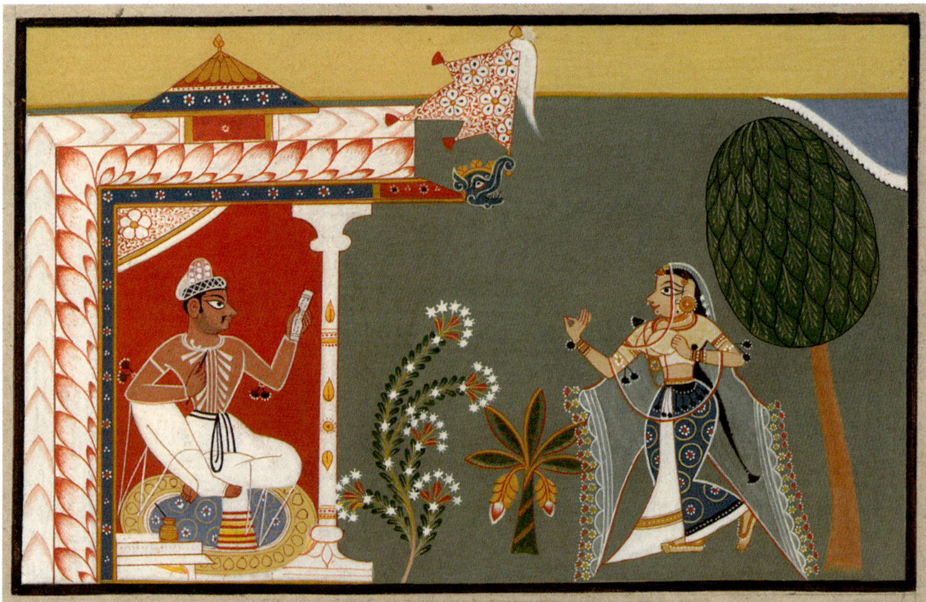

Bilhan's *Chaurapanchashika*. Painting by Vijay Sharma

by the same name, the paintings of *Chaurapanchashika* retain a remarkably native and earthy Indian romantic ethos and are undoubtedly, a product of a Hindu court and culture, both in style and content. Even though they incorporated some pre-Akbari Muslim artistic styles they can be considered the first truly Indian art of post-classical northern India and leaves, no doubt that there was both in the Indian *kavya* and *kalam* a strength and a joy in expressing the many colours of sensuality. Champavati, the heroine in the painting seems self-assured and poised with an undercurrent of passion, moving with a dancer's grace and poise, and in her, the Indian artist invented perhaps his most enchanting symbol of feminine coquetry, demure and studied, at the same time advancing and in retreat. There is in these paintings a declaration of frank sensuality and moments of uninhibited romance that seem to resonate Bilhana's hauntingly nostalgic refrain *adyapi*, even now. The assured line depicting a square face, a large backward sweeping eye, a large triangular nose, a sharp protruding chin which curves softly down into the neck, well endowed breasts that intersect, cut away *choli*, the triangular lower projection of the *patka*, the diaphanous *odhni* that balloons over the head, the *chakdar jama*, colourful Gujarat textiles, a vivid palette with the intense red and green background, have all come to be recognised as the signature of the Chaurapanchashika style. The most important innovation however, of the Chaurpanchashika artists, was the turning of the head in full profile and dropping of the farther projecting eye, one artistic idiom that was to give more freedom to the artist, not only to narrate a story, but even more importantly to convey the many moods of the *nayak* and the *nayika*. From the *dedh chasme ka chehera* the face was now *ek chashme ka chehera*, the face with one spectacle, a face that could do justice to the many colours of love and romance, and the miniature artist could give full play to the eye, especially of the romantic heroine, and was thus able to match the romantic poet in depicting the language of the eyes, so important in a romantic transaction. The artist, the poet and the characters in the painting were speaking the same language.

The Chaurapanchashika style, after the *Vasanta Vilasa* and the *Balagopalastuti*, emerges in the 16th century as the landmark of the most eloquent and elegant Indian representation of *shringara rasa*. In the *Gita Govinda* (1525–1570) of our Museum we have a romantically vivacious, sensually evocative, self assured and spiritually aware *nayika* that would be worthy of the love of Krishna. The artists of the Chaurapanchashika style maintained the *pothi* format even though they were painting on paper but created an artistic space that resonated with the love of Krishna; it was a two-dimensional space that touched the many dimensions of love, a few square inches that covered the whole universe of the romantic heart.

The 16th and 17th centuries saw the emergence of the Mughals, and with it another aesthetic of *shringara rasa*. While Babur (1483–1530) was a keen observer and Humayun (1507–1556) was responsible for bringing Persian artists to his court, it was in the ateliers of Akbar (1543–1605) and Jehangir (1569-1627) that miniature painting and the production of texts were to reach a high watermark, and this was to play an important part in shaping the artistic sensibilities of Indian painters both in the ateliers of the Mughals and, by osmosis, those artists who were working in the Rajput courts. This captures the essence of the Mughal artistic sensibility which was fostered by Akbar who was largely responsible for forging a distinct Mughal identity and steering it away from the Persian and the European style. Jahangir continued his father's tradition. The Mughal penchant for naturalism and portraiture, its desire to record accurately history and court proceedings, its need to treat space with rational perspective and the production of lavishly adorned and illuminated visual books, was an important development in the history of Indian painting, and endeared it to Persian and European aesthetic sensibilities. However it is the very strength of the Mughal idiom that distanced it from the Hindu ethos of Krishna *bhakti* of the Rajput courts. The sensuality and the spirituality of Krishna *bhakti* demanded a very different attitude and *kalam*, an ability to portray sensuality and move it to spirituality, and this the Mughal artists were not able to provide and this was present in a seminal form in the 15th century in the Western Indian style, which was to come fully in the mature Rajput style of painting in the 17th and 18th centuries. The Mughal palette, though refined artistically and with its insistence on rational perspective and naturalism, lacked the throbbing passion and spontaneity that the loves of Krishna demanded, and although its effects were pervasive no artist in Rajput courts was immune from the Mughal influence, the Indian artist was searching for a style and an idiom that could do justice to the many hues and colours of Krishna's love, and this was to come in the 17th and 18th centuries with the development of the fully mature Rajput style which we could call totally and fully Indian and uninfluenced by the Mughal, Persian or European trends.

In the 17th century, even though the *chitravali* with vertical loose leaves had established itself as the preferred format for expressing the love of Krishna, the nostalgia of the *pothi* of the 15th and 16th centuries remained in the minds of the artist for several hundred years. This is seen clearly in the 1630 Mewar *Bhagavata Purana* where the text has been given more prominence than the image, and while this is reminiscent of the Jain manuscripts the images are clearly of the 17th century vintage. The two early 17th century leaves from the *Bhagavata* from Gujarat are good examples of the ability of the Gujarat artists to balance the text and the images not only to effectively narrate the story of Krishna from the *dashama skanda*, but create lively figures contained within simple outlines and set in a basic, but strongly monochromatic background. There is in these *chitravalis* a primitive charm,

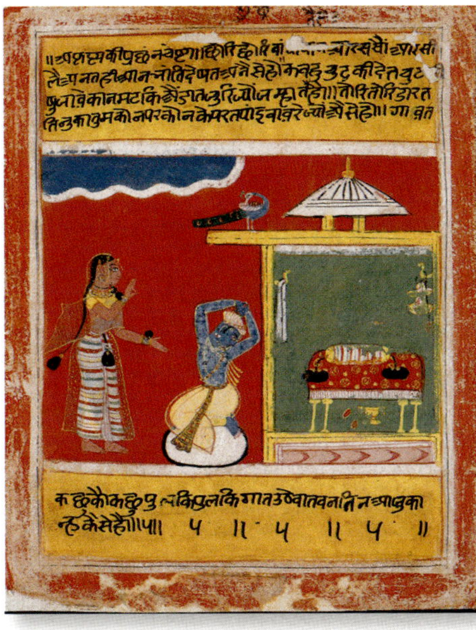

Rasikapriya. Malwa, 1634 CE

a statement that one did not have to turn to Mughal and Persian styles but just to dip into indigenous resources of *kavya* and *kalam* to create a pleasing picture. Here, we have a coming together of sacred words and sensuous images which sums up the ethos of Krishna in its unpretentious way, a Krishna that was loved and venerated in homes and *havelis*, by the *raja* and the *praja*. Chaurayasi Vaishnava ki Varta is a 1701 manuscript from Nathadwara that illustrates this point further. In a large vertical format it narrates the devotional stories of Vaishnava merchants from Gujarat and intersperses it with small illustrations mainly from the Shrinathji tradition. It not only attests to the strong Pushtimarg tradition of Vallabha that prevailed in Gujarat and Rajasthan in the 17th and 18th centuries that touched not only the *havelis* of Krishna, but equally the laity and especially the business classes but also to the indigenous ethos of the primacy of the written word and the illustrations serving mainly to embellish the text. Even through the *chitravali*, as form of painting was well established at this time, the desire to narrate a story or create a text remained strong.

In a slightly later leaf from the *Gita Govinda* the Mewari artist of 1714 creates a *chitravali* in the *pothi* format and attenuates the text to a few lines at the top giving enough room to display, not only human figures in their romantic dalliance but, equally, the luxuriant landscape in which this romantic emotion is being played out. Even though the courtly ambience of *ritikal* had established itself, the verdant Vrindavana always beckoned, and especially when it came to the *Gita Govinda*, there could be no other locale. The sacredness of the *pothi* and the sensuality of the *chitravali* seem to come together in these 17th century creations emphasising that Krishna has both a sacred and a secular presence, that within the lush sensuality the sacred was hidden but not lost.

The next step in the evolution of the *pothi* to *chitravali* in the *shringar bhakti* of Krishna was to come with the rise of the Rajput courts in the 17th and 18th centuries, and the development of the mature Rajput style. The proto-Rajasthani style of the 16th century that had developed in Western and Central India had given the Indian artist the confidence to handle a two-dimensional space and make it come alive with the many and variegated colours of love, and this had ensured that they had the skills to produce a lively painting that was capable of expressing the *shringara rasa* of Krishna in all its nuances and splendour. In their account of the development of Rajput paintings art historians write about issues of patronage after the decline of the Mughal ateliers, and the pervasive influence of the Mughal style in Rajput paintings, and talk of the Rajput ateliers in the debt of the Mughlas. While it cannot be denied that artists of the Rajput ateliers were influenced by artists of the Mughal courts, or from centres of Popular Mughal painting, and in particular learnt about modeling and shading creating the perfect human figure, yet that artistic perfection of form was inadequate in containing the many colours and hues of *shringara rasa* of Krishna. It cannot be forgotten that there was a refreshingly vibrant Hindu ethos in the Rajput courts and this was to stem mainly from the Pushtimarg *shringar bhakti* of Krishna, reflected in song and dance, and the paintings that came out of this milieu were to reflect the music and the rhythms of the poetry and song that celebrated the love of Krishna and which were a part of rich ambience of the

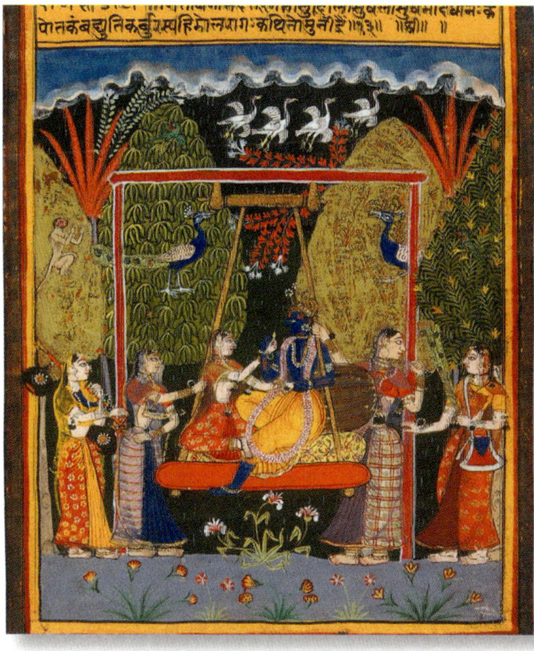

Raga Hindola, Kota. 18th century

Rajput courts. It has been suggested that the painters who could nor keep pace with the rapidly-evolving Mughal style were released from the ateliers to seek work elsewhere. Could it be that they felt uncomfortable with the Mughal idiom and wanted to return to more indigenous modes of expression particularly of *shringara rasa*? The mature Rajput style of the 17th century is best represented by the work of Sahibdin of Mewar, who created beautiful paintings of the *Rasikapriya* where the courtly figures of Krishna and Radha were in harmony with the lush landscape and elegant architecture, which clearly speaks of Sahibdin's indigenous lineage despite this awareness and even training of the Mughal *kalam*. Sahibdin's work leaves no doubt that when it came to the *shringara rasa* of Krishna the earthy indigenous *kalam* reigned supreme. Rajput painting, whether in Rajasthan or the hill states of Punjab, saw the resurgence of the Krishna of love in the native *kalam*, a Krishna that was already celebrated with a distinctively indigenous flavour by poets in Eastern India in the *Bhagavata* and the *Gita Govinda*. Rajput patrons assured the centrality of Krishna in the celebration of *shringara rasa* and this needed a very evocative *kalam* distinctly different from that of the Mughals. To the Rajput psyche, amorous feelings could not be separated from the flute of Krishna, the sensuousness of romance was tied intimately to the sights and sounds, the aroma and the ambience of the enchanted forest of Vrindavana or the elegance of the courts where Radha and Krishna dallied, the joy of belonging and the pathos of longing could only be understood through the various moods of Radha, and one could only experience the depth of *shringara rasa* by recreating Vrindavana within one's heart. All of this required the passionate Hindu *kalam*, and not the rational Mughal style. If *shringara* for us has *madhurya* it is only through Krishna, if *viraha* is *adhyatmika* or spiritual it can only be through the mind of Radha and this was best brought out by the creations of the Rajput ateliers working with the indigenous Rajput, rather than the Mughal *kalam*. Radha and Krishna are particular and universal, human and divine, secular and sacred at the same time, all features of Pushtimarg Vaishnavism which was the credo of the Rajput courts. This is the reason why the love of Radha and Krishna is so central, so meaningful and played an important part in Rajput courts, and it needed, not the historically accurate and rationally correct Mughal eye but the poetically sensitive and passionately earthy Rajput mind to depict it in paintings. In partaking of their love, through the paintings, we bring something of their sweetness into our own lives, in remembering Vrindavana we bring some of its enchantment in our own minds, in enjoying the various *lilas* of Krishna there is a reminder, that within the Krishna of love is also a child given to pranks, and in letting their abundant love touch us we are bringing boundless joy into our own little lives. It is because of this that the Rajput courts gave a new dimension to this very rich and magnificent love through the many evocative paintings, whether they were of the *Bhagavata* or the *Gita Govinda* or the *ritikal* creations of Bihari and Keshavdas set in a courtly ambience and used their own artistic techniques creating the uniquely evocative Rajput *kalam*. The songs and the stories, the poetry and the Puranas took on a visual and palpable form in Rajput courts and *havelis*. One could hold and feel the paintings and enjoy them in elite company, enjoy the *kathakars* or story tellers as they recounted the deeds of Radha and Krishna and exult in the sensuous dances that brought alive their many dalliances. If Jayadeva had created an enchanted Vrindavana, the Rajput artists painted magnificent courts and *havelis* that resonated with the love of Krishna, if Jayadeva wrote evocative poetry, the Rajput artists in their ateliers created visual poetry, if Jayadeva's words were music to the ears, the Rajput painted creations were a visual feast, and the Rajput *kalam* was a testament to the proud and self-confident Rajputs, who may paid military obeisance to the Mughals but who were not going to give up their pride in their native religious and artistic traditions.

The Rajput courts continued the ancient Indian tradition of tying visual art to textual sources and creating paintings that were not only sensually rich but spiritually evocative, but they broke new ground and inaugurated a new era in Hindu art, when they chose to represent visually, the many nuances and shades of romantic love, and especially that of Radha and Krishna and relegate the text to a few lines at the top or at the back of the painting. In many cases the painting reflected a romantic theme but was not related specifically to a verse or a *doha*. In the Rajput courts a new chapter in the aesthetics of Vaishnavism was being written. Besides creating paintings of the *Bhagavata Purana* and the *Gita Govinda*, Rajput artists produced refined and visually charming paintings from the *Rasikapriya*, *Rasamanjari* and *Satsai*. Ragamala and Barahmasa were another favourite texts of the Rajput ateliers. In placing romantic love within the myriad taxonomies offered by the *ritikal* poets, Rajput artists moved romantic love from the idyllic Vrindavana to the *havelis* and courts. It has been said that in satisfying the spiritual and aesthetic needs of their Hindu patrons and placing Radha and Krishna in a courtly ambience, the artists who created these Rajput paintings, whether they were Hindus or Muslims, were working within a conceptual and emotional framework that was well established centuries before their time.[20] It is worth noting that although there were sharp doctrinal and religious differences between the Hindus and the Muslims, however, when it came to painting, Hindu and Muslim artists worked together and harmoniously in many Rajput ateliers. Some of the finest paintings with a Hindu theme have been painted by Muslim artists such as Sahibdin in Mewar and Ruknuddin in Bikaner. In great measure this was due to the culture of tolerance that prevailed in many Mughal and Rajput courts. In the exuberant Vaishnava ethos, religious differences were put aside in the celebration of Krishna. What mattered most was to capture on canvas, the spirit of romantic excitement and ecstasy of Krishna and Radha. Ancient texts such as the *Kamasutra*

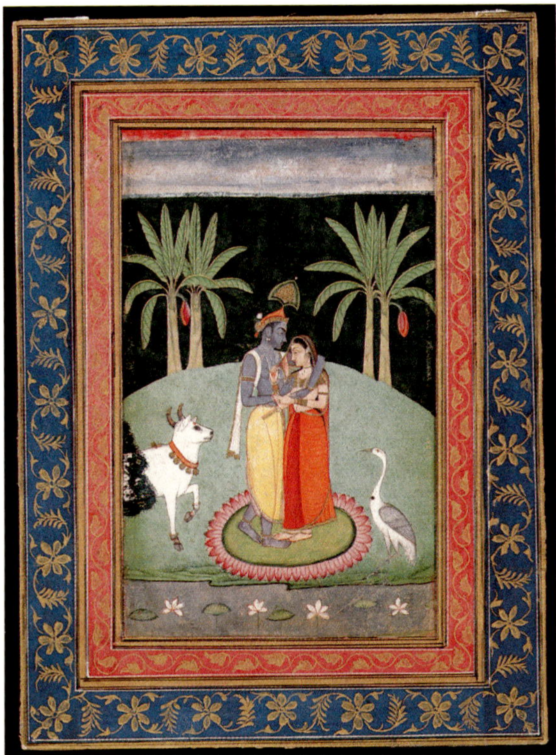

Bikaner, 18th century

stipulate that the cultured elite should be well versed in the art of painting. While agreeing in principle with these statements we would like to emphasise that while the artistic idiom of ancient India in the visual arts was sculpture, and that while this was able to depict feminine eroticism and fertility with finesse, the sensitive and elegant visual depiction of *shringara rasa*, the romantic sentiment, reached a high watermark only in the paintings of the

Rajput courts, and that this art stemmed from the Indian earth and was not fostered either by Mughal or Persian aesthetic sensibilities. Another aesthetic feature for which the Rajput ateliers must be given credit is the boldness and sensitivity with which they used colours. If a *chitravali* had to function on its own in conveying a certain mood, it did not always have a text to fall back on, and therefore had to use the language of colours and the aesthetics of space and this they did with finesse. The artists of the Rajput courts excelled in the art of colours and letting it speak the language of love. Pal is right in saying that "the most compelling aspect of Rajput painting is the primacy given to colours, chosen more for their intrinsic qualities and emotional values than for their fidelity to nature".[21] This was an important factor in the success and brilliance of the *chitravalis* where the text was minimal or absent and the figures could speak for themselves. The Indian mind has deep reservoirs of passion and lyricism that were to emerge through the artists of the Rajput courts; both in Rajasthan and the Pahari regions in Rajput paintings the arbor of the assignment bursts into flower, line becomes rhythmic, colour begins to glow.

The Rajput artists created a female form that was emotionally evocative, sensually rich, romantically heart-warming and aesthetically pleasing, and in this they owed no debt to the Mughal or the Persian traditions. The face had already turned to full profile even before the Rajput courts embraced the *shringara rasa* of Krishna. However, the artists of the Rajput courts introduced one important development in the creation of this, and that was the *lata rupa*, the form of a vine of the *nayika*. Anand Krishna traces this to the depictions of beautiful women in early Sanskrit literature. He cites this passage from Kalidasa's *Kumarasambhavam* where the poet is referring to Parvati:

> Her entire body displayed amour as if like a newly sprouted
> Kadamba blossom,
> as she stood before Shiva,
> having large eyes,
> she looked prettier as she stood with her face
> turned in the *sachi-krita* attitude.[22]

The tender loving *nayika* was developed more fully in *ritikavya* where Bihari speaks of the delicate feet of the *nayika* under which spring up soft *dhupariya* flowers as she walks. Anand Krishna[23] feels that the *paravritta ardhamukha* depiction of the *nayika* brought out her sensuality and helped in igniting romantic feelings in the *nayaka*, and the artist of the Rajput courts turned often to this artistic technique. If Indian sculpture depicts mythic figures in their iconic splendour using the full frontal view which facilitated a religiously powerful *darshana*, Indian painting on the other hand converts the frontal representation into the profile making it a perfect vehicle of romantic lyricism for aesthetic delight. While the icon stands on a lotus pedestal expressing its majesty and divinity, and is a vehicle of *darshana* or transfiguring vision, the lissom *nayika* assumes the form of a winding, swaying lotus creeper that twists and turns as she expresses her tender, wistful feelings of love. Traditionally a woman's sensuality is tied to the sap of the trees and creepers. While the *salabhanjika* in sculpture offers her fecundity to the Ashoka tree the *nayika* in *shringara rasa* paintings identifies herself with the lotus creeper as she responds to the touch of her beloved or wilts when she finds his absence unbearable. The romantically-sensitive and sensually-aroused heroine in the hands of the Rajput painter is like the lotus creeper, when she expresses and experiences her sensuality, the life that animates her is no different from the sap that informs the creeper and thus it is that the *shringara rasa nayika* and the creeper are trans-substantiated. This remains the most significant creation of the Hindu mind, and the painters of the Rajput ateliers gave it their best artistic representation. An equally important artistic innovation of the Rajput ateliers was the creation of the arational aesthetic space in preference to rational perspective, a space that reflected with fidelity the mind of the *nayika* in her state of love, for that mind was driven not by rules or reality but had a logic of its own, a mind like that of the *abhisarika nayika* that defied society and security in search of her beloved. Goswamy is right in stating that:

> "The whole philosophical view that the culture takes of matters like time and space becomes reflected in the painter's oeuvre...One senses that in rendering a moment the painter is not losing sight of the moments that have gone by and those that are yet to come... the manner in which the painter changes his point of view within the same painting, manipulates

the elements of space, not treating them as fixed or immutable…nothing of this kind happens in Mughal painting which insists on a more rational view of things and stays within the limits of naturalism".[24]

One can speak of the Hindu way of seeing, *drishti*, that reflects the Hindu view of life, a view that eschews linear time and rational space and in the small dimensions of a painting the Rajput artist is able to reflect the state of the mind. This is the most significant contribution of painters in the Rajput court of Rajasthan of the 17th century.

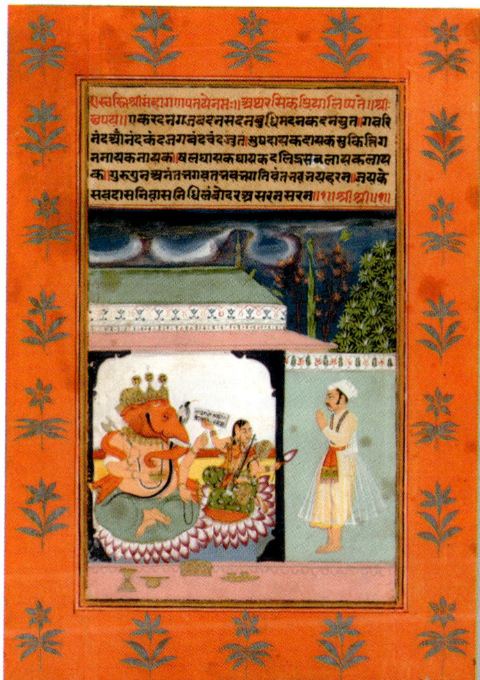

Mangalacharan, *Rasikapriya*, Mewar, 18th century

While the 17th and 18th centuries saw the emergence of the mature Rajput style and a golden chapter in Indian art was written in the plains, the Raput ethos of Krishna *bhakti* travelled to the Himalayan hill states through trade routes, upon which merchants and musicians carried the love of Krishna from the plains to the mountains. The Pahari area was sheltered from the conquests and invasions that the rest of the country suffered, and therefore the Mughal influence in these kingdoms was less marked, and this was responsible for the creation of a unique Pahari style that combined both artistic finesse and devotion to Krishna and remains unique in the history of Indian painting, and more importantly, is able to bring out delicate nuances of the love of Krishna. An early manuscript of the *Devi Mahatmya* of 1552 attests to the presence of a Devi cult in the 16th century in these hill kingdoms and the presence of the Charupanchashika artistic idiom, in but the 17th and the 18th centuries saw the emergence of the unique Pahari style of *shringara bhakti* of Krishna in

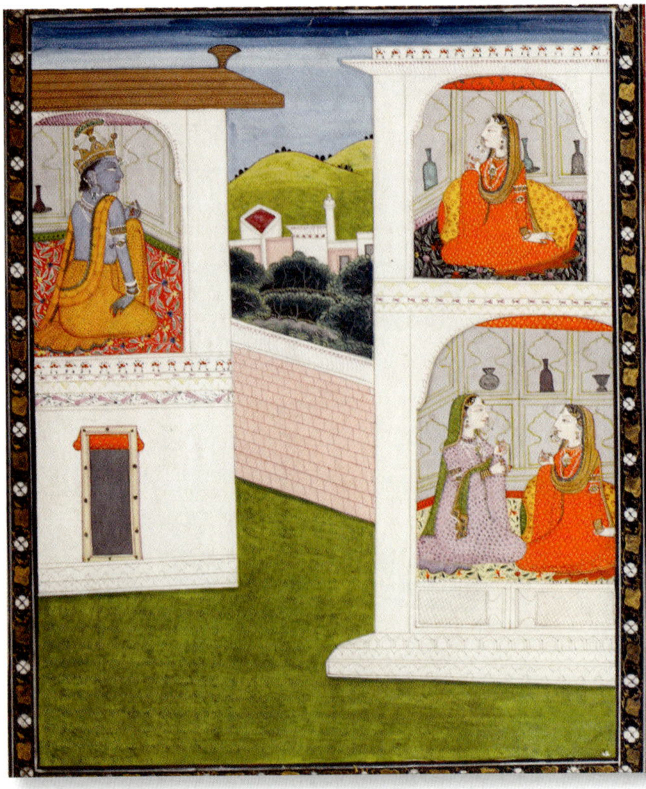

Satsai. Kangra, 1830–40

the Pahari kingdoms which was richly expressed through paintings.
While Rajput painting of Krishna *bhakti* in Rajasthan saw the complete experimentation and evolution from *pothi* to *chitravali*, namely the movement of the early manuscript illustration to the fully evolved and refined miniature painting, it appears that Pahari painting did not go through

this transformation. Rajput ateliers in Rajasthan had fully developed the motifs and the metaphors of the Krishna of love, and although the essence of the text always underpinned their creations, the written text gradually got attenuated to a few lines at the top and then only at the back of the painting. This is because the paintings had enough artistic strength to stand on their own. The Pahari artists took these artistic accomplishments a step further; to the already well developed motifs and metaphors, the forms and the figures of Rajasthani painting they added a softer, lyrical touch to create endearing compositions befitting the mellifluous love of Krishna. The strong monochrome backgrounds reminiscent of the Rajashtani *kalam* were preserved in the Basohli *kalam*, but this was gradually given up in favour of the lush landscape and distant horizon. Another feature of the Pahari *kalam* was that there was greater homogeneity between the output of different kingdoms, unlike Rajasthani paintings, as artists from one kingdom frequently travelled to another, and it was the family of the painters that determined the style more than the geographical situation of the atelier. Pahari painting confined itself throughout its comparatively short history to the realm of the beautiful. This underscores the fact that Pahari art, was not a court art in the Rajput sense, and even more importantly patronage of Pahari art was more enlightened compared to Rajasthani art as it not only gave the artists total freedom in their work but rewarded them handsomely, and gave them an elevated social status.

Broadly speaking three phases in the development of miniature painting in the Pahari *kalam* can be recognised, the early beginnings in the kingdom of Basohli, the middle phase in the Guler, and the late phase in Kangra. Basohli was an ancient state and its present capital was founded in 1630, and it was Raja Kirpal Pal who was born in 1650 and ruled from 1678 to 1695 who inaugurated the first atelier of Pahadi painting in his state of Basohli and commissioned a manuscript of the *Rasamanjari*; and he must therefore be considered the father of the Pahari *kalam,* and the *Rasamanjari* the prototype of Pahari art. The Basohli atelier had artists from Kashmir and possibly even from Nepal as well as *tarkhans* or carpenters who were proficient in architectural drawings and wood sculpture, and this explains the unique style that developed in the atelier of Basohli which incorporated all these influences. Besides the robust, ethnic and primitive human figures that are a signature of the Basohli *kalam*, the use of shiny green beetle wing particles on jewellery was its feature. Equally the unique architecture of the love pavilions of the Basohli *Rasamanjari* with turrets, mythic animals, ornamentally-adorned interior and set in a lush landscape are special features of the 17th century *Rasamanjari*. Raja Kirpal Pal was a learned ruler and, like Akbar, he developed a fondness for possessing illustrated manuscripts on a variety of subjects. Raja Kirpal Pal was aware, not only of Mughal styles and sensibilities of the Aurangzeb period, but equally of Rajasthani tastes, particularly that at Mewar. Besides the *Rasamanjari,* which was the favourite text of Kirpal Pal, the *Bhagavata Purana* and *Gita Govinda* were also illustrated at Basohli, and Krishna had a large presence in all of these manuscripts. Throughout the 18th century Basohli rulers showed a special fondness for *Rasamanjari* and this kingdom was to produce some of the finest illustrations of this romantic text by Bhanudatta. Even though it is entirely possible that artists from neighbouring states may have played a role in the development of the so-called Basohli style, the style remains unique and is one of the finest artistic expressions in miniature painting of the 17th and 18th century, with its characteristic ethnic types, bold colour schemes, wooden architectural motifs, large and staring eyes, and frank and robust figures. Artists from Basohli migrated to other states and to Nurpur in particular, and also to Mankot, Bilaspur, Kulu and Chamba, where they continued the Basohli *kalam*.

The second phase of the development of the Pahari *kalam* was to take place in the kingdom of Guler. Geography as much as patronage was responsible for the development of the Guler *kalam*. Founded by Hari Chand in 1405 Guler is located south of Kangra by the river Beas and, since it was easily accessible from the plains it was subject to outside influence. It was Govardhan Chand (1743-1773) who founded and patronised the atelier at Guler. However the Guler style was mainly shaped by Pandit Seu and his illustrious sons, the older Manaku and the younger Nainsukh. Information gleaned from *bahis* at pilgrimage centres suggests that Pandit Seu and his family came originally from Kashmir and were Raina brahmins, and his initial training was in a Mughal atelier of Muhammed Shah. Pandit Seu brought these skills to the Guler court of Raja Dalip Singh and it was thus that a new Guler *kalam* was inaugurated. Nainsukh was born in 1710 and had prodigious skills, and after working initially with his father moved to Jasrota in 1740 where he attached himself to Balwant Singh, a young prince who belonged to a breakaway branch of the ruling family. There is some debate whether Balwant Singh belonged to Jammu or Jasrota. Nainsukh brought a certain delicacy, refinement and lyricism to Pahari painting, which is in sharp contrast to the earlier Basohli style. The Alakananda river which flows through Guler had a special fascination for the Guler artists. Nainsukh and his brother Manaku left an indelible stamp on Pahari painting, and it would be no exaggeration to say that their creations rank as one of the highest achievement of Indian

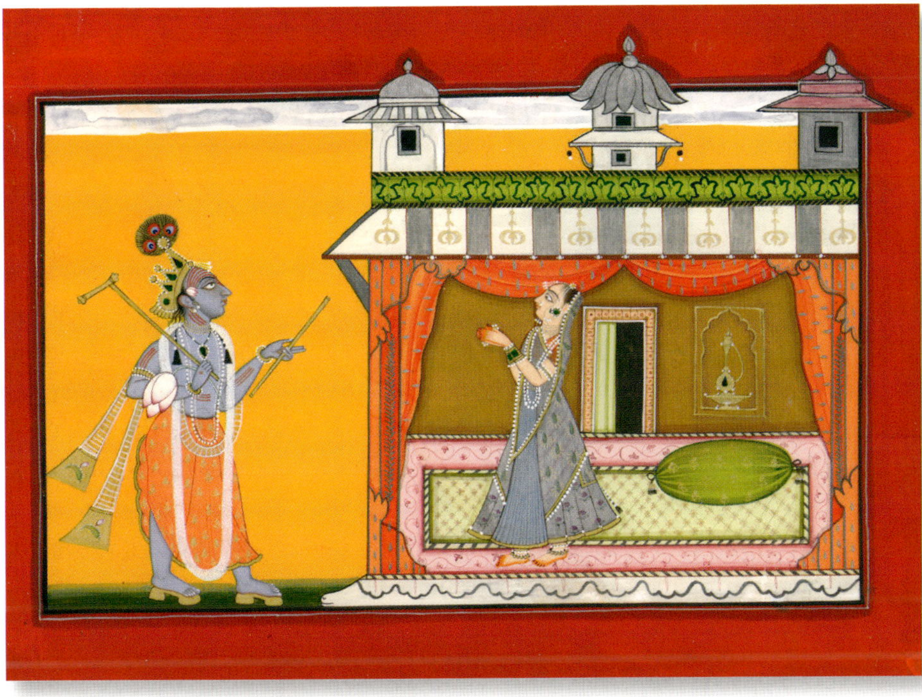

Rasamanjari, Painting in Basohli style by Vijay Sharma

art in the 18th century. In its lyrical lines, subdued colours and a charmed landscape Krishna's mellifluous love for Radha is almost palpable and one can hear, as it were, the sweet whispering of their conversation. In 1780 the fully evolved Guler *kalam* was taken to Kangra and in that state, under the patronage of Raja Sansar Chand (1775–1823), miniature painting reached perfection in the late 18th and early decades of the 19th century.

The psyche of the people was also conditioned by the geography of the environment and the history of the prevailing times. Kangra was blessed with an idyllic landscape, with blossoming trees and verdant groves, sylvan hills and distant mountains, picturesque meadows, fragrant flowers and chirping birds, flowing brooks and a clear sky that provided a canopy to the enchanted world below. There was here none of the harshness of the Rajasthan deserts or the sweltering summers of Gujarat, the courtly intrigue of Rajasthan courts or the enforced privacy and distance of the Mughal harems. Although there was political intrigue in Kangra there were no major wars or military strife, the rulers were benevolent and patrons of the arts and leisure and culture flourished both with the *raja* and the *praja*. There was a certain joyousness and sensuality in the 18th and 19th century Kangra court, as is seen in the accounts of Western travellers like Moorcroft. It is not surprising that the Kangra artist was to incorporate this ethos in their *kalam* and used it to portray the *madhurya* of Krishna. It has been rightly said that Kangra painting is characterised by a lyricism, a patrician elegance tempered by a simplicity and warmth of feeling, a refined earnestness plus a suavity of form. These paintings are *kavyamaya*, suffused with the lyricism of poetry, *layamaya*, full of the delicacy and softness of dance and *gitamaya*, resonant with the sound of music. Emotion is almost palpable, tender feelings of Krishna and the *gopis* are visible, and the music in the air is audible in these beautiful paintings, but only to those who have the sensitivity to go beyond the surface and partake of the nuances and suggestions of Krishna's romantic moments with the *gopis*. In their time these paintings must have been celebrated in elite and cultured company, in sophisticated and elegant surroundings, with the accompaniment of song and dance, with flowing *madira* and smouldering *hookahs*, and not silently watched in the sterile ambience of a museum or in the mute pages of a book like this.

It has rightly been said that Kangra painting is the superb lyricism and the melody of the sweet love of Krishna made visual. The landscape in the paintings which is inspired by the bucolic and luxuriant Pahari terrain is assimilated to the mood of the personages through a symbolism that is very transparent in its poetic suggestion. While the Kangra *kalam* exudes a refined sensuousness and lyrical grace, drawing its inspiration not only from its idyllic landscape but equally by the living presence of the Krishna of love in the courts, it is in the depiction of the graceful and elegantly sensuous *shringara rasa nayika* that it reaches its greatest heights of artistic finesse and mastery. The Modi *Bhagavata* and the Lambargaon *Gita Govinda* rank as the highest watermark of the magnificent Kangra *kalam*. The Kangra *nayika* of painting not only has an elegant and sensuous charm, a luminous elegance and unsurpassed beauty, but a refined romantic sensibility, whether she was experiencing the pain of pathos of the pleasures of love, and in the genre of romantic figures that Indian artists have produced, she represents the most beautiful and the most exalted. There is in her, not only the charm of romantic sensuality but the serenity of a woman in love, who is also aware that her sensuality is the doorway to spirituality. As Coomoaraswamy has said "The Kangra *kalam* is indeed a feminine art, intrinsically an art of sentiment rather than of passion."[25] Among the Pahari ateliers other than Basohli and Kangra mention must be made of the Garhwal atelier which was dominated by Mola Ram (1743-1833), who in his long life produced some scintillating paintings imbued with life and colour and resonant of Krishna. Mandi was yet another important centre, and the Mandi artist had a fondness of depicting the *doha* that informed the painting in a fly sheet with a floral border and this created a nice effect in a *chitravali*.

Thus from the tentative but evocative paintings of the Balagopalstuti of the 15th century, through the sensually charged representations of the Chaura, the monochromatic and passionate spaces of Mandu, the evocative figures of the Chawand Ragamala and later the mature creations of the Rajput ateliers in Rajasthan where *shringar rasa* of Krishna and Radha was evocatively represented, and culminating in the charged lyricism of the Pahari *kalam*, the loves of Krishna are transformed from poetry to a charmed pictorial space, painted with both passion and piety, where *shringara* and *bhakti* become a seamless whole, where amorous moments of longing or belonging with Krishna are brought alive with an artistic finesse and romantic sensitivity, where Radha emerges as the prototypical romantic heroine, self-assured but yet gentle like a creeper, ecstatic and effusive in moments of heightened love but at the same time dignified and demure in her *viraha,* and holding all these charmed and magical moments of love together, like an invisible *sutra*, is the mellifluous love of Krishna, who ensures that while affirming and celebrating romantic sensuality, that same love moves to the rarefied domains of spirituality.

There has thus been an evolution in the style and format of paintings as the loves of Krishna move from *pothi* to *chatravali*. Changing historical conditions, political patronage and foreign artistic influences were responsible for these changes. But underpinning it at all times was poetry which was responsible for a certain vision of Krishna, equally there was piety which demanded that *shringara rasa* be transformed into *shringara bhakti* and even more the power of the indigenous *kalam* to celebrate and recreate the passionate and earthy sensuality of Krishna, a sensuality that did not need to conform to the dictates of rationality or be confined to rational order, but which answered only to the sweet love of Krishna and delighted in his *krida* and *lila* and which partook of his *madhurya* and suffered in his *viraha*, to create the beautiful and heart throbbing paintings of Krishna over five glorious centuries, leaving behind for us a visual treasure, a feast of colours, a painted festival of his love, so that we who participate in that love can enrich our lives and make Krishna come alive in our mind and ensure that we will hear his flute, and along with the *gopis* wait under the Kadamba tree for that charmed rendezvous; when we do hear that flute the world around us will be Krishnamaya, full of Krishna, and in that magical moment we will find ourselves and the journey will have reached our destination.

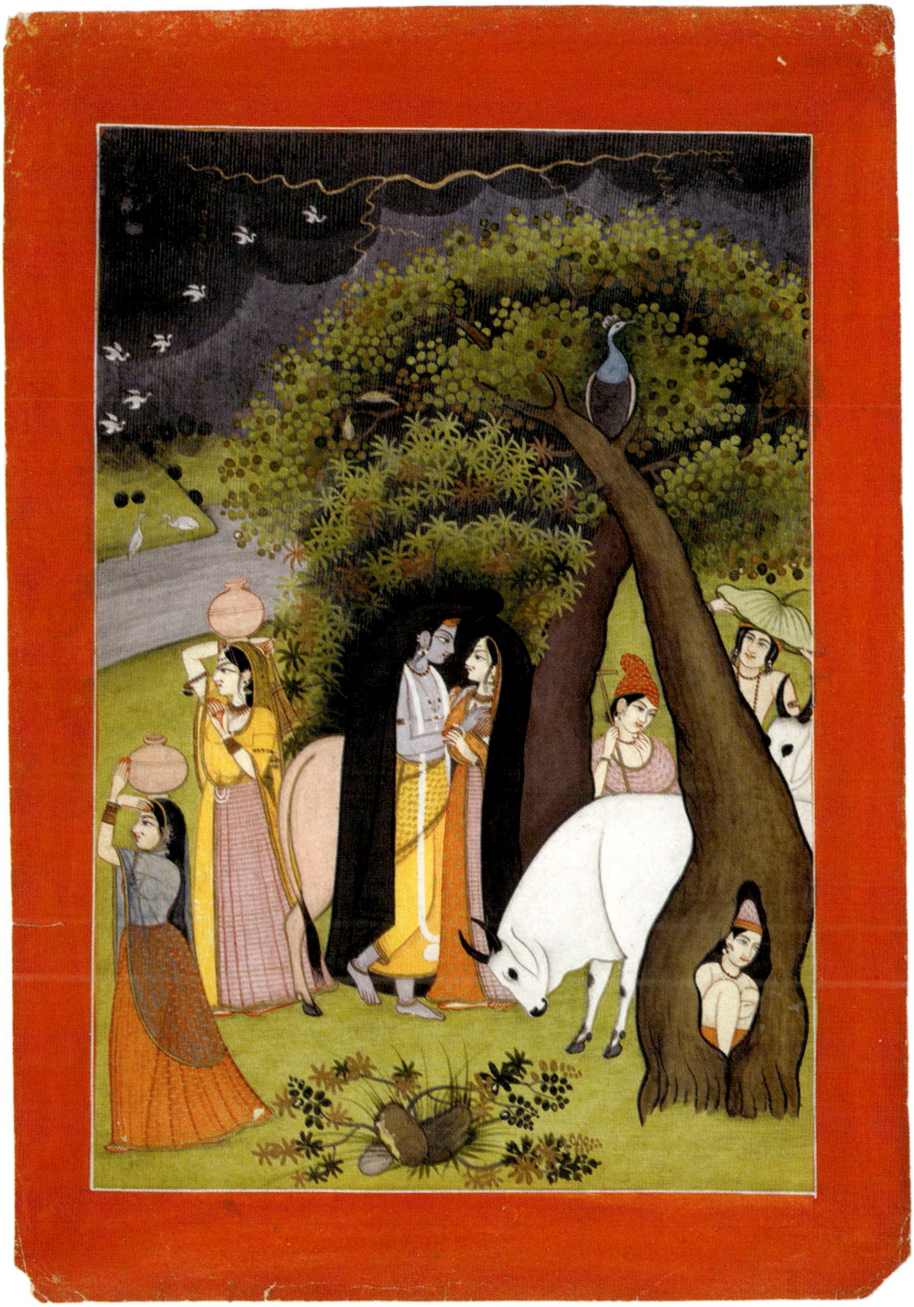

Kangra, 1820–30

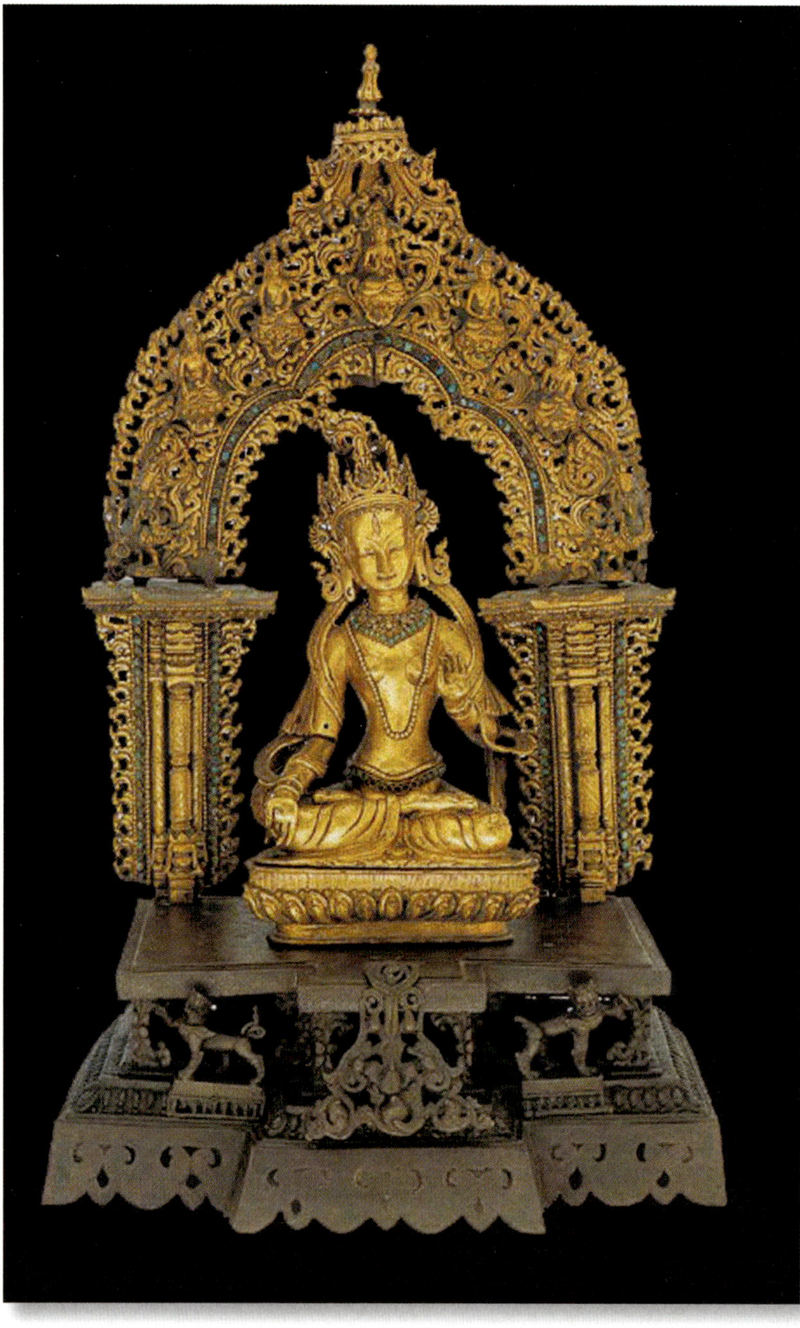

Tara. Nepal. 18th century

Gods of Our Shrines

Beauty of Bronzes

Bronze (*kansa* in Hindi) casting is an ancient, prehistoric, art in India as is evidenced by the enigmatic bronze icon in the Indus Valley artifacts. Bronze is an alloy of copper and tin and was the preferred material in ancient India, as it was not only malleable and therefore easy to sculpt but also more permanent than wood. In the 20th century silicon was added as an additional component. Copper and tin were not found in the same place and therefore the creation of bronze required trade, and this would explain the history of bronzes. Bronze icons from the Kushana and the Gupta periods have been found. The Chausa hoard of 18 Jain bronzes is the first known bronze discovered in the Gangetic valley thus named after the place of discovery in the Buxar district of Bihar.

While this art must surely have continued in many different ways, not only for making images but also for tools and utensils, the next significant development comes with the Iron Age where iron was replacing bronze as this was not dependent on material being available through trade. The south of India seems to have missed this early Bronze Age, and it is only with the Cholas creating magnificent bronzes, both as icons for the *garbha griha* as well as *utsav murtis* that bronze returns to India. These Chola bronzes remain as timeless expressions. not only of our southern monarchs, but of the entire

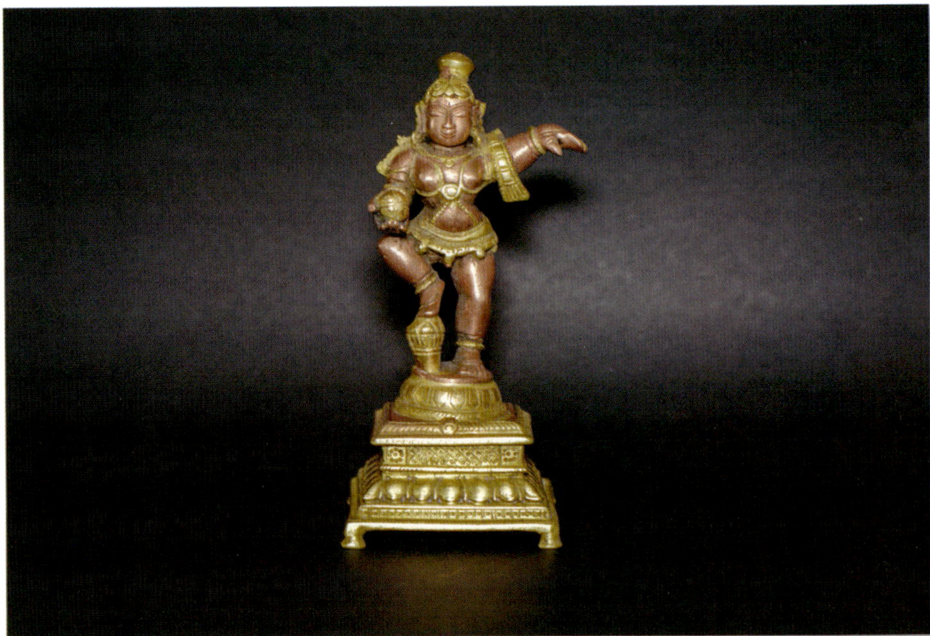

Navnitpriya Krishna, Karnataka, 18th century

Indian civilisation. If we were to choose only one bronze that can speak for our entire civilisation it must be the Nataraja. However, we will bypass the glorious tradition of Chola bronzes to look at the equally significant chapter of the small bronzes, which in some ways are more beautiful. Not only are they pan-Indian, but even more, they find a place in the home shrines of both the *bhaktas* and the shelves of *rasikas*.

If for the *bhakta*, life is bound by divine forces, that for the *rasika* is defined by concepts and expressions of the beautiful, and for both purposes a visual image that we can hold and touch and see is important. Small bronzes are ideal for that purpose. For the wealthy there would be a prayer room in the home, and for the not so privileged the home shrine is usually in the kitchen or in a niche in the wall. These bronzes are of our gods and goddesses, major and minor, and in being small they are accessible and close to us. We bathe them in the morning and apply either sandalwood or *kumkum*, offer flowers and food which then becomes our *prasada*.They are a part of our quotidian life, we talk to them, we venerate them, we open our hearts to them and tell them of all our earthly problems, they participate in our *samskaras* and festivals, we feed them and clothe them as if they were humans, but never forgetting for a moment that they are divine. With these small bronzes the border between human and divine is seamless. These bronzes are portable, and on journeys or pilgrimages they travel with us. Sometimes we strap them to our body in a special container, for unlike the grand icons in temples we want to be close to our gods at all times. The gods of the small bronzes do not reside in a distant heaven but in our hearts.

Sometimes we have divided our gods into the great and the little traditions, or the *margi* and the *desi*, and while this may be upheld by scholars and curators, when it comes to the little bronzes this artificial distinction disappears. The small bronzes belong to the high and the low caste, the rural and the tribal, the Brahmanical and the folk, for they respond to our emotions and not to the *shastras*.

We must fast forward from the grand age of Chola bronzes to the 16th century of small bronzes. The *bhakti* movement which started in the South had spread to the West and the North and was catching momentum. The time for the grand temples had passed, the Muslims had a significant presence in the country and were expressing their anti-iconic beliefs in temples, and the Hindus sought solace in small gatherings in their own home away from the Muslim gaze. The need for small images of our gods and goddesses was strong. While terracotta images were available, they could not be used for worship which involved *abhishek* with water, milk or honey. A *bhakta*, unlike a *rasika*, felt comforted with the ritual worship of icons, and not just a silent contemplation of its beauty. Even more these small icons could be hidden in the ground, if the need arose. This explains why even today gold coins and bronze images are found by farmers or archeologists. This was the time of small bronze images which could satisfy the need for Hindu households, and its creation proliferated from Kashmir to Vijaynagara and everything in between and beyond.

As we have noted, the great and little traditions meet when it comes to the small bronzes, and this is seen particularly in the tribal or *adivasis* of India. While not formally part of the Puranic tradition of gods and goddesses, Lakshmi is adored and icons of Lakshmi are given as dowry, along with other objects such as oil lamp, boxes and measuring bowls for rice. The Kondhs are the largest tribal group of Odisha and the tradition of these bronzes is very strong. Once these bronzes became collector's items the Kondhs started hiding them in bamboo baskets, their loft, and the smoke from their hearths covered them in a dark brownish sooty patina.

Bastar in Chattisgarh is another important centre of bronzes. The first bronze figures were introduced into Bastar by the royal family of Warangal in the 15th century. Bastar bronze casters follow a variation of the cire-perdue method. The images are initially fashioned out of clay, not wax. This clay core is then completely encased in a series of thin wax threads *(mom sutta)*. There is a long tradition of creating icons such as Radha Krishna, the *saptamatrika*, shrines of goddesses, spirit riders on a horse and animals, and often a family would commission a icon for offering to the village goddess. The pride of place in Bastar goes to the tutelary deity Danteshvari, and at the annual festival thousands of people congregate and it seems that it is Danteshvari that brings them all together. Unlike Puranic gods, the gods of the *adivasis* do not have a fixed iconography. It is said that the *adivasis*, gods convey their wish to the bronze, caster in their dreams. As he bestows the invisible god with a visible form the metal caster assumes a great responsibility.

Gujarat is home to Vaishnavism for centuries and it not surprising that some of the finest bronzes are those of Krishna and Radha Krishna. The signature of the Gujarat Krishna bronzes is the square base and the hair tied in a knot at the back. The commonest figure is that of Venugopala or the fluting

Krishna deriving its inspiration from the *Bhagavata Purana*. While not following any canonical dictates, these Gujarat bronzes of Venugopala draw their inspiration from the many illustrated manuscripts of the *Bhagavata* which were created in Gujarat in the 16th century. It is noteworthy that while Shrinathji at Nathadwara accompanies the main deity of Gujarat it does not translate into bronzes. Equally the strong presence of Jainas did not lead to the creation of bronzes, as the Jain *tirthankaras* were celebrated with illustrated manuscripts like the Kalpasutra. These charming Venugopala bronzes would invariably be part of the home shrine and venerated with ritual worship and singing of *bhajans*.

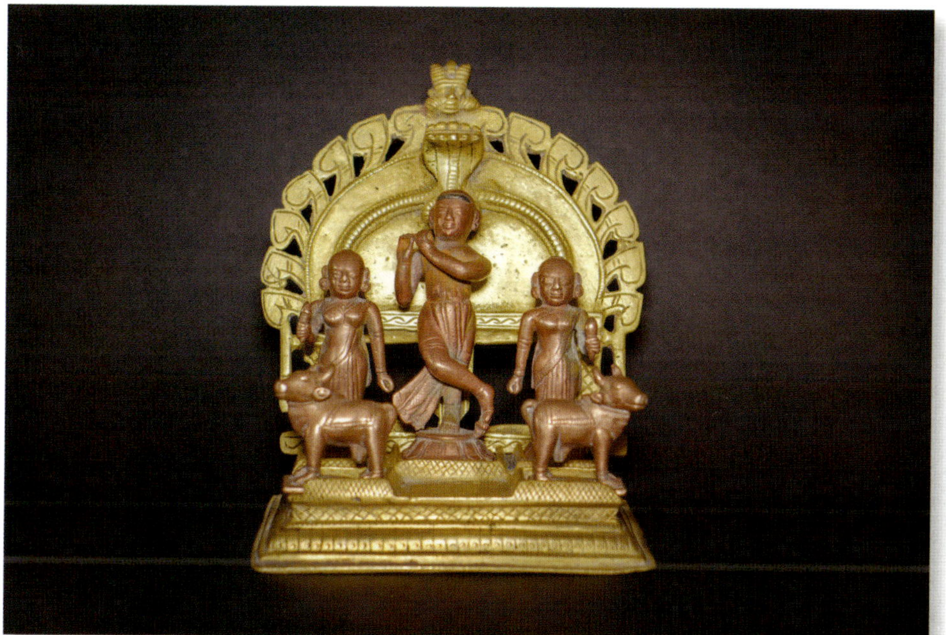

Krishna and Gopis, Karnataka, 18th century

When we come to Karnataka and Maharashtra it is the Balagopala, or the crawling Krishna, that is the most popular icon. Possibly inspired by the *Balagopalastuti*, the infant Krishna is celebrated by rite and ritual, song and dance. Made both of brass and bronze and sometimes adorned with silver eyes, the child Krishna is popular with young mothers and is the centrepiece of their home shrines.

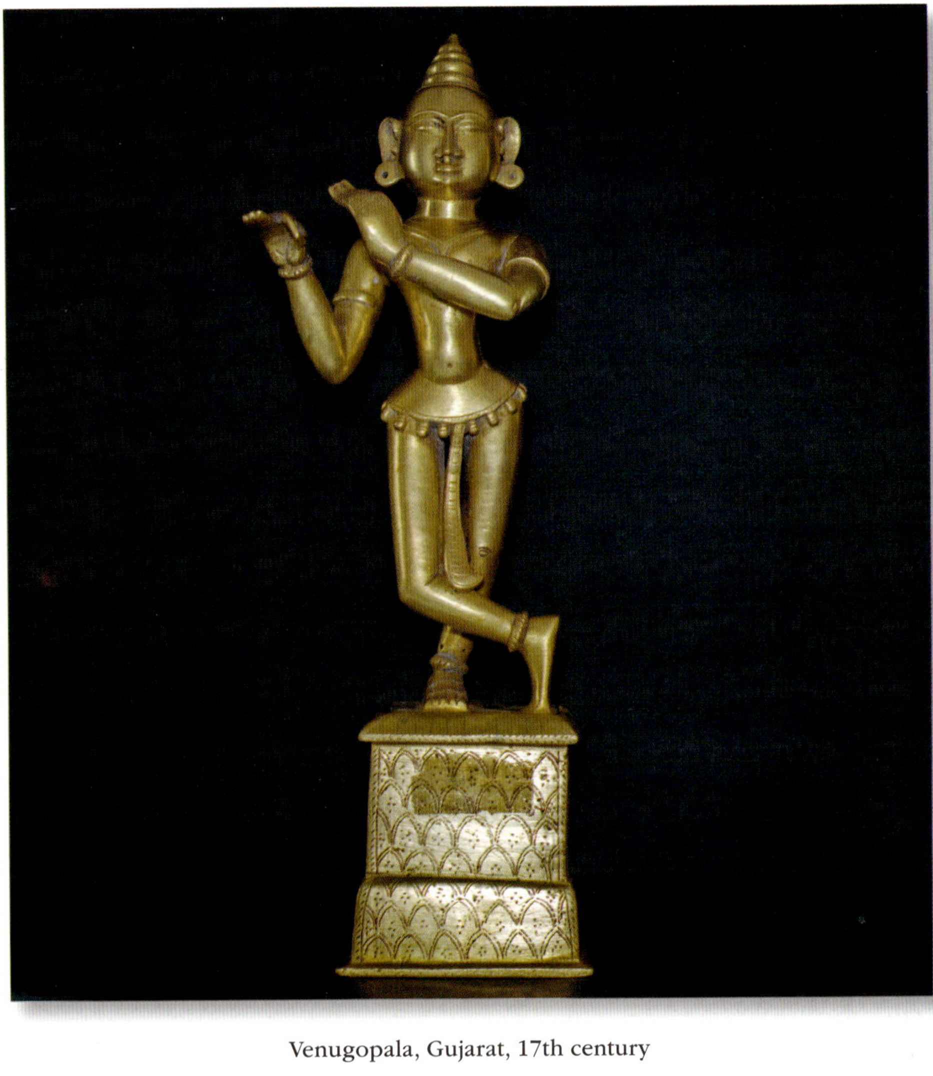

Venugopala, Gujarat, 17th century

If the *Bhagavata Purana* is the inspiration for Gujarat bronze casters, it is the *Gita Govinda* that drives Krishna art, whether it is painting, song, dance or bronzes. Orissa bronzes tend to be diminutive but exude an extraordinary charm with both their physiognomy, stance and the signature flute held pointing to the right. One can only imagine that the worship of these bronzes in the home shrine must have been accompanied by the singing of *asthapadis* of Jayadeva.

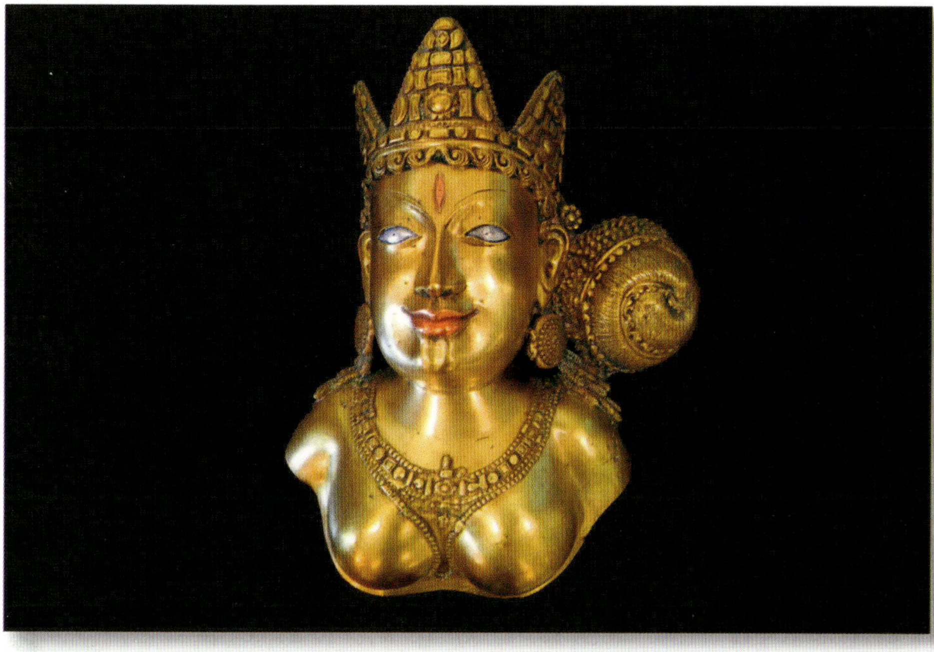

Mohra of Parvati. Himachal. 20th century

Nestled in the Himalayas, Himachal Pradesh is privy to many trade routes from Iran, Central Asia, Tibet and China and therefore has been influenced by many traditions. Of special significance to Himachal Pradesh are their *mohras* or masks. In Kulu, Mandi and Shimla we see a strong tradition of *mohras*. Wrongly translated as masks, *mohras* are surrogate icons of the cult deity. Mounted on the shoulder of devotees these divine proxies call on the homes of their devotees to bestow their blessings. Their processions grace two grand festivals, Shivratri at Mandi and Dassera at Kulu. In Mandi the royal patron is Madhav Rai or Krishna, in Kulu it is Raghunath or Rama. Most of the Puranic deities are worshipped in Himachal in the form of *mohras*. Fashioned of silver, alloy of various metals, or even gold, the *mohras* of the *deotas* are not sculptures in the round but cast or beaten sheets. While records of *mohras* being made date back to the 11th century, it is only after the 16th century that we have an unbroken history of *mohras*. The principal deities are quite content being lodged in their shrines, but their *mohras* take great delight in being in the open air outside the temples, and on the move, surrounded by their people.

One cannot complete our's journey of small bronzes without considering Vijayanagara. Called the connecting link between the North and the South, the artisans of Vijayanagara inherited their artistic skills from the Cholas and created small bronzes, that could not equal the Chola bronzes, but yet were graceful and had a charm of their own. A Vijayanagara bronze in the home shrine must have brought visions of the empire of Krishnadevaraya and the grandeur of Hampi under his reign. The Sanskrit name 'Tara' is derived from the Sanskrit word *tarika* which means 'deliveress' or 'saviouress.' She first appears as an attendant to Manjushri in the *Manushrimulakalpa* and, later, as an enlightened figure in her own right, in the *Taramulakalpa*, which was likely authored sometime in the 7th century. The present figure, a commanding image of the all-knowing goddess Tara, is a product of the valley of Kashmir.

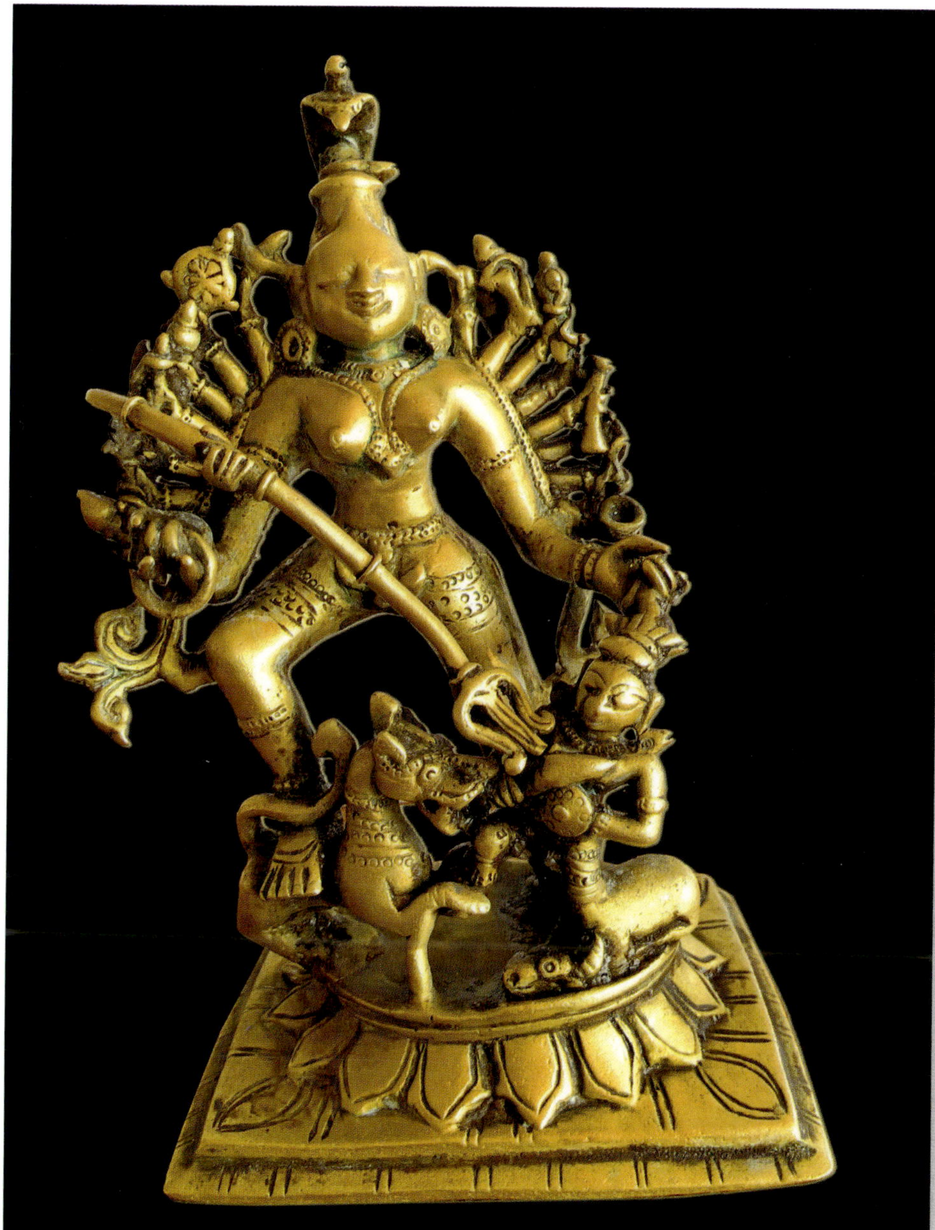

Mahishasuramardini, Bengal, 19th century

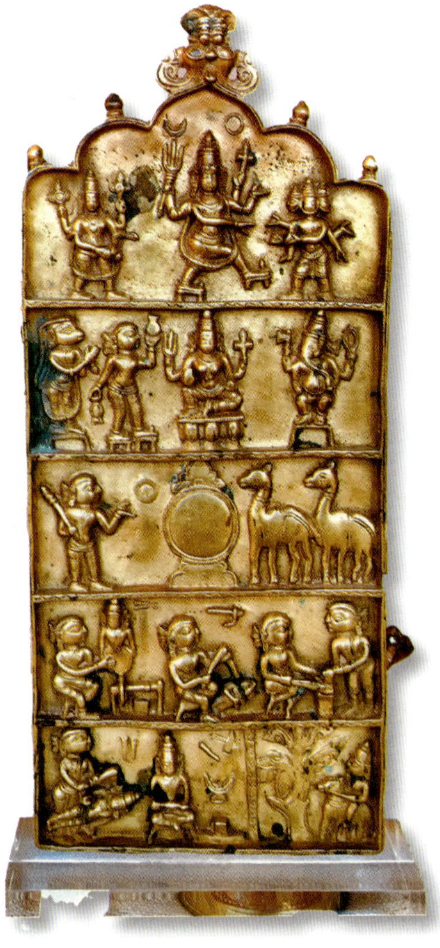

Vishvakarma lord of the arts,
master of a thousand handicraft,
carpenter of the gods
and builder of their palaces,
divine fashioner of every jewel,
first of craftsmen
by whose act men live
and whom, a deathless god,
they continually worship.
Mahabharata. X. 15.2 [26]

Celebrating The Quotidian

Beauty of Everyday Objects

It is not without reason that the Indian linguistic tradition of Sanskrit does not have a specific word for art, art objects, art activity or even artists. Neither does it set up a dichotomy within human creativity of the classical and the folk, or art from craft, or artists from artisans, all of these taxonomies being modern art historical constructs. Rather, the tradition subsumes under the rubric of *sunder* or beautiful, everything that human creativity encompasses, whether it is language or music, dance or sculpture, painting or architecture, ritual and even everyday objects. The creation of what was sensually beautiful, and equally incorporating that into one's everyday life and experiencing the sense of beauty from that creation, was considered an integral part of radiant life and noble living. Even the word *sanskriti*, understood generally as culture or refinement, carries with it the concept of something that is well created or nobly crafted. and is therefore not far from beauty as it is commonly understood today. To be cultured was to uphold and appreciate beauty in many different ways.

While relating human creativity to *sunder* or what is objectively and sensually beautiful is fundamental to the Indian world view, the subjective, contemplative and inward experience of that beautiful creation or *saundarya* is equally important as a philosophic principle. In emphasising both *sunder* and *saundarya*, we in the Indian tradition recognise that there is an inner reality of beautiful objects, a reality that is dismissed or overlooked by modern sociologists and art historians. These modern custodians of the arts seem to

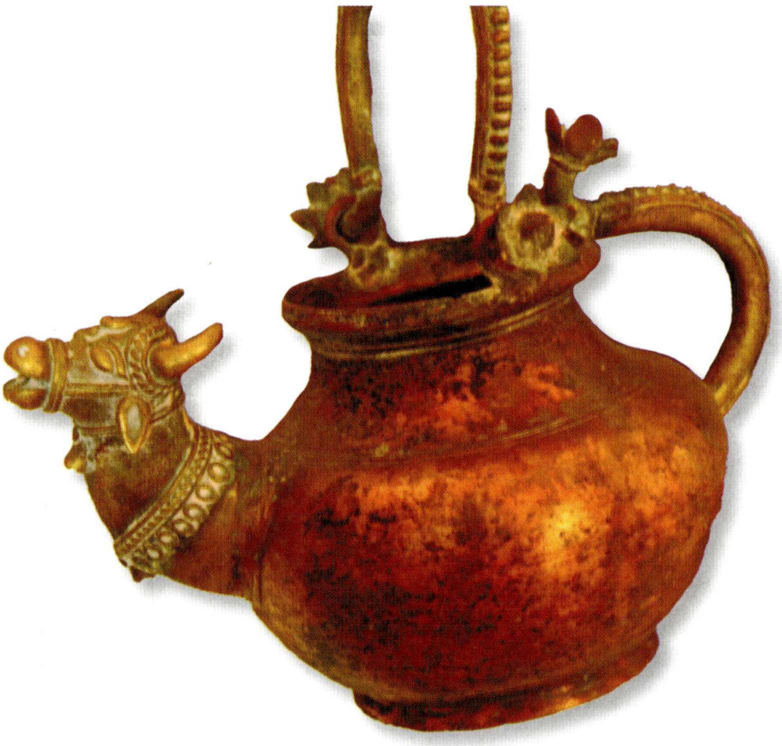

Abhishek Vessel

be carried away by forces such as patronage and market value of these art objects. While not denying the importance of these socio-economic forces that play on human creativity, there is however a still centre, a *bindu*, of beauty and an inner reality, at the core of the object, which is homologous to *brahman* or what is ultimately real, emphasising that human creativity is similar to cosmic creativity, and that mankind approaches the divine when he is creative.

Sanskrit words for design, *akriti* and *rachana*, both imply a creative process and signal an exalted human activity, an activity that requires not only skill but creativity, not just moral discipline but a spiritual outlook. The Upanishadic dictum *purnam adha purnam idam purnad purnam udachyate*, asserts that it only out of the fullness of beauty that the beautiful can arise. Creation in its best sense stems from a sense of joyousness, it comes within the purview of *dharma*, it is born from a desire to produce something in the likeness of the creator, a desire also to replicate the cosmos in smaller terms, and creativity therefore arises from a need to give form to the formless, and thereby give shape to something beautiful, that can then take its rightful place in the world we inhabit. It is thus that an object that is created is not just an object but something more than itself. It has been correctly observed that in India, all forms have a hint of the formless, all sounds lead to silence and all movement has in it the seed of stillness, for has it not been said *rupam rupam pratirupam babhuva*, all forms are a replica of the primal form.

The creation of forms, the making of objects and the design of spaces, all have an ancient pedigree for us in the Indian tradition, and we can trace it back to pre-history. The Indus Valley produced forms in terracotta such as pots and Mother Goddesses, and seals from this civilisation had animals and trees which more than of passing interest, as they signal the making of primal shapes and forms. The Vedas were essentially oral and even though we do not have a history of plastic objects ,they enunciated seminal ideas that were to shape our aesthetic sensibility. The Upanishads that followed used evocative languages point to metaphysical truths, and the Puranas like the Vishnudharmottara actually give directions to painters and sculptors. Through trackless centuries these have informed and inspired Indian craftsmen who have created beautiful forms and have ensured that *akriti* is a pointer to *sanskriti*.

In the *antara hradaya akasa*, the realisation of beauty in perfect form, a perfect concord exists between viewer and viewed. Perfect form is the model of his inner vision to which he then seeks to give expression through visual or aural forms.. The Indian artist's concern is with design imbued with a consciousness of the totality. He gives this form many forms, always bearing in mind the inner state in which he saw the perfect form. Conscious of mundane living, he built a superstructure of refined feeling and sensibility, where a continuous process of distillation, sophistication takes place. Where the empirical and the metaphysical are held together as an organic whole. Concepts underlying Indian architecture, sculpture and painting bring us back to the image of Man, the Purusha and the Purusha of Upanishadic thought and the *yajna* of the *brahmanas* in more explicit terms.

The *Vastusutraupanisad* rightly says, *tad shilpa jnanad divya jnanam bhavati*, that is, the knowledge of sculpture results in divine knowledge. This Upanishadic injunction can be enlarged to understand *shilpa* as any object that has been thoughtfully and lovingly made and therefore embraces *akriti* or design in a broader sense, and the knowledge that a contemplative person derives from this object then becomes divine knowledge. The onus then is on both the *shilpi*, the maker of the object, and the *rasika* or the connoisseur of that object so that *akriti* can progress to *sanskriti*.

The first principle in designing an object is that the object be functional, efficient and safe, and it is only when these basic design requirements are met that aesthetic concerns of the *akriti* can start. Utility is, of course, important but it cannot limit or exhaust what a sensitive person demands from an object. *Artha* or material satisfaction is a basic and primal need and this must obviously be fulfilled. This is the first order of designing an object. But there is within us a need to go beyond the banal and the material and surround ourselves with things beautiful, to have not only the means but a meaning to life and living, to nurture not only *artha* or materiality but the *kamana* that is at the very core of our being, for it is there that emotion and imagination are experienced, it is there that the joy of participating in what is sensuously beautiful becomes a *rasadhara* and flows like a stream, it is there that the various *rasas* are tasted. It is *kamana* that leads our mind from the mundane and the banal to the exalted and the sublime, and ushers a sense of grace and dignity to our daily living and brings joy into our quotidian tasks. For the human mind is not satisfied with mere *dharma* and *artha*, or utility and efficiency. There is, in the human condition, a desire for *kama*, a need for us to use our breath to sing songs and not utter mere words of commerce, a need to make our bodies a vehicle of grace and not of mere function, a need in our environment for adornment and not mere expediency, a need for the beautiful and not mere utility, a need to use our hands not only to work but to touch the stars, to grow not only food that nourishes the body but to plant flowers that will touch our spirit. All of this is the function of design and designers, and equally of *rasikas*.

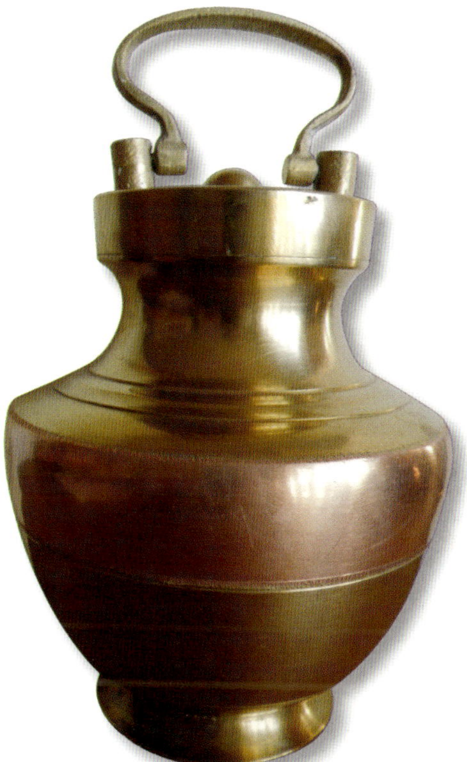

Ganga Jamuna Lota, Maharashtra

Thus, the function of design in essence is to create the beautiful so that the mind that tires in the world of daily commerce can rest in realms of beauty. As Tagore rightly states "The consciousness of the real within me seeks for its corroboration the touch of the real outside me."[27] Implicit in this statement is the supposition that our inner reality becomes known to us on account of the reality of the beautiful around us, that the infinite that is at the core of our being is awakened by an understanding of the finite that surrounds us, that our subjective self must find and feel the objectively beautiful to fully realise itself, and ultimately the *purusha* needs *prakriti*. Thus there are two levels of reality, one outer and the other inner, the one that is defined by *prakriti* or the beautiful and the other that is defined by *purusha* or beauty. "We become aware of a profound meaning of ourself at the consciousness of some ideal of perfection, some truth beautiful or majestic which gives us

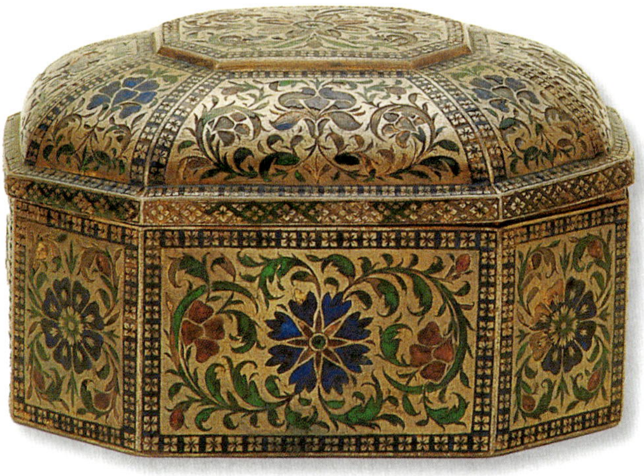

Minakari Pan Daan, Jaipur, 20th century

an inner sense of completeness, a heightened sense of our own reality".[28] There is, for Tagore, an inner logic and reality of things that are outwardly beautiful. Tagore reminds us that the world of objects in which we live, a world of lines and forms, colours and shapes, textures and cadence, words and movement, express vastly more than what they appear on the surface. Therefore, an object that is beautiful does not remain merely an object but it leads the contemplative person to a journey of inner discovery. In Tagore's words "They open the windows of our mind to the eternal reality of man."[29] Tagore's position places *akriti* securely within a metaphysical grid of Indian thought and moves it away from the merely psychological or superficial. *Akriti* then takes its rightful place in the domain of Indian Aesthetics and is a window to visual knowledge, and it therefore behooves us to develop a discourse of Indian design, not just in empirical but in philosophical terms. We must view design not just from the point of view of the practitioner or the marketer but from the vantage point of the philosopher as well. It is not sufficient to talk about design in either commercial or psychological terms, to merely refer to it as something that pleases the eye or to look upon it as a source of mental excitement, or one that sells well in the markets of the world. Sensual pleasure and excitement are indeed the first response to a beautifully-designed space or object, for that is its *raison d'etre*, it exists to satisfy those primal needs, but the beautifully designed object goes beyond itself, and expresses in its mute and hushed language, a vision of the culture that defines us, it is in its own silently eloquent way a pointer to our cherished values of the tradition that shape us, and is a testament to the *pratibha* or creative imagination of the artisan who made it and for us who partake of its beauty. It is because of this that it can qualify to be a source of *divya jnana*.

The adjective *sunder* or beautiful is intimately related to the abstract noun *saundarya* or beauty, just as *shabda* or a word is related to its *artha* or its meaning, or as Shiva is tied to Shakti. And still within the domain of linguistics it is worth remembering that traditionally the adjective *sunder* was never used as a metaphor; thus in Sanskrit one never said *iti sunder vicharaha*, this thought is beautiful, once again emphasising that the beautiful is what is sensually appealing and attractive. The concept of *sunder* or what is beautiful is not only purely sensuous, but even importantly secular, and it occurs predominantly in *kavya* or poetry, rather than in *shastras* or doctrinal literature. While what is beautiful is available to the *samajika* or the proletariat one and all, the subjective experience of beauty stemming from the beautiful object requires contemplative analysis and therefore is a prerogative of the *rasika* or the cultivated aesthete. Our journey in this book is directed mainly at the *rasika*. It is worth pointing out that there is, in Sanskrit, no verb for the predication of beauty, suggesting that the creation of beauty is an unknown or perhaps an unknowable process, a creative act akin to cosmic creation, that is to kept sacrosanct and not open to meddlesome probing, and even if probed will yield only psychological insights. It is important to give this preamble from the stand point of language to understand the Indian concept of what is beautiful, for language is the ultimate foundation, and the first expression, of not only all our doctrines and ideas, but even more importantly, our enunciation of the beautiful and the decorative, and it is therefore that *nadabrahman* or primal sound is quintessentially the repository of beauty. *Vak* or exalted speech is not just uttered, but sung with melody and rhythm, and this gives vocal music a primacy and makes it the foundation of the edifice of all our creations, and all that we consider beautiful rests on the perfect creation and enunciation of sound. That uttered sound or *shabda* is an active performance, not a passive creation, it requires participation, and not mere idle involvement.

Participation thus becomes the first order of what is beautiful in the Indian tradition, and one must go beyond the modern art historian's inability to interrelate beauty and utility. The primal objects of beauty for us in India, are objects that we can see and touch, objects of daily living such as kitchen utensils and toys, accessories for adornment such as toilet boxes and mirrors, terracotta and metal pots, and textile wraps and coverings, and many others. These objects of daily living which are commonly called handicraft, are neither art objects in the conventional sense, nor industrial objects in the modern sense, and obey no rules or formulae, and do not answer to any *shastra* or *mantra*, but arise from the sheer pleasure of the hands of the creator be he, a potter or weaver, a blacksmith or a woodworker. Kamaladevi Chattopadhyaya is right in saying,

> "We must recognise that craft is as much an expression of the human spirit in material form, which gives delight to mankind, as any of what are termed fine arts. Craft has always been a basic activity in human society; in fact it is considered more cohesive and permeating in human relationships than even language, for it can penetrate many barriers to communication."[30]

In creating objects of daily living where utility and the beautiful co-exist, there is the oneness of the creator, the created and participant, in that joyful creative process. These beautifully-made daily objects enhance life and are evocative of the magnificence and meaning of gracious living, where the immediate and the ultimate are connected by the living reality of beautiful objects, where the beautiful is received by direct participation and not by detached observation, and joy and delight are not reserved for a later contemplative moment, but are in the here and now. Through these objects the common becomes the cherished and joy giving, and the beautiful is not only what the eyes can see

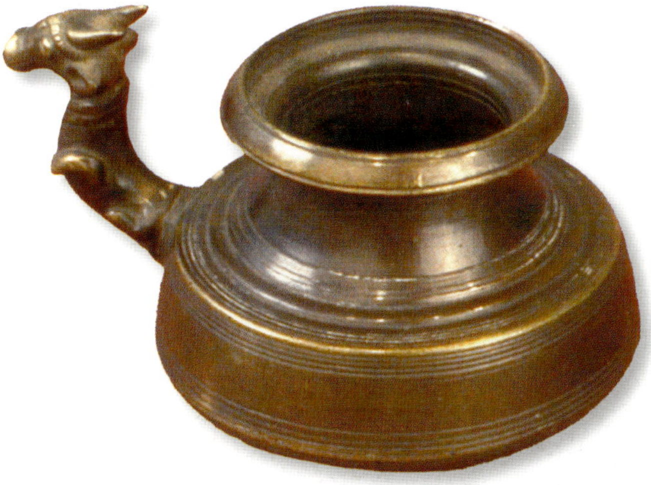

Container for Holy Water, Andhra

but what the hands can feel. Colour and texture, shape and form, line and colour, all participate in that sensual experience of the beautiful object. The making of these daily objects was considered a noble act, and the creator of these objects traced their origins to Vishvakarman or the divine architect. In traditional society these makers of objects were also considered *prajapati* or social leaders, and given a pride of place.

If utility is the first order of beauty, ritual is the second. Through ritual a correspondence is established between the microcosm and the macrocosm, between the world of humans and that of gods, between chaos and order, between temporality and eternality, and between death and immortality. Ritual action is an ancient way of knowing, and since water is the basis and substratum of life and creation, many ritual objects were connected with water, objects such as a *kalasha* or the ritual pot, the ritual spoon, a container for ritual water and a dispenser for sacred water. These ritual objects were beautifully and decoratively made with one or more metals, with spouts that resembled the mouth of a cow, and motifs of snakes and turtles. Fire and light are equally important in rituals, and a variety of beautifully-made

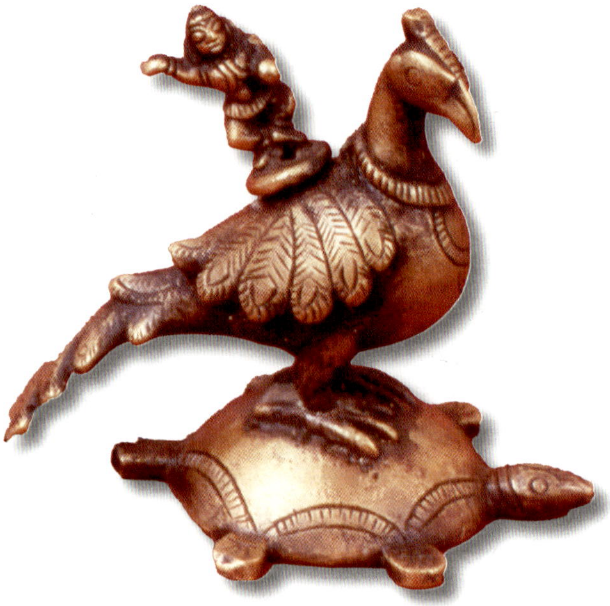

Perfume Container, Karnataka

oil lamps are an important part of every ritual. What is beautiful in ritual defines itself not through a refined aesthetic sensibility, but through its ability to create that living correspondence between the basic elements of the macro-cosmos on the one hand and the same elements of the world of mankind on the other. These rituals are an attempt of primal man to control a mysterious environment and render it tangible through the visible and the palpable. Ritual also includes votive objects such as clay votive horses that form so much a part of tribal and folk worship, and the making of these horses is an important function of the village potter. These votive horses are offered to the deity and left at the shrine, where they stand and perish with time, and return to the soil from which they were made, and when the potter makes another horse he takes this soil and a horse is created again, thereby emphasising a metaphysical principle of life and death and rebirth.

After utility and ritual come adornment, where once again beauty is realised through participation. Adornment is a special activity which operates at more than one level. Adornment starts with one's own body, then moves on to the home, and then ends with adorning the deity in the home shrine. A woman adorns herself with the traditional 16 adornments, and all her oils and unguents, perfumes and pastes are held in beautifully-made containers. Her clothes are a special part of that adornment and not only the texture but the colour and the decorative motifs of what she wraps and drapes constitute an integral part of beauty. An important part of adornment is the self-assurance that comes through the mirror, and mirrors therefore become an important part of the paraphernalia of adornment. For the romantic heroine, adornment is an offering to the beloved, for ultimately it is for his eyes that she adorns herself. and when she sees that glint of pleasure in his eyes she feels truly fulfilled. If personal adornment is the expression of a woman's self assured beauty, adorning the home converts one's dwelling into a cherished space. Every part of the home from the threshold to the kitchen, outer and inner walls, are decorated with designs and motifs, that are not only beautiful but which are as it were visual prayers as they invite divine presence, express a certain world view and sanctify the home. Of special importance are doors and windows as they are at the border of the limited space within, and the vast space outside, and no Indian door is complete without motifs sacred or secular, marks of vermillion and festoons of flowers and decorative banners or *toranas* creating the gods of our thresholds. Adorning the deity in the home shrine is a special part of daily worship, and binds the devotee and the deity in a personal relationship, and makes the icon come alive and creates a living presence of one's chosen god in one's home. A number of objects for adorning the deity are part of every household.

These objects of beauty which enrich daily life and living are part of the many living traditions of India. Despite the inroads of urbanisation and the supremacy of machines, many of these still continue to be made and used. In fact, with the advent of post-modernism and the nostalgia that has come in its wake, the value and appreciation of these traditional objects is enjoying a comeback. These simple objects of beauty seem to provide a respite from the fatigue of modernity. It must be admitted, however, that the post-modernist approach tends to needlessly romanticise these objects and take them out of context, and make them into art objects, or decorative objects on the coffee table, which they are really not. It must not be forgotten that quintessentially these objects were objects of daily living, that the maker of the objects was very much a part of the society in which these objects and their users lived, and it is important they not be considered as art objects but regarded as *vastu* or objects of beauty. For the concept of art brings with it its own baggage, its biased and historical discourse, its hierarchies of art and craft, its view of what is art and what is not, its museums and curators, and all of this would needlessly distance these objects from their unique position as objects of beauty in the everyday life of traditional and present day India. To call them art objects would draw attention to the objects, take them out of context and fragment the wholeness of life, but to consider them as objects of beauty, would underscore the fact that the creation and enjoyment of beauty through these objects was an ancient way of knowing and of realising, of being and becoming, through conferring dignity and nobility to daily living.

There are two valid questions however that should be asked about these objects, questions that would take us into the domain of aesthetics and away from art history, cultural anthropology and sociology. First, why do we consider these objects beautiful, and second how does the beauty that inheres in those objects become *saundarya* or the subjective state of beauty and lead to *atmajnana* or ultimate knowledge. Unless these questions are answered, a proper aesthetic discourse cannot develop and these objects will stay relegated to the folk or the craft. To claim that these objects are beautiful for purely post-modern nostalgic reasons, or that they adorn the modern home and bring with it ethnic charm is not enough. To reconstruct the times and the methods which led to their creation is anthropologically interesting, but does not take us to the core of the aestheticians's concern which is epistemology. These objects, and our enjoyment and celebration of them, needs to be brought into the investigation of what constitutes beauty for us in the Indian tradition. These objects suffer from a double misfortune. In the times in which they were made and used, they were an integral part of beautiful and gracious living, and therefore did not have an elevated status of their own. With modernity they were downgraded to the status of folk art and craft, and as with other features of the little tradition, did not generate an aesthetic discourse. The time has come to move away from both these positions, even though the patronage for such objects has changed, but those who are concerned with *saundarya* or beauty and not just the *sunder* or

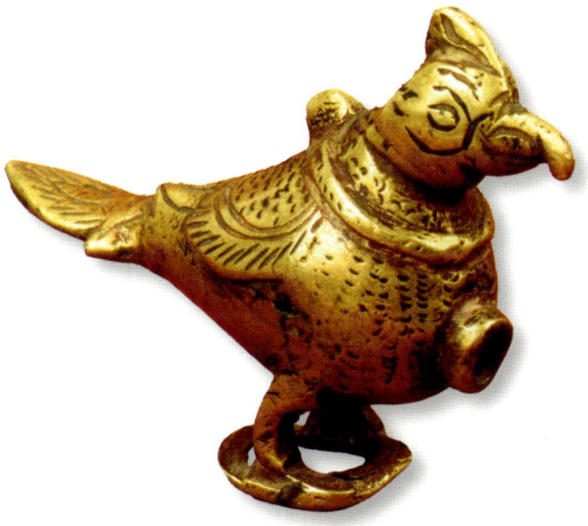

Oil Container, Karnataka

the beautiful, must bring them into the mainstream of Indian aesthetics. In their time these objects were sold in *bazaars* or traded within the prevailing barter system, but today, especially in urban India, they adorn urban homes and have moved to the living room and on coffee tables. The making of these objects, whether it is a pot or a door, a toilet box or adornments for a home, does not follow any canons or doctrines, nor does it arise from prescribed methods or the dictates of a royal patron. It stems from that uninhibited joy of creation, spontaneous craftsmanship, the desire to cater to the needs of the ordinary people amidst whom the creator lives, the freedom to follow the heart rather than the mind, and a well honed skill that has developed over many years by observation and practice, not through *shastras* or ready made molds, and passed down orally and visually from father to son and mother to daughter. It is that joy and pleasure of creation that passes from the maker to the user through the object, it is that satisfaction that utility has not constrained creativity and a rejoicing from the realisation that form has exceeded function, that makes these objects beautiful in the first instance. There is in these objects a *rasa* of creativity, a *rasa* not formally recognised by Bharata, but which must be considered a *rasa* in its own right. Secondly, beauty resides objectively in the physical and sensual form of the object, and when that beauty results in the subjective feeling of joy and self-assurance through the sensuality of the object it is then that the joy of sensuality is converted into knowledge understood as *ananda*. That joy is an ancient way of knowing and results in the knowledge of being integrated in the world of everyday objects around oneself, a joyous self-awareness of one's place in that world, and ultimately a realisation of the nobility, beauty and dignity of life itself. There is in the creativity of these objects for the creator and the re-creativity of the same object for the user, a sense of *purnatva*, wholeness and fullness, a breakdown of the dualities of the human ratiocinative mind, an integration of the fragmentation of the mind that inevitably results in dealing with modern life and living. A third way in which these objects bring home the concept of beauty, is by bridging the sacred and the secular, and in so doing connect the microcosm to the macrocosm. The living objects of beauty in incorporating motifs from the world of trees and blossoms, birds and rivers, suggest, in its typically non-doctrinaire style, the inter-connection of the world in which we live, reminding us that the sap that flows through the vegetative world resonates with what animates us. Many examples of this can be cited. A kitchen shredder or grater shaped in the form of a tortoise is not very far from the *kurma* of Vishnu, a cup for making medicines with Ganesha and Kartikeya as its handles invokes the presence of Shiva, a vessel for pouring sacred water shaped like the human *yoni* reminds one that just as life begins in the *garbha* of the mother, one is re-born in the sanctum of the temple, the *kalasha* for storing water becomes special with the image of Ganesha inscribed on it, and countless such objects which move us from the sacred to the secular and the other way around emphasising that the sacred and the secular are one continuum and not two opposites ends of the human experience. The fourth way by which these objects lead us to an experience of beauty is through the motifs they employs such as the circle which represents the sun, the vine, mango or the leaf which come from the tree of life, the parrot and the fish which suggest fertility, the checkered pattern on textiles which is none other than the sacrificial *vedi* and many such motifs which when understood are not mere decorative but lead us to a greater vision and reveal a world view, and thus become sources of beauty. And finally in the words of Octavio Paz these daily objects of beauty not only "teach us how to live but also how to die."[31] For these objects have no pretense to be immortal or everlasting, they are time-bound and eventually they do perish and decay, and when they do so they return to the elements that they came from, and it from the same elements that another object will be lovingly made, and thus the cycle of creation, death and recreation continues through these objects, and the humble but beautiful object reminds us and teaches us, in a simple but elegant way, of that cycle of life and death of which we must all be a part.

In fostering a sense of beauty through its unpretentious but self-assured presence these objects assert that beauty exists even outside what are conventionally called art objects, and that there is a *rasa* in them even beyond the prescriptive canons of Bharata in the *Natyashastra*. The joy of creativity is a *rasa* in its own right and must be considered as such in the post modern times in which we live. These objects of beauty are in the end a celebration of the creativity of human hands and seem to resonate the primal Upanishadic thought that creativity arises from joy, and into joy it leads us.

These simple and unpretentious objects of beauty are a silent testament, not only of the need for the beautiful in our everyday life, but equally of the inherent capacity of that ordinary but beautiful object to lead us to the subjective and ultimate state of beauty. The object participates in the movement from *sunder* to *saundarya*, which is the essence of an aesthetic experience. Understood in this sense these objects of beauty can take their pride of place in the treasure of beauty in the Indian tradition. It has rightly been said that "When craft is withdrawn from its context it becomes an object. Released into its own environment it becomes a process of living.[32]

When we enter the Decorative Arts Gallery we do so with some reservations. Most of the objects in this Gallery are objects of daily use. Should we call them art objects? The craftsperson who makes these objects, whether he is a potter or a metal smith, takes a special pleasure in creating these objects which are utilitarian at one level, but beautiful at another. The psyche of that craftsperson is touched by the universe in all its abundance and multiplicity of life and form. This world is inhabited by plants and creepers, birds and blossoms, the stars and the planets, mountains and rivers, and all these are an integral part of our life in India. Human consciousness and the awareness of the universe around it are interrelated and interdependent and always transmutable. It is this awareness that inspires a great variety of motifs in Indian art and craft. These are naturalistic, beautiful and spontaneous on one level and imbued with symbolic significance on another. The two move concurrently, they are not just symbols but living visual metaphors. It is this that confers upon the *akritis* a reality and beauty of its own.

Beauty beyond utility is the hallmark of our objects of daily use. We touch them, caress them, lovingly clean and polish them and live with them. They bring a certain amount of grace in our daily life. Art is in our every day life and not for museums.

One of the first questions that comes to mind is what do we mean by decoration. Is decoration merely adorning or beautifying a space or an object? If that is the case, then decorative arts do not have a place in a Museum like ours. We in India adorn and decorate with a passion and a purpose, a dedication and a meaning; whether it is our homes or bodies, our *havelis* or palaces, our shrines or temples, our fabrics or our many objects of daily utility. While adornment creates a state of superficial beauty this by itself is not saying much. When we understand adornment, either as a metaphor or as a visual prayer, it takes on a different meaning. The *nayika* adorns herself for the delight of the beloved and it is her offering or *arpana*, the housewife adorns the threshold of her home to sanctify it and seeks divine blessings, and even the truck driver adorns his vehicle with protective motifs of fortune and prosperity such as the *kalasha*. At one level adornment is beautification but it is equally a statement of our world view, where the beautiful is cherished as a value, perhaps even a *purushartha*. In our world view adornment spreads and bestows auspiciousness around it and therefore it is *mangalmaya*, and by its very presence or *sannidhya*, the adorned object, whether it is a deity or a woman, the threshold of a home, the palace or a *haveli*, the *rangamandapa* of a temple or an object of everyday use, every adorned space or object resonates with a utilitarian radiance, it trembles with aesthetic energy and exudes a joyous affirmation of life.

Adornment is clearly more than just beautification, it is an opulence both of matter and mind. That Indian mind values and celebrates opulence and luxuriance not only for its own sake, but because adornments understood aesthetically can be either a metaphor or prayer. Understood not only in its material and physical aspects, although these are important too, the concept of luxuriance for the Indian mind goes far beyond the material and the sensuous.

Luxuriance for the Indian mind is to adorn our deities, whether it is in a temple or our home shrine, the pleasure of decoration on our everyday objects, the flourish of colour in our homes and surroundings, the penchant for rich and beautiful fabrics, the pleasure of wearing sparkling and radiant jewellery and endless other ways in which we bring opulence and lushness to our surroundings. Luxuriance is to indulge sensually but it does not stop there and is carried forward to a higher state of mind. Even more importantly luxuriance is a mental attitude that stems from our affirming and enjoying our *avkash* or environment and surroundings, it is to luxuriate with our thoughts and feelings, to let the mind roam in vast and majestic vistas, create timeless tracks and infinite spaces, all of this is luxuriance as well, which is part of the Hindu view of life.

Adornment is not just for the artist or the craftsperson. The grammar of adornment for the housewife is made up, not only by the motifs and metaphors which she either embroiders, or paints on her walls or floors, like the *kalasha* and Vishnupada, the *swastika* and the mango, the sun and the moon, *lata* and *vriksha*, but equally important in adornment are the various colours which evoke distinctive feelings.

Robust, charged and evocative colours are an important part of our sense of beauty and joy, and colours therefore form an important part of our lived lives. The word *rang* is etymologically related to the word *ranj* which means not only colour but also states of mind, hence the word *manoranjan* or a state of mental excitement. A beautiful phrase heard and found particular in *shringara kavya* is, "I am coloured by your love," which makes the word *rang* polyvalent and stresses the importance of colours as an important part of our living and being for us in the Hindu tradition. We refer to inner states of mind as *antarang*, an inner colour. Whether in song or dance, colours for us speak and whisper, sing and dance, and express our moods and feelings better than words. Drawing their inspiration from the lush and luxuriant natural world around them, the world of bird and blossom, earth and sky, gems and stones, we use colours not only to beautify and adorn, but equally to create a certain feeling and a luxuriant ethos. On fabric or canvas, mud wall or floor, sculpture or pots, colours for us have a language, a *raga*, a *rasa* and a *tala*.

This prelude should change our *drishti* as we engage with objects in this gallery. One almost hears whispers of the housewife as she proudly and lovingly places her objects of daily use back in the kitchen or in the rest of the home, reminding us once again that these are not art objects.

Let us study two objects in this gallery: the Jade bowl and the Bidri *huqqa* bowl.

Jade is an ancient stone and jade beads have been discovered in the artefacts of the Indus Valley Civilisation. The earliest literary reference to jade in India goes back to the 7th century CE, to Chinese traveller Hsuan Tsang's description of an 8-foot-high statue of the Buddha in blue jade at Samatata in Bengal. However, the use of jade started with the Mughals, initially with Akbar (r. 1556-1605) but did not achieve its full efflorescence as an art-form until the reigns of the two great aesthetes of the dynasty, the emperors Jahangir (r. 1605-1627) and Shah Jahan (r 1628-1658).The Timurids of Central Asia were one of the greatest patrons of jade, and for the Mughals, who descended from Timur himself, this beautiful green stone became a way of reclaiming their Central Asian legacy. Jahangir, in particular was a pleasure-seeking emperor and he played a key role in the development of the Mughal jade working tradition; a number of elegant jade drinking vessels engraved with his name and imperial epithets survive.In support of the epigraphic documentation, Jahangir is also portrayed in at least one extant portrait as prominently holding a white jade wine cup as one of his symbolic royal attributes. Our information of the Mughal atelier comes from the Aini-Akbari by Abul Fazl and from portraits of Mughals. It appears that the Mughals got their jade from Kashgar in Central Asia. The artisan working on jade was called Zarnishan or gold inlayer, who was an expert in cutting and shaping jade and insetting

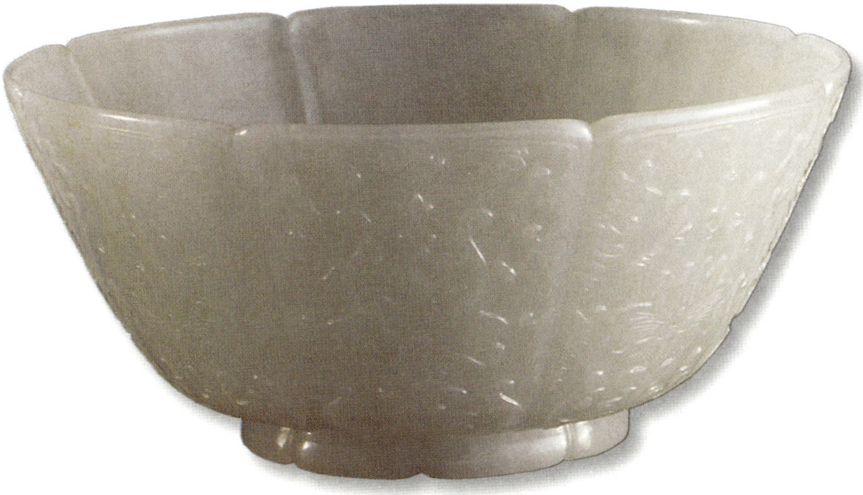

Jade. Mughal, mid-18th century

precious stones in it. These artisans created objects in jade that could rank among the highest in the world of art which not only had a visual aesthetic but a palpable caress as well. Artists drew their inspiration from a wide variety of flowers, foliage, and animals, which were often combined to create fantastic hybrid forms. Decorative elements and design used in Mughal architecture in stone and marble were beautifully used in jade. Jade formed an important material with which small objects like thumb rings, wine cups, plates, trays, boxes, *huqqa* bowls, dagger and sword hilts and the like were fashioned and decoratively enriched with various designs.

The Mughals referred to jade by its Persian name Yashm. They had workshops and factories where these artistic objects were manufactured in a refined style and encouraged artists-craftsman and artisans to come to their courts to receive honours and grants. The imperial workshops were maintained as part of the emperor's household. Abul Fazal describes the imperial household containing "one hundred workshops, each resembling a city or rather a little kingdom."[33]

Whether judged by their degree of technical difficulty or level of aesthetic accomplishment, or merely by the number of surviving high quality examples,

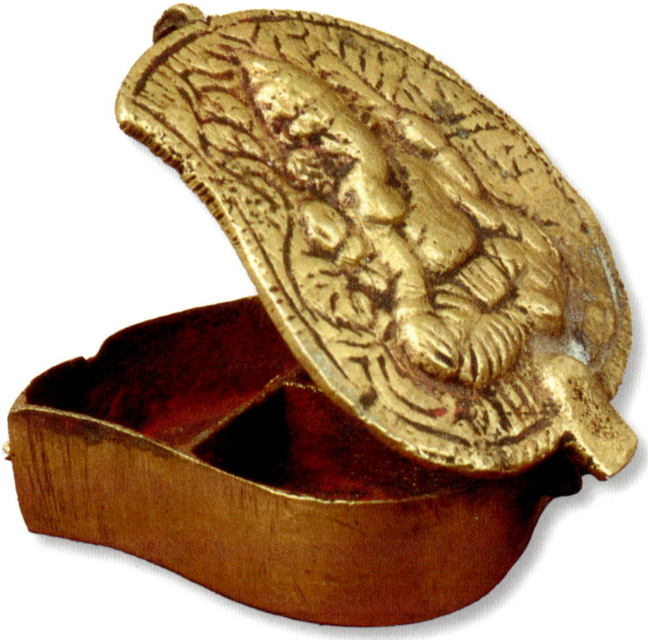

Kumkum box, Gujarat

Mughal jades clearly represent a zenith of artistic achievement in the rich visual heritage of South Asia. The details of how jade objects were made need not detain us here. However, let us transport ourselves to the *darbar* of Jahangir and listen to Narmada Prasad Upadhyaya.

"The welcoming note from the *naubat khana*, the ceremonial chamber at the top of the entrance arch, was announced. A loud voice came forth: Sultanul Islam Amir Ul Momanin Mirza Nuruddin Beg Mohammad Khan Salim Padshah Jahangir Gazi is arriving with a splendour. At hearing this sound all courtiers stood up with heads bowed and in a few minutes the king placed his foot on the threshold of the throne. We were in the presence of a resolute monarch, who had a tawny brown body dressed in a resplendent silk robe with a cap that he himself had designed and came to called Jahangiri *pagdi*. Around his neck there were necklaces full of *basra* beads, diamonds and precious stones. The monarch, of the lineage of Timur and Chugtai walked regally and sat gracefully on the jewel-embedded throne. Jahangir was the fourth descendent of the Mughal dynasty and his name meant the protector of the world. The entire court bowed in reverence to his splendour. Mirza Aziz Koka, Mahavat Khan, Abdulla Khan, Governor of Kashmir Muhammad Yusuf Khan, Raja Basu, ministers of various regions of the Mughal empire and prince Khurram, later to become Shah Jahan, were all present. Also present was Sir Thomas Rowe of Britain who had met Jahangir in Ajmer. The emperor asked the courtiers to sit down and called his son Khurram and grandson Shuja and blessed them. The agenda for the day was read out, the emperor gave his judgements on legal matters. It was further announced that the emperor along with Nurjahan, the queen of Hindostan would go for a holiday to Lahore and then to Kashmir. Accompanying them would be artists Mansour and Govardhan who would create paintings of Kashmir and present it to the emperor daily. The next day the emperor and his consort in a palanquin, along with his retinue, left. Jahangir who was madly in love with Nurjahan did not want to be away from her even for a minute. The retinue halted at a town called Preetnagar, near Lopake village, not far from Amritsar which was a favourite of Jahangir. In this idyllic place with gardens and dense trees and a pond he had built a palace here. He, along with Nurjahan, would come here often for rest and relaxation and lose themselves in romantic pleasures. The court had already been established here and everyone was in anticipation of the soiree that would follow. Jahangir was a pleasure loving person and he would often say, 'If one has one liter of wine and a half a pound of meat then what does it matter if my kingdom is in favour of Nurjahan or against her.' The emperor's wine was specially brought from saffron-washed Kabul, and was cooled by ice from Kashmir. It is now night and lamps were lit and

Pritinagar came to life. The emperor came and sat on the throne, and next him was Nurjahan on a smaller throne. The musicians started to sing *dhrupad*. Rakkasa came and started to dance. At Nurjahan's gesture, two gem-studded carafes containing wine from saffron-washed grapes from Kabul were placed on a platter. On another platter was an exquisite jade cup. This cup created by Saida-ye-Gilani in 1603 has a prayer inscribed on it in Persian and is preserved at the Victoria and Albert Museum. The inscription says "Through the world-conquering Shah, the world found order/ our time became filled with light by the radiance of his justice/ from the reflection of his spinel-coloured wine may/ the jade cup be forever like a ruby." Nurjahan lovingly lifted this cup and poured wine from the carafe into it and moved it from under her eyes to the lip of Jahangir. Jahangir looked at Nurjahan, and as he took a sip there was a whisper of a gazal in the air, "The cup of wine that the bartender gave was only a drink. But the real wine is drunk by the eyes."[34]

While still in this gallery let us visit the Deccan. Bounded by the Vindhyas and the Narmada in the north and the ocean on two sides, the Deccan is a unique part of India and was divided into three regions: Maharashtra, Karnataka and Tilanga-Andhra. The Bahamani Sultanate of the 14th and 15th century is considered the origin of modern Deccan, for from this Sultanate arose the five kingdoms of Ahmednagar, Bidar, Berar, Golkonda and Bijapur. These Deccani states had a mixed population of Muslims and Hindus, but also had immigrants from Turkey, Persia, Arabia and Africa. Sufis, men of letters, merchants and soldiers migrated to the Deccan from all over the Middle East, lured by the generosity of the wealth of the sultans. All this was to last until the onslaught of European culture in the 19th century. The Deccan had a distinct Islamic culture which displayed more direct contact with the Middle East than with north India. Most of the Deccani sultans were patrons of the arts. The Deccan was home to temple building as in Vijayanagar, Kalamkari as in Srikalahasti, Bidri work in Bidar, and above all it patronised miniature paintings.

The Deccan is a region shaped by the Sultans, and while it is tied to the Indian ethos it has a unique aura of magic and mystery, alchemy and arts. The Deccani psyche is characterised by charged colours and hybrid forms resulting from its mixed demographic of Hindu and Muslim, Indian and

Persian sensibilities. If one were to paint the Deccan in broad strokes one could say that the Sultans of the Deccan were both learned and pleasure-loving patrons of the arts and architecture, given to music and mysticism. We cannot talk about the Deccan without listening to Mark Zebrowski:

> ...the emotional content of Deccani art is unique. Whereas Mughal art has a generous dose of logic and verisimilitude behind its glamour...Deccani art revels in dream and fantasy. Paintings pulsate with restless lines and

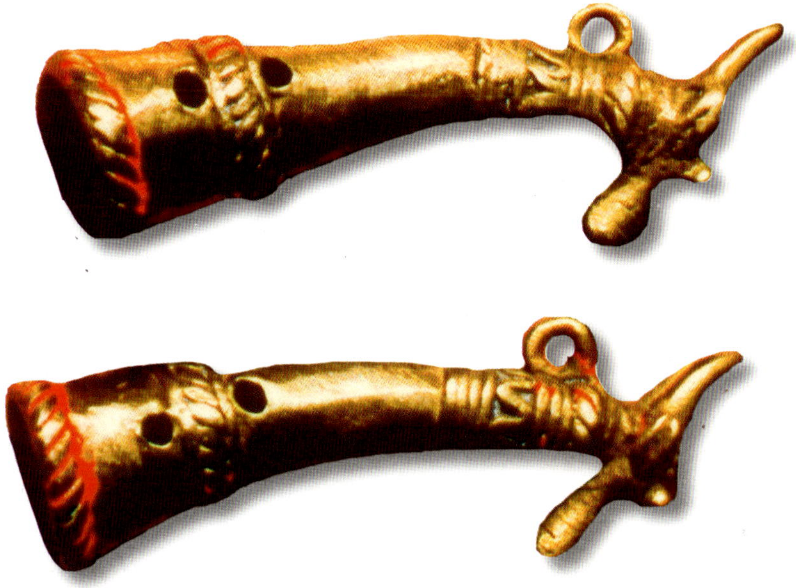

Ornaments for a bull's horns, Maharashtra

> riotous colours...opulent excess reigned unchallenged and produced some of the most lyrical images in Indian art.. Palaces and tombs in the Deccan invigorate us with exotic visions of the Middle East, a fantastic Arabian Nights atmosphere..in its brilliant architecture we sense a yearning for the domes and minarets of the Muslim heartland... Few Deccani paintings record historical events...instead princely portraits predominate, which aim to establish a gently lyrical atmosphere, often one of quiet abandon to the joys of love, music, poetry or the just perfume of a flower...moods

are established through fantastic colour...we are admitted into a private world of feeling...reflection and reverie triumph over dramatic action... they worked in styles that combined the delicate rhythms of Persia, the lush sensuality of south India and exotic elements taken from Europe and Turkey. Deccani art revels in dream and fantasy. Paintings pulsate with restless lines and riotous colours. We may well ask if Deccani painting ever attained to a classic phase, with all the restraint and power which such a phase implies. Perhaps it did, but only for the briefest moment at the courts of Bijapur.... and Ahmadnagar ... At most other times opulent

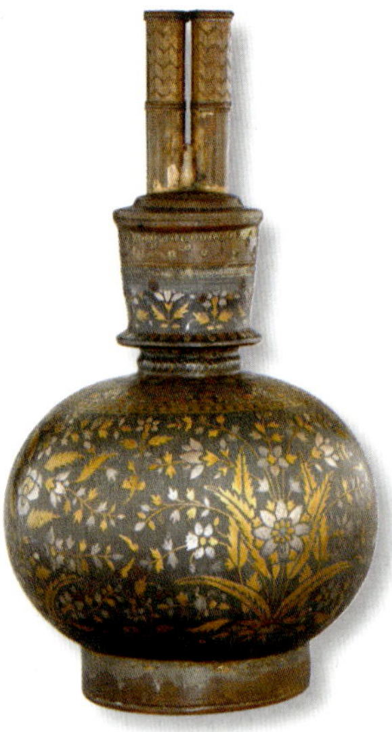

Bidri. Deccan, 19th century

excess reigned unchallenged and produced some of the most lyrical images in Indian art."[35]

Geographically, the Deccan was a plateau and much of its landscape is marked by stones and boulders. Also the soil of the Deccan is rich with minerals, and this is what leads to the charged, saturated and robust colours whether it is on fabric or paper. The coastal areas of the Krishna river delta were particularly well-suited to the cultivation of a weed called *chay* which was a source of a brilliant red dye. The delta area had also had abundant flowing water for rinsing dyed cloth and was rich in calcium from decomposing sea shells which helped to fix the dye. In addition to this, Indigo was readily available, and because of this the Deccan was home to some of the most brilliant and saturated colours which we see both in painting and Kalamkari.

The Deccani artist has a fondness for ornamented, sinuous, rhythmic patterns which he introduces into artistic spaces. Along with this the Deccani penchant was for stylistically ornamented textiles and carpets. Their language sees a coming together of Persian and Hindustani, and the emergence of Urdu literature was born in Bijapur and Golconda in the late 16th century, almost two centuries before its full development in North India. Politically even if there was a clash of the Marathas and the Sultans, the region was generally peaceful, and this was conducive to the development of the arts. It has been said that the rhythmic delicacy of Persia, the lush sensuality of South India and the restraint of European and Ottoman Turkish art is the hallmark of Deccani painting.

One patron in particular stands out, and that is Sultan Ibrahim Adil Shah II of Bijapur (1579-1616) who was influenced by the mysticism of his uncle Ali Adil Shah and his aunt Chand Bibi. Ibrahim's entire world was saturated with melody and it would be correct to say that if there is lyric and joyousness in Deccani art it comes from music. A description of this Sultan from a painting of his from the 17th century sums up the Deccani style:

> "A certain majesty surrounds the image. One notices the sumptuous dress, the golden turban, the gold thread wrapped shawl wrapped around his shoulders, the fine muslin *jama* through which the salmon pink of his pyjama trousers shimmers, the finely patterned *patka* which falls lazily over the hips, the rich jewellery and the easy self-confident posture, with Persian looking flowering trees alive with pairs of loving birds and the twists and curls of Chinese clouds in the gold filled sky."[36]

A decorative object of the Deccan is Bidri. The origin of Bidriware is usually attributed to the Bahamani Sultans who ruled Bidar in the 13th–15th centuries. Abdullah bin Kaiser, a craftsman from Iran was invited by the Sultan to work on decorating the royal palaces and courts. According to some accounts,

Kaiser joined hands with local craftsmen and this gave birth to Bidriware. Since then, the craft has been handed down succeeding generations mostly among the local Muslim and Lingayat sects. Bidriware is manufactured from an alloy of copper and zinc by casting. The zinc content gives the alloy a deep black colour. First, a mould is formed from soil made malleable by the addition of castor oil and resin. The molten metal is then poured into it to obtain a cast piece which is later smoothened by filing. The casting is now coated with a strong solution of copper sulphate to obtain a temporary black coating over which designs are etched freehand with the help of a metal stylus. Bidriware in the 17th century relied heavily on soil in the unlit portions of the Bidar. The Bidri designs are usually patterns such as the Asharfi-ki-booti, stars, vine creepers and stylised poppy plants with flowers. Traditional designs include the Persian Rose and passages from the Quran in Arabic script.

The earliest extant Bidri objects are from the first half of the 17th century. Inspired both by Mughal and Chinese motifs, Bidri features floral arabesques. The poppy flower was particularly favoured. The flowers twist and turn as if caught in a whirlwind. Bidri objects whisper the royal dignity of the Deccan, and remain an important object from that part of India and a reminder of the penchant of decorative objects in their courts.

Whether it is the *raja* or the *praja* jewellery for us is both ornamental and sacred. Reference to precious metals for us are ancient. In the *Chandogya Upanishad* is found this verse:

> In the beginning this universe was non-existent.
> It turned into an egg.
> The egg opened, one part was of gold which was the sky
> the other of silver which became the earth.
> 3.19.1-2[37]

Jewellery conjures up a world of gold and glitter, gems and grandeur but behind all this is the innate Indian penchant for adornment and equally of human artistic creativity. The Indian mind values and celebrates opulence and luxuriance as it is a part of what is beautiful for us. Understood not only in its material and physical aspects, although these are important too, the concept of luxury for the Indian mind goes far beyond the material. Luxuriance for the Indian mind is to adorn our deities, whether it is in a temple or our home shrine, the pleasure of decoration on our everyday objects, the flourish of colour in our homes and surroundings, the penchant for rich and beautiful fabrics, the pleasure of wearing sparkling and radiant jewellery and endless other ways in which we bring beauty, opulence and luxury to our surroundings. But even more importantly, luxuriance is a mental attitude as well, for to luxuriate with our thoughts and feelings, let the mind roam

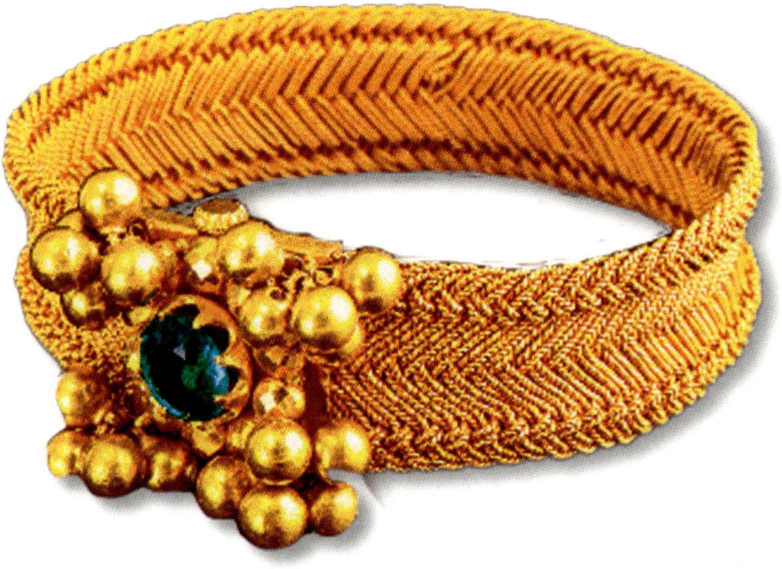

Bracelet in Gold Filigree

in majestic vistas, entertain beautiful emotions, enjoy poetry and narratives, suck leisurely on notes of music, create timeless tracts and infinite spaces is luxuriance as well. Luxuriance is both material and emotional, and bridges the gap between the sensual and the spiritual, and is one of the signature of what is beautiful for us in India. Jewellery is the crown jewel for us in the world of adornments.

Ornamental beads made from semi precious stones like Carnelian, Jasper and Agate are found in the Indus Valley Civilisation giving jewellery a pre-historic antiquity. These beads were exported and were found as far away in Mesopotamia. Medieval India was known for its gold and gems, the Mughals love of ornaments was legendary, and even today jewellery shops are the brightest in the market. Temple sculptures in stone and bronze, miniature paintings and chronicles of travelers, are sources of the history and designs of jewellery.

While we adorned gods and goddesses in the temple and the royalty and the nobility of the courts, it is the ordinary woman of India, with almond eyes and lotus feet, who is the most adorned. The bejewelled woman is both *ramaniya* and *mangalmaya*, not only beautiful to look at but one who bestows auspiciousness to everything around it, and we have created ornaments for her from her tresses to the toes. Of all the peotic women in our tradition the *shringara rasa nayika* is the most evocative. Our *sutradhar* reminds us that for that *nayika* each ornament creates the perfect romantic ambience.

The head ornament is where romantic thoughts arise
the *kesphul* brings beauty to those thoughts
the nose ring adds fragrance to those thoughts and makes them poetic
the earrings create a certain movement so that those thoughts
begin to dance
the *mala* is a reassurance that every heart beat carries his name
the *bajubandh* holds the melody and the lyrics of the dance together
the bangles jingle and make sure that there is a sonorous rhythm
the rings on the fingers are meant for the beautiful *abhinaya* of *shringara*
the cummerband adds a lyrical gait
the anklets announce as she walks towards her beloved
Thus every ornament on the *shringara rasa nayika*'s body has a role
in ensuring that *shringara* be celebrated joyously and beautifully.[38]

The act of creating a piece of jewellery is sacred, and skills were passed down from father to son through long periods of apprenticeship. Techniques varied from region to region, and included lost wax casting, *kundan* or pure gold, *minakari* or enamelling, *nakashi* or repousse, *tarkashi* or filigree, *rawakam* or granulation, use of moulds, stamping, and so on. As in other *akritis* the Indian jeweller and goldsmith drew their inspiration from the luxuriant world of leaves and flowers, birds and blossoms, the sun and the moon and therefore traditional jewellery designs reflect this association with nature. Gold and gems are considered to have magical properties and afford protection to different parts of the body, and by the same token buying gold on certain days like the *akshaya tritiya*.

Decorating the hair with fragrant flowers, like *mogra*, *chameli*, *malligai* (jasmine), *genda* (marigold), *sarangi* (*Mammea suriga*), *bakuli* (Spanish cherry) *kewra* (screw-pine), *kanakambaram* (firecracker), *gulab* (rose), and *champaka* (frangipani), was an indispensable aspect of personal adornment and started even before we had jewellery. Over time, these flowers were replicated in metal and took the form of *veni* and *gajra* (garlands), hair pins, combs, and coverings for the braid. Hair ornaments were believed to activate the energies in the *sahasrara chakra* (thousand-petalled lotus), located on the crown of the head, optimise energy, strengthen memory, awaken consciousness and enhance intelligence. Stylised over time, they are symbols of miraculous generators of life, fertility and birth. Bangles were like amulets affording protection and were talismans worn around the neck. Certain jewellery was associated with marriage rites and rituals while some others like the *payal* had romantic connotations.

Jewellery functioned as symbols of rank and position, and as articles of faith and protection. Every piece of jewellery speaks a metaphorical language. Shells, beads and feathers, thorns, flowers, and leaves are all imbued with magical powers; and, mystic symbols and images of guardian deities assume extraordinary properties when they are worn on different parts of the body. Jewellery more than any other beautiful object-endows the creator and wearer of magico-religious benefits. In an *abhang* Sant Narhari, a 13th century poet, refers to his profession as a *sonar* or goldsmith, and calls himself a goldsmith who works in the name of God. He says that his body is the melting crucible for His soul of gold; he pours the molten gold of God into the mould made of the three *gunas*, goodness, passion and darkness (*sattva*, *rajas*, *tamas*); he hammers out anger and passion; with scissors of discernment, he cuts out in gold leaf, the name of God, and weighs the name of God with the balance of spiritual enlightenment. Narahari Sonar, the devotee of God, meditates upon Him eternally.

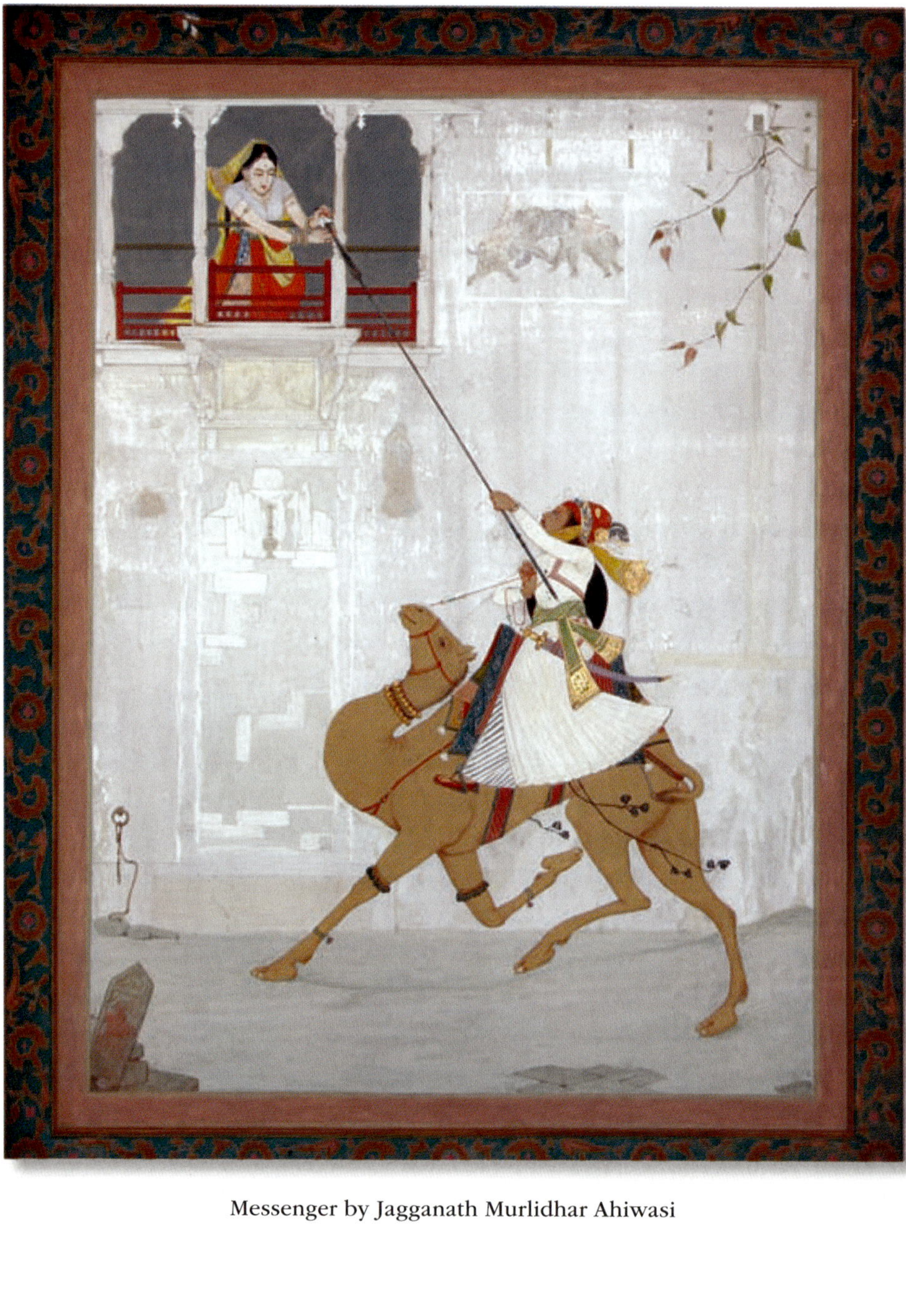

Messenger by Jagganath Murlidhar Ahiwasi

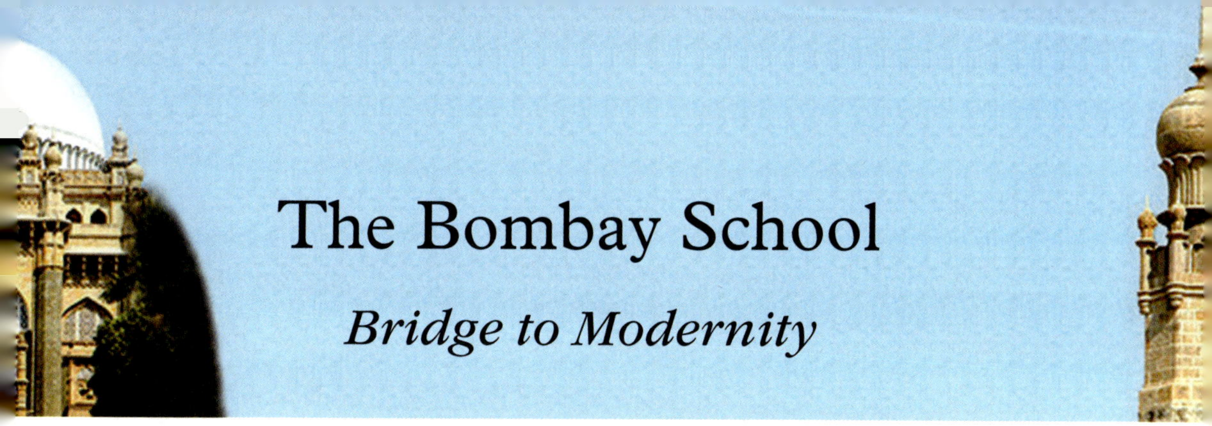

The Bombay School

Bridge to Modernity

If there is one bridge that can take us from the traditional to the modern in India, it must be Indian painting. At the dawn of the 19th century, the era of majestic temple building was long over, and even the many centuries of painting from cave painting, as in Ajanta to Rajput miniature painting, had come to an end with passing of Sansar Chand of Kangra. Our British masters in the 18th and 19th centuries, in an attempt to modernise us, felt that our artists should be taught the Western academic style of painting, while some wanted us to revive our traditional arts and crafts. Revivalism in painting was never complete as some degree of realism did creep in. Some have called this romantic revivalism as we were not far from our gods and goddesses. The early 20th century should perhaps be called a time for ecclectic styles Most Indian artists of the time vacillated between an earlier India's art of affect (or imaginative recreation of experience), and the exactitudes of the physical eye, such as the academics represented. This distinction may well be expressed in terms of what may be called the subjective or the objective artistic intellects: The objective intellect being one which is eminently impersonal, and the subjective equally personal. The former disengaging itself as much as possible from its own prepossesions, striving to see and represent objects as they exist; the other viewing all objects in the light of feelings and preconceptions. In the year 1790, James Wales started training a few students at Shanvarvada in Poona at the request of Peshwa Sawai Madhavrao but this was short-lived. At Madras in 1850, Dr. Hunter started a polytechnic for reviving Indian art. A similar institute was established in Calcutta in 1854. These were early beginnings of art schools in British India.

Bombay was the *Urbs Prima in Indes*, the first city of India, and even though it was a cosmopolitan urban city, a major trade centre and a port of entry into the country, it did not surprisingly attract British artists who had come to paint picturesque India. Another surprising feature of artists in Bombay at that time was they were not touched either by the World Wars or the freedom struggle. Bombay in the 19th century was blessed with philanthropists, and it was on 2 March,1857 that the Bombay School of Art was established, with a gift of One lakh Rupees from Jamshetji Jeejeebhoy. The JJ School, as it was

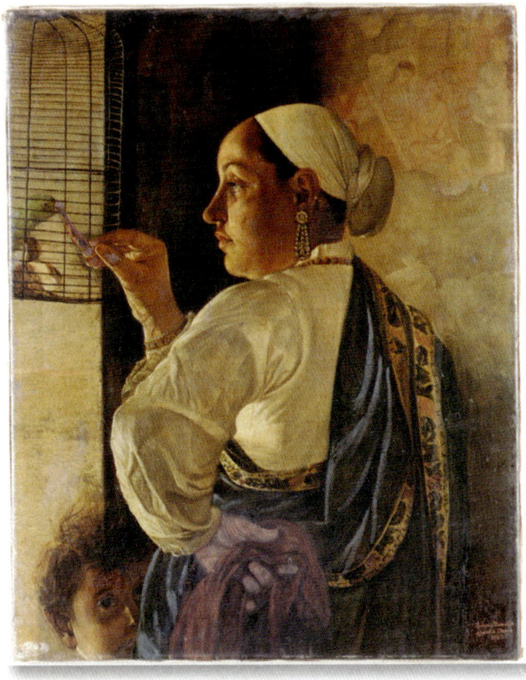

Feeding The Parrot, Pestonjee Bomanjee (1882)

called, was a crucible of artistic trends, where Revivalism was pitted against Modernity and art against craft. Tradition in painting, for the British teachers, meant only the Ajanta frescoes and Rajasthani miniature painting, while being blissfully unaware of the many beautiful genres of painting in ancient and medieval India. The school's first class was in drawing and began on 2 March, 1857. The building of the school was designed by architect George Twigge Molecey in neo-Gothic architecture. In 1866 the Government of India took over the management of the School and at that time Lockwood Kipling, who was an architect and sculptor, was one of the professors of the school and also its Dean. Rudyard Kipling, his son and noted author was born in 1865 on this campus. John Griffiths, in 1868, organised the teaching schedule at the school and he was instrumental in starting a class that copied paintings from Ajanta. William Ewart Gladstone Solomon (1880–1965) was the Principal of Sir J. J. School of Art from 1918 to 1936, as well as the Curator and on the Board of Trustees of our Museum, from 24 January, 1921 to 25 March, 1937. Solomon later, and foresightedly, acquired most of the Bombay School paintings for this Museum, which shall remain a great legacy for generations.

The Indians who completed art education at the JJ School needed an art organisation. The efforts of certain Indians as well as the British Officers and their wives who painted as a hobby, resulted in the formation of the Bombay Art Society, which was established in December 1888. The annual exhibitions of the Bombay Art Society soon became the main attraction in India, as the major artistic event of the year. Artists from all over India aspired for the Governor's Prize or the Society's Gold Medal to establish themselves as professional artists.

The late 19th century was an axial period in the history of Indian art. We were still under British rule, and while our colonial masters were keen that we learn the Western academic style of painting, at the same time they were equally keen that we do not give up our many centuries of tradition in painting. Initially, the syllabus of the JJ School was adopted from the School of Industrial Arts of South Kensington in England. The first phase,1885-1900 of education was to train Indian artists to draw, paint and sculpt from a live model, a practice that continues even today. Artists trained at this time were able to find jobs at princely courts like Kolhapur, Hyderabad and Aundh to do royal portraits. The next phase of 1896-1918 was that of landscape painting, and this mainly due to Cecil Burns who encouraged the artists to create naturalistic landscapes. All along realistic painting in the Western academic style remained foremost, and a number of students emerged in this genre. The most noted in this field was Pestonjee Bomanjee.

Among the portrait painters of the Bombay School, the name of Pestonjee Bomanjee (1851-1938) stands out. He was drawn to painting even as a child, and he entered the JJ School at the age of 13. His initial training was under John Griffith recreating the murals of Ajanta. And it was during this period that he painted the iconic Parsi Lady feeding a parrot, the lady being none other than his wife Jilubai. Pestonjee painted the daily and religious life of Parsis in Bombay, and this attracted a number of Parsis to his studio. Pestonjee's portraits are marked by strong lines, a soft colour palette and detailed depiction of the background. He used round brushes and delineated microscopic details like draperies. His colour schemes were pleasant and the colour of the figures was unmistakably Indian, unlike some other painters in this period who painted Indian figures with European complexion. Feeding the Parrot is a portrait of his wife and remains an iconic testimony to his talent.

Another noted student in the same genre was Mahadev Vishwanath Dhurandhar. Following the success of Raja Ravi Varma, Dhurandhar embarked on creating realistic portraits. His education at the Institute helped him develop a sense of realism as well as the classic technique of chiaroscuro, wherein light and shadow are used to create three-dimensional portraits. He was the first Indian gold medal winner of the Bombay Art Society in 1895. Dhurandhar's work is mostly known for his documentation of city life, his paintings of the Indian mythological figures, and most importantly his depiction of Maharashtrian women navigating the realms of the private and the public sphere.The artist is known to have spent hours by the promenade, sitting with his sketch pad, observing the people as they carried on with their mundane activities. He would try to capture the essence of their activities in his intricate drawings. Later in life, Dhurandhar returned to the JJ school as a teacher, and in 1930 he became the first Indian Director of the Sir J.J. School of Art. He exhibited his paintings widely, and it is said that Queen Mary of London bought one of his paintings. Dhurandhar developed a habit of regular sketching from his student career. He always carried a small sketchbook and has left behind about 100 small sketch books. He was an avid writer and his book *Kalamanchiratil Ekkechalis Varshe* is a virtual history of the JJ School. In retrospect, Dhurandhar's work also gives us an insight into the sartorial sociology of Maharashtra.

The pride of place among the students, in its early days, goes to Jagganath Murlidhar Ahiwasi. He was raised by his father in a cultured and religious environment, and the art of Nathadwara had a great influence on him in his early years. He entered the JJ School in 1924 and completed its diploma in 1926. Ahiwasi was drawn to the tradition of miniature painting from the early Jain right up to the Kangra schools. Prof. Solomon was quick to recognise Ahiwasi's talent and asked him to head a class on traditional painting. True to his character, Ahiwasi insisted that students sit on the floor

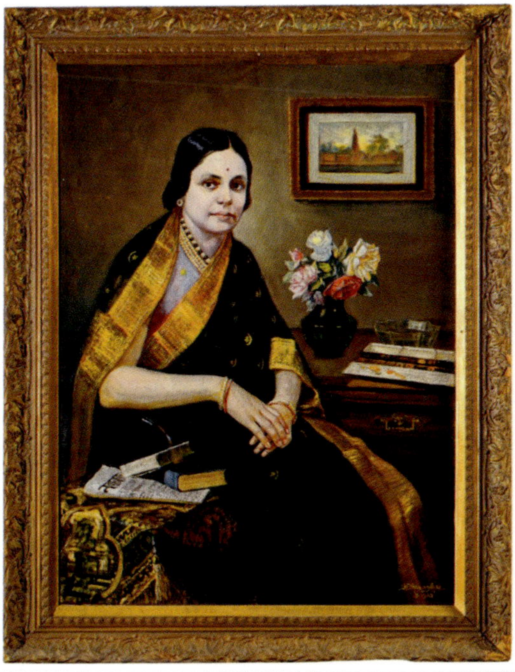

Lady in Chandrakala Sari, M.V. Dhurandhar

as they painted, as he believed that traditional painting should be created in a traditional atmosphere. Ahiwasi, it is said, painted with lyrical lines and minimal colours to create truly outstanding works of art like Messenger and My Father, both of which are in our Museum. Ahiwasi inspired painters like Hebbar, Almelkar, Palshikar, and he remained a beacon of traditional culture both in his paintings and personal life. As a tribute to Ahiwasi, Palshikar painted a portrait of him. However, the winds of modernity were blowing in the JJ School and Ahiwasi faced opposition, not only from other teachers in the school but also from emerging painters like Souza, Tyeb Mehta, Muqbool Fida Hussain and Sadwelkar. After retirement, Ahiwasi joined the Benares Hindu University. He was also a good writer and his books *Rekhanjali* and *Chitra Manjusha* are testament to this. Ahiwasi will always be remembered for his faith in tradition even in the face of modernity.

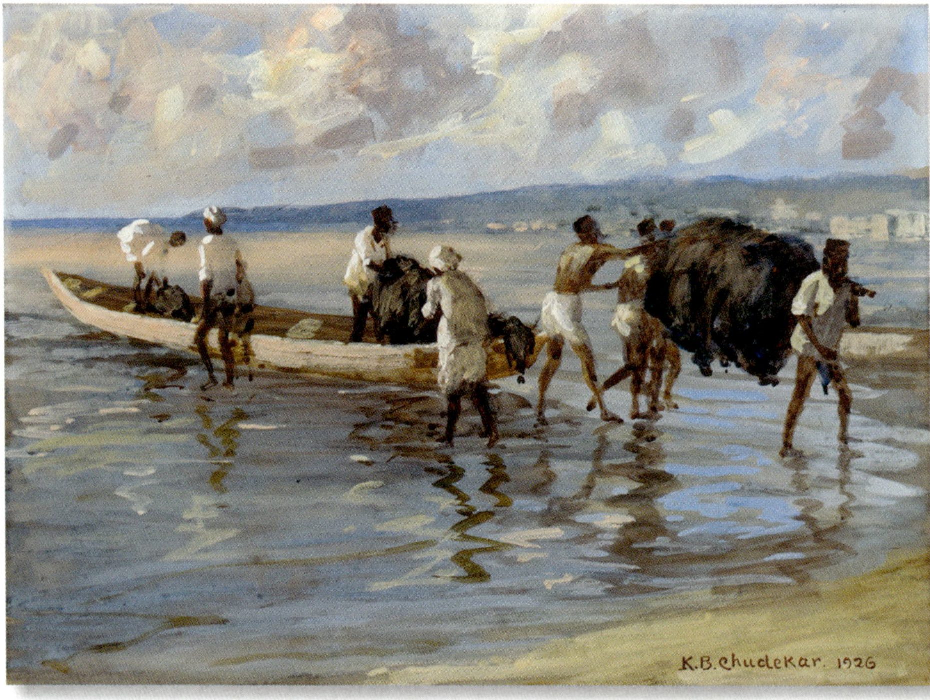

After Fishing, Keshav Bhavanrao Chudekar (1884–1971)

Seeking to bring the effect of light into their works, artists gradually ventured into the open air to draw impressionistic landscapes. The interest in watercolour landscapes was stirred by Cecil Burns, Principal of JJ School from 1898–1918, who excelled in the form. One of the foremost artists in this genre was K.B. Chudekar (1884–1971). Chudekar painted with strong strokes, and colours for him were spiritual.

The life and work of Y.K. Shukla would seem to provide an exact illustration of the workings of the artistic spirit on the Indian art scene in the 20th century.

It is artists like Shukla who brought the newer methods, content and media from both the occident and the orient to India. They helped enlarge the ambience of art, in terms of greater possibilities and choices.

Shakuntala by Raghunath Dhondopant Dhopeshwarkar is a beautiful rendition which almost brings to life Kalidasa's drama. One sees strong suggestions of Revivalism even though Shakuntala has not been painted in the past.

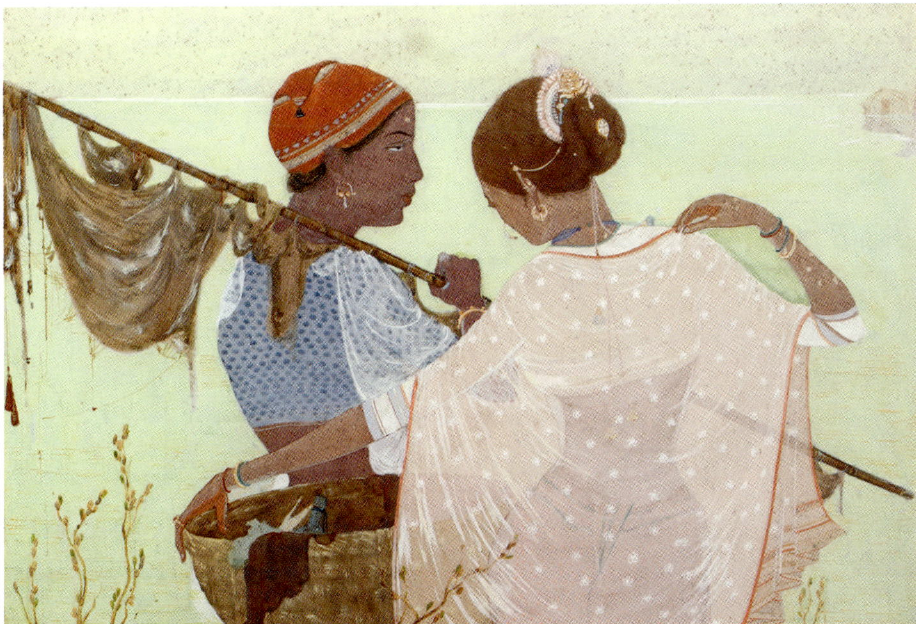

Sweet Hearts, Y.K. Shukla (1907–1986)

Connected with the Bombay Art School was the so-called Progressive Art movement with names like Souza and Raza who were students briefly at the JJ School but felt uncomfortable and decided to embark on their own. They had support from Rudy van Lyden, Walter Langhammer and E. Schlesinger. These European art connoisseurs even purchased their paintings and Schlesinger, before his retirement, wanted to donate these paintings to our Museum, but our Museum refused. Nonetheless they went on to become highly successful artists, both artistically and financially. JJ School of Art has given India some of its revolutionary artists making a global impact on art, like Vasudev Gaitonde,

Akbar Padamsee, Tyeb Mehta, Jeram Patel, Prabhakar Barve, Prabhakar Kolte. As we look back nostalgically on the beginnings of the art movement at the JJ School, one wonders whether Revivalists like Ahiwasi are still remembered and recognised, or whether they have become footnotes in the history of paintings in Bombay of the 20th century.

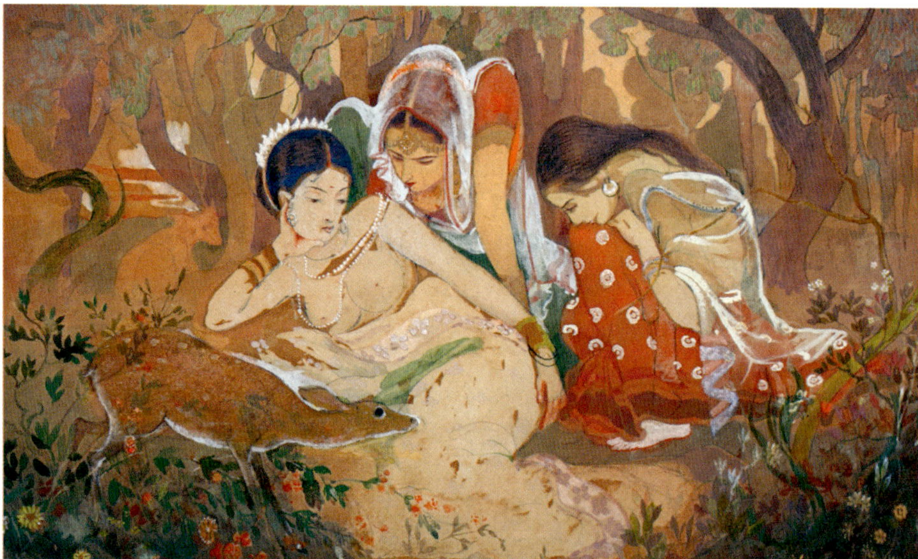

Shakuntala, Raghunath Dhondopant Dhopeshwarkar (1931)

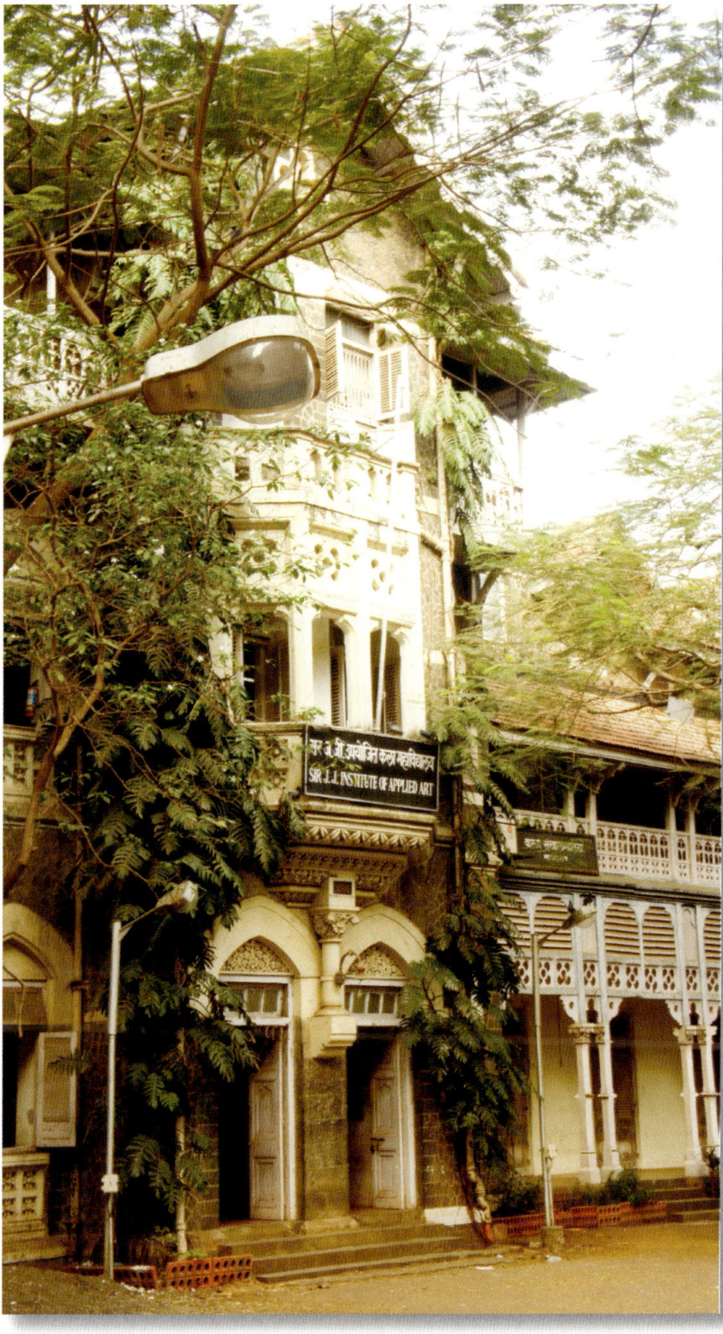

JJ School of Art. Photo by Vijay Kothare

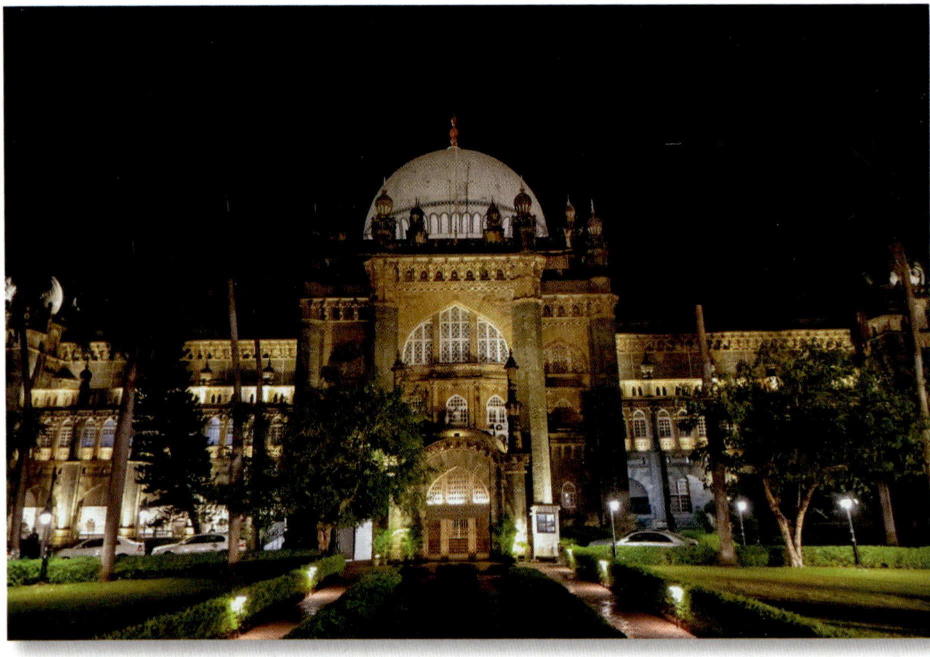

The Museum at night. Photograph by Sneha Mestry

Vidai

As we Take Our Leave

As we take our leave of this Museum the animated voices of the potters and the painters, *shilpis* and *sangeetkars*, that we heard are now hushed. The gods and goddesses that spoke to us are asleep. The *raja* and the *praja* that had come alive through *patas* and paintings, will go back to rest. Under the moonlit sky, the Museum will be silent. The words of Tagore come to mind, "when I sing a song I want you to complete it." This is our responsibility, namely that the many images that we saw must now be converted to visual knowledge, *shabda* must be transformed into *shabdabrahman* and the *rupa* to *rupabrahman*, the various metaphors must be decoded, and the many *akritis* that we saw should lead us to our *sanskriti*. As contemplative visitors to the Museum it behoves us to do just that.

Museologists tells us that museum objects must be celebrated aesthetically and not venerated or worshipped. While this may be true academically, we as Indian musuem-goers cannot accept this totally. While we may not venerate a museum object with religious rites and rituals, how can we forget that, most if not all, objects were originally in a temple, home shrine, stupa or a Jain *bhandara*? In their original liocation these objects were sacred and therefore worshipped. The rubbed off forehead of a bronze, the marks of vermillion on a manuscript, archival photographs and our collective memory, all remind us that the distinction between sacred and secular does not hold for an Indian mind, and for objects that are lovingly created. When we are looking at the manuscript of the *Bhagavata Purana* or the *Devi Mahatmya*, even as we are struck by the beauty of the painting or the erudition and wisdom of the words, we cannot forget that these manuscripts were in their original state objects of veneration, and the two features, the sacred and the secular for us are a continuum and not dichotomous.

What should touch us is the beauty and grandeur of human creativity, how thoughts and feelings, inspirations and *shastras* were transformed into shapes and forms that we could see and touch. At the root of human creativity is the hand.

The hand is central in any artistic creation and even the word *akriti* incorporates the word *kar* which is the hand, suggesting that it is the hand that is at the main tool of human artistic creativity. Evolutionary biologists pay great attention to the detached thumb and hence its prehensile ability to hold objects, such as weapons and the brush, the pen and the chisel, and this is the key to human creativity. A traditional morning prayer is:

karagre vasate Laxmi
kar madhye Sarasvati
kar mule tu Govindam
prabhate kara vandanam.
Laxmi resides at the tip of my hand
and Sarasvati in the middle
at the bottom of the hand is Govinda
and this morning I venerate that hand.

The words of Kabir come to mind:

How many know the world weaves who spread the warp?
Earth and sky the two beams of his loom.
Earth and Sky the two beams of his loom.
Sun and moon two shuttles filled and ready.
He takes a thousand threads.
He spreads them lengthwise.

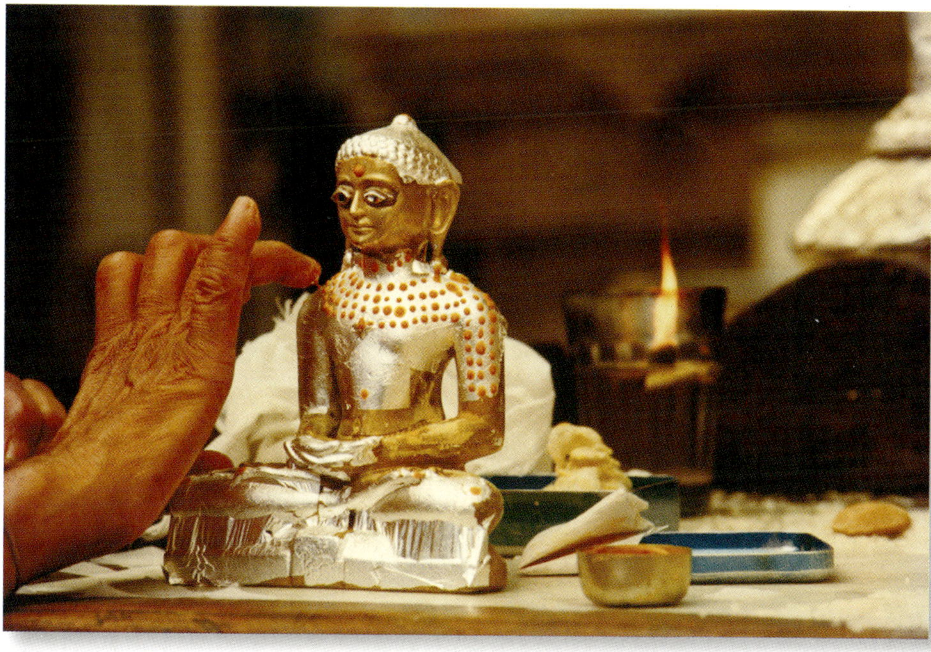

Adorning the Jina. Photograph by Rajesh Vora

Watch him as weaves today.
The length end is still far away, most difficult to reach.
Says Kabir: *karma* with *karma*, woven with unwoven threads.
How well this weaver weaves.
The potter takes a lump of earth
and encloses the sky within
as he makes a *ghata*
and when the *ghata* breaks

the sky is still the same
only the potter knows
where is the earth and where the sky
from the voice of those who drank from the *ghata*
is still heard.[39]

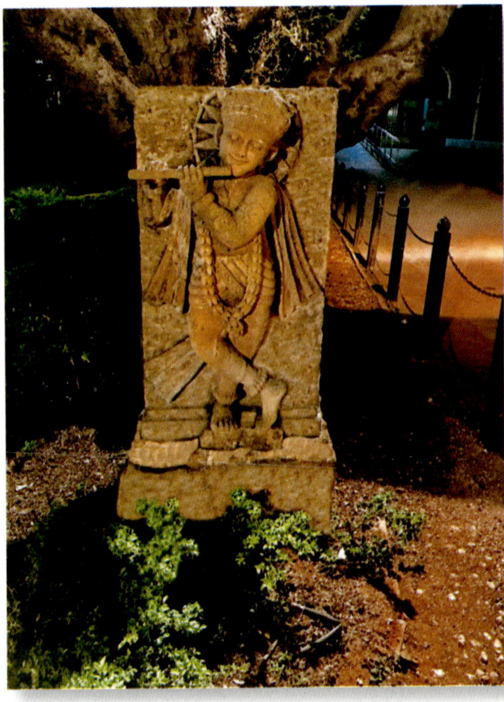

Krishna under the Champa Tree. Gujarat. 19th century

Shruti , what is heard and *smriti* or what is remembered, are traditional sources of knowledge, and the spoken word enjoyed a primacy and validity in ancient India in times ancient and does so even now. The written word came later and we owe this to the Buddhists and the Jains, but even when written, the textual tradition was mainly oral, as texts were read aloud and even chanted. From about the 6th century BCE, texts were produced on copper plates and then on palm and birch leaves. The textual tradition remains of prime importance as sources and transmitters of knowledge. However we shall bypass them in this Museum in favour of *drishti* or visual sources of knowledge.

It is useful to begin with some basic concepts in Sanskrit that revolve around the words *drishya* and *pashya*; *pashyati* is a verb that denotes the simple optical act of seeing. *Drishti* however, is a noun and means more than the act of visualisation or seeing; it is rather perceiving, feeling, knowing, insight and then ultimately realising, and therefore *drishti* is undertaken in a second more contemplative moment. And then there is *najar* in the *bhashas*, which is a type of vision and has a variety of meanings which include the romantic glance and even the evil eye. Etymologically related to *drishti* is *darshana*, and while Sanskrit does not differentiate between *darshana* and *drishti* Prakrit and the *bhashas* considers *darshan* as the transfiguring vision of a deity and *drishti* as enlightened vision. *Darshana* or transfiguring vision of an icon is fundamental to the religious experience, whether it is in a home shrine or a temple. Equally the icon gives aesthetic hints that an adept *rasika* or aesthete picks up and assures himself of a rich aesthetic experience. However *drishti* can be understood even in a museum in a wider context and is not limited to *darshana* or the transfiguring vision of icons, and can go much beyond the narrow confines of an organised temple or even a shrine and can occur in everyday spaces in the lived lives of the *samajika* or the common people. The gods and the motifs and symbols of these visual representations, as well as those who hold them sacred, are simple and unpretentious, but yet dignified and self-assured. Whether it is a tree that is held sacred or a naturally-occurring stone that is revered, a river that is considered the embodiment of divinity itself, an ancestor that is worshipped, a fabric that is simply draped but considered sacred, a simple roadside shrine on a busy street or a votive terracotta horse that is lovingly made and offered, a narrative scroll that holds its audience spellbound, here is visual knowledge at work that is as spontaneous as it is intense, as visual as it is oral, charged with faith, fervor and commitment, now private and now shared, that forms an integral part of the lived lives of these common people, be they rural or urban, tribal or traditional. The rituals and practices for these visual creations are neither scripted nor canonised, but what they may lack in grandeur, erudition and ceremony they more than make up in the faith and feeling that they generate, and going beyond all of these become a source of non-didactic knowledge. In a civilisation which has encountered majestic truths and erected grand temples, these visual representations and expressions of the ordinary people which are in the Museum tend to be sidelined or dismissed by scholars as well as the world at large, as minor or lesser gods, or mere adornments worthy of curiosity, but not of serious study; but it is important to remember that they have a beauty and presence of their own in the pluralistic Indian tradition, and that it is through them that knowledge is available visually and outside sacerdotal rites and rituals and scholarly texts. In other words *drishti* understood as the perception, understanding and realisation of these simple visual forms becomes a parallel knowledge system in its own right. This underscores the fact that while scholarly texts and their erudite commentaries are an important part of the Indian tradition of textual knowledge systems, they are not the only source of knowledge and that *drishti* offers an alternative and parallel system of knowledge, through everyday visual representations. These other sources outside the textual tradition are probably more ancient and perhaps more pervasive than *shruti* and *smriti*. *Drishti* therefore should be given a honoured place in the epistemology of knowledge.

Gesture and signs must have been the earliest form of communication, even before language evolved. Recent findings at Bhimbetka and at other sites leave little doubt that visual representations may predate even the spoken word. The Indus Valley seals have left hieroglyphics and primitive images such as that of a cross-legged yogi or a woman within a Pipal tree which are obviously more than decorative motifs, but markers of a world view. *Drishti* thus is able to claim a pre-historic pedigree.

Visual forms transcend and bypass the limitations of rational language, it uses images and not words, its grammar and lexicon are made up of forms and shapes, its canvas is not just palm leaf or paper but mud walls and scrolls, its logic is the inner essence of form and not a formal idea, it creates forms only to break out of them, it suggests but does not impose, it leads and does not insist, it creates vistas of meaning rather than give didactic instruction, it is beautiful in its own right but subtly leads to visions of beauty, its impact is immediate and direct but its message is the ultimate that is realised in a later contemplative moment.

Visual knowledge for us in the Indian tradition has a special place, for it conveys more than what meets the eye. Whether it is a mural in a cave, or a wall painting in a nuptial chamber in Madhuban, or an adornment on a mud wall or a decoration on the threshold of a home, motifs and patterns embroidered on a fabric, a visual image that we see in the Museum performs many functions. It adorns and beautifies, it gives a certain sanctity to the space in which it exists, but it equally serves a magical function and confers to the space and the environment it occupies a protective charm. Above all visual motifs and metaphors, images and forms bring a direct perception of *jnana*

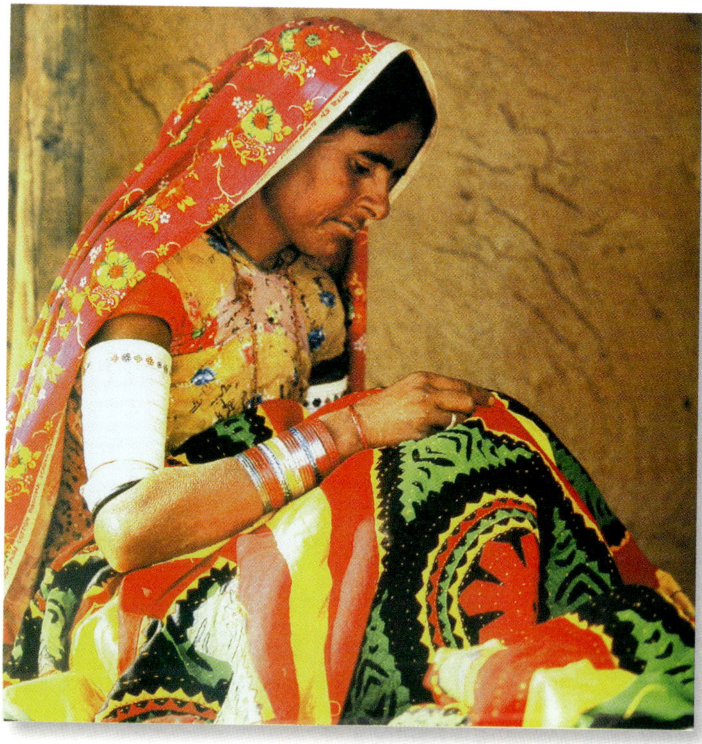

Kutchh. A Rabari Woman.

or knowledge, both to the *rasika* who has a cultivated and trained eye, and to the *samajika* to whom it conveys an intuitive sense of *purnatva* or fullness.

The visible and the palpable representation of divinity is an important, almost defining, part of the Indian Hindu, Buddhist and Jain traditions, and the creation of visual motifs and symbols is an integral and important part of that.

These visual markers belong both to the sophisticated and the unlettered. If the spontaneous and widespread public representation of the sacred and the divine is a feature of Indian religions, mainly Hinduism, the creation of visual motifs and symbols, and their presence in the everyday lives of the people are an equally important part of Hindu living, and are a testament to the sensitivity and awareness of philosophical truths by the unlettered and untutored in their own unique and unlettered way. These symbols are more than static and inert symbols, they are living visual metaphors, generally

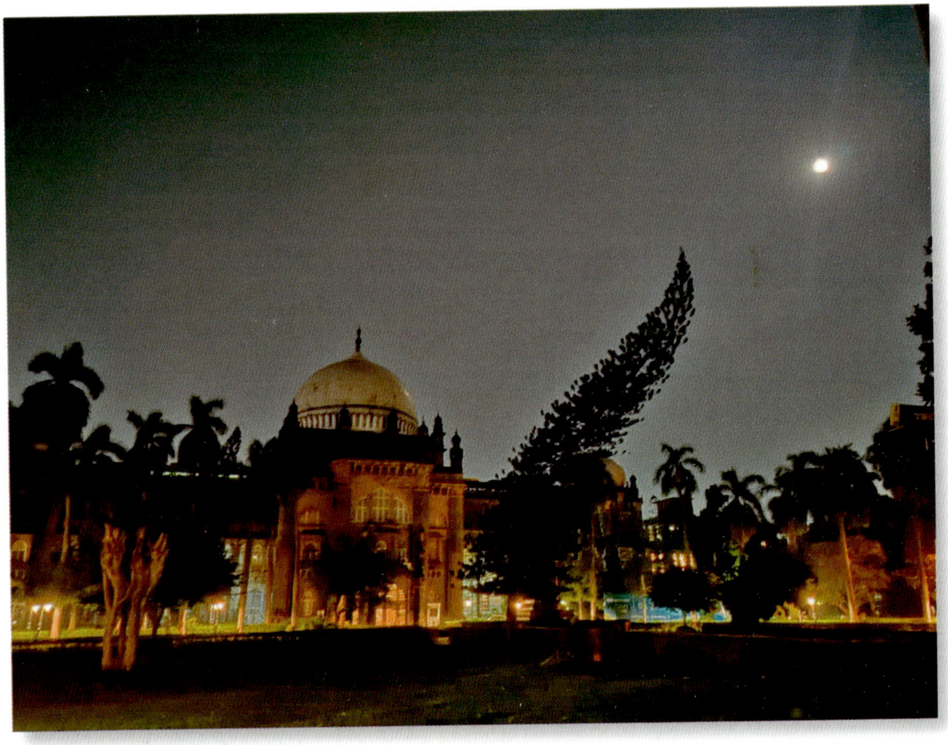

Under a full moon night it is as if we hear the flute of Krishna inviting the *gopis* to participate in the *rasa lila*.
Has our journey in this Museum not been like a *krida* with Krishna?

transmitted from mother to daughter, through trackless generations, and stem from ancient memories, memories that are a storehouse of fundamental and distilled truths, of Puranic stories and folk legends, and where time-tested philosophical truths survive in songs and images, where a handful of earth can hold more knowledge than countless pages of erudite and hoary palm leaf manuscripts. In these simple and everyday visual representations, the beautiful and the sacred come together through archetypal and primal forms, they beautify and they inform, they protect and purify the daily spaces in the lived lives of our people.

It has been said that *rupam rupam pratirupam babhuva*, every form is a replica of a primal form. Running like an undercurrent of subterranean streams underneath the many beautiful folk forms, be they in our homes or *havelis*, fabrics or festoons, is the primal myth of *samudra manthan* or churning of the ocean, which locates many beautiful forms in the ocean, from which they are churned out and emerge as the *ratnas* or the jewels of the ocean. Underpinned by this important myth various forms arise, and like branches of a tree interlock and intersect and provide us with motifs and metaphors, designs and patterns, and like archetypes go deep into ancient memories and are transmitted from mother to daughter, potter to poet, artist to artisan. These beautiful forms adorn and decorate, they add grace and dignity, but above all they inspire and chasten our minds and are transformed into visual knowledge. It has been said rightly that *yatha drishti tatha shrishti*, *drishti* leads to *shristi*, and this *shrishti* is the creation of visual knowledge. The visual presence of these beautiful representations assures the *raja* and the *praja* like, the king and the subject, not only of pleasing surroundings but to the aesthetically sensitive person it is an invitation to explore these objectively beautiful forms so that he can experience the inward serene subjective state of beauty. This is the end point of *drishti*.

In a civilisation that is mainly agricultural, both in rural and urban spaces, growth and fertility are not only important economically and socially but become a measure of the beauty and meaning of life itself, and provides a world view and a frame of reference. To grow is to live, to prosper materially and flourish emotionally, to ensure the continuity of life and creation but equally in the understanding and representation of that growth and fecundity it is to realise the movement and circularity of time, for what grows must change with the seasons and eventually perish, but from its seeds life will start all over again, and thus this points to the eternality of time even in the face of human impermanence.

Many are the journeys we undertake
some for pleasure, other for commerce
some with family, other with friends
but a journey to a museum should be a pilgrimage
where we engage with beautiful objects
lovingly made and fondly cared for
and as we are touched by their sensual features
we must not forget to move sensuality to spirituality
we must move from objectivity to subjectivity
from the outer to the inner
and then we will be touched by human creativity
a creativity that expresses itself so that it can find itself
in the *ananda* of *saundarya* in the spaces of this Museum.

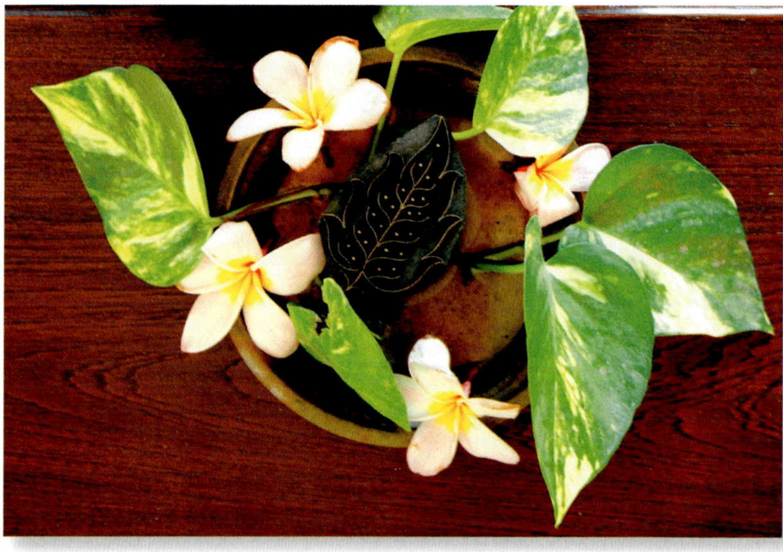

This pagination logo was created with Champa flowers and leaves from the Museum garden.

Endnotes

1. Pal, P. *Sensuous Immortals* (Los Angeles: LACMA, 1977), p.14.
2. Dehejia, Harsha V. *The Advaita of Art* (Delhi: Motilal Banarsidass, 1996), p.43.
3. Kalidasa, *Abhijnana Shatuntalam* (Delhi: Motilal Banarsidass, 1969) 4.3.
4. Dehejia, H. *Romantic Moments in Poetry and Painting* (Ahmedabad: Mapin, 1995), p.54.
5. Dehejia, Harsha. *Amarushataka: A Centennial of Love Songs* (Delhi: DK Printworld, 2017), p.48.
6. Ibid.
7. Randhawa, M.S. *Basohli Paintings of the Rasamanjar* (Atlantic Highlands. N.J.: Humanities Press, 1981), pp.10–70.
8. Dehejia, Harsha V. *Painted Words: Kangra Paintings of Matiram's Rasraj*. (Delhi: DK Printworld, 2012), p.69.
9. Bahadur, K.P. *Bihari: The Sat Sai* (Delhi: Penguin Books/UNESCO, 1990), pp.228–240.
10. *Taittriya Upanishad*. II.3.
11. Anand, Mulk Raj. *MARG*. XXXII. No 1. p.33.
12. Tagore, Rabindranath. *Creative Unity* (Delhi: MacMillan & Co, 1922), p.95.
13. *Bhagavata Purana*. X. 50.1.
14. Dehejia, *Bhartrhari* (Delhi: Motilal Banarsidass, 2020), p.11.
15. Foreword in *Saree*, Redpepper Books, 2012.
16. Parekh, Soha. Ibid. p.124.
17. Miller, Barbara Stoller. *The Gitagovinda of Jayadeva* (Delhi: Motilal Banarsidass, 1977), p.71.
18. Hacker, personal communication
19. Losty, J.P., in Dehejia, H.V. *Celebration of Love* (Delhi, Roli, 1999), p.158.
20. Pal, Pratapaditya. *The Classical Tradition in Rajput Painting*. p.10
21. Ibid. p.28
22. Kalidasa. *Kumarasambhavam* (Delhi: Motilal Banarasidass, 1981), 4.15-16.
23. Krishna, Anand. Personal communication.
24. Goswamy, B.N. Notes taken at a lecture delivered by Dr B.N. Goswamy at CSMVS.
25. Coomaraswamy, A.K. *History of Indian Indonesian Art* (New York: Dover, 1927), p.132.
26. Vatsyayan, Kapila. *Metaphors of Indian Art* (Delhi: DK Printworld, 1999), p.56.
27. Tagore, Rabindranath. *Creative Unity* (Delhi: MacMillan & Co, 1922), p.82.
28. Ibid., p.91.
29. Ibid.
30. Chatopadhyaya, Kamaladevi, *IIC Quarterly*, June 1995, p.32.

31. Paz, Octavio. *In Praise of Hands, Contemporary Crafts of the World* (Greenwich, Connecticut: New York Graphic Society, 1974), p.22.
32. Basham, A.L. Personal communication.
33. Devi, Priya. 'An Introduction to Aditi', *Marg*: Continuity and Change. Volume XXXV. No 4. p.70.
34. Upadhayaya, Narmada. Personal communication.
35. Zebrowski, Mark. *Deccani Painting* (England: Sotheby Publications & Berkeley: University of California Press, 1983), p.10.
36. Daljeet. *Deccani Painting* (Delhi: National Museum, 1985), p.42.
37. Swahananda, Swami (tr.). *Chandogya Upanishad* (Madras: Sri Ramakrishna Math, 1950), p.44.
38. Nene, Manisha (CSMS). Personal Communication.
39. Singh, Sukhdev. *The Bijak of Kabir*. (Delhi: Motilal Banarasidass, 1983), p.43.

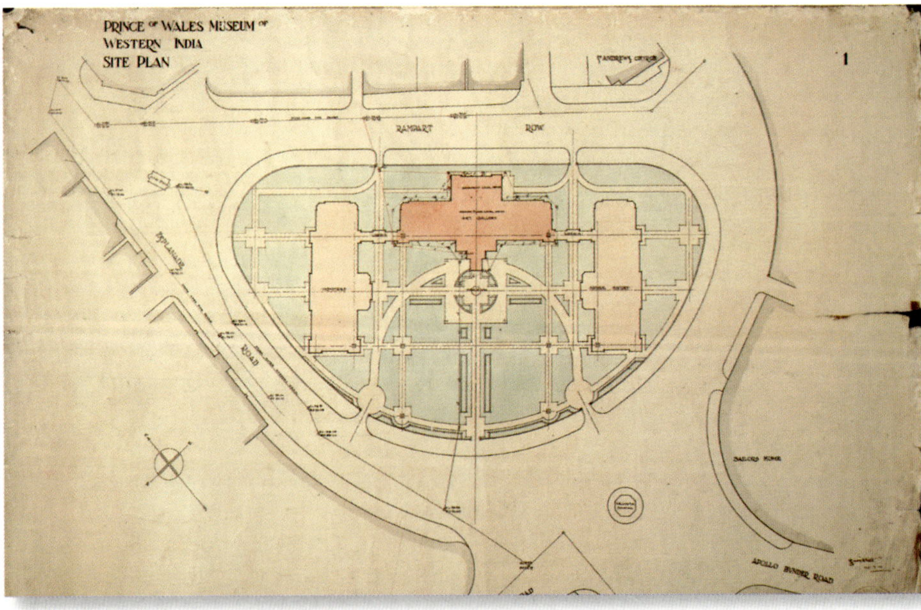

Site Plan of the proposed Prince of Wales Museum.

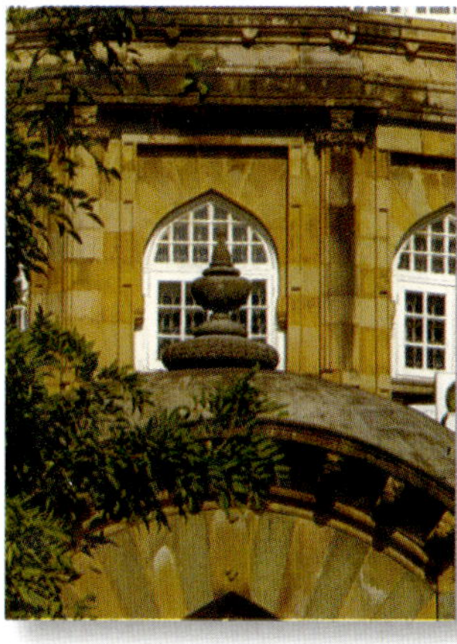

George Wittet's master stroke is the porch of the Museum
where he creates a Bangla curved roof on top of which is the amalaka.
These are unmistakeable signs of a temple.
Does he suggest that we should enter this Museum
as we enter a temple, cleansed of mind
and ready to receive the bounty of beautiful objects that await us within?

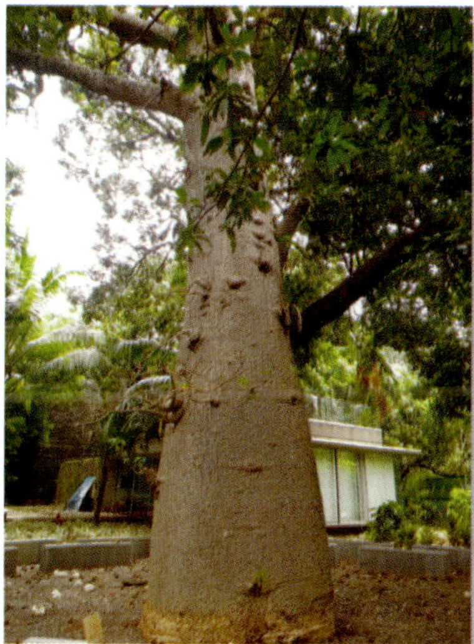

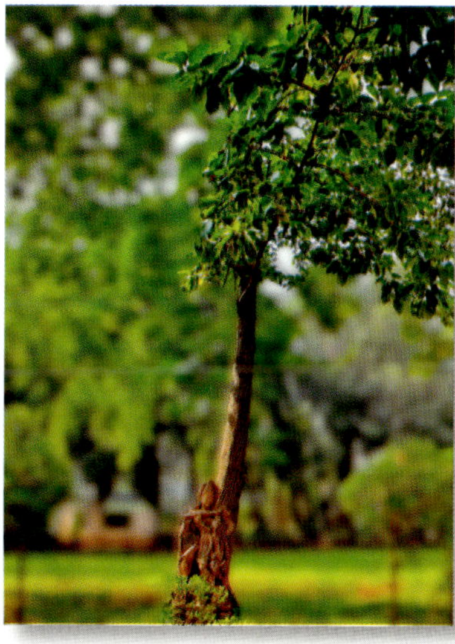

The Museum is blessed with many trees. Ancient trees and blossoming trees, trees that speak to us and sing for us, trees that have ancient memories and trees that change with seasons. Time spent in the company of trees are meditative. That is why we say *vriksha rakshati rakshitah*.

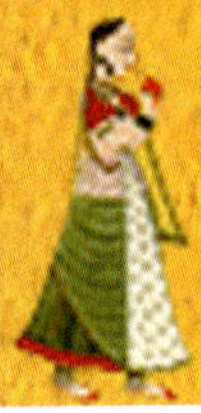

Acknowledgements

As we Begin: Meeting the Sutradhar—To Vikas Dilawari, Rahul Mehrotra and Christopher London my gratitude for leading me through the nuances of architecture. When I needed help I would turn to Anupam Sah, the Conservator par excellence, whose smiling face would solve the problem.

Alap: The First Notes—I would particularly like to thank Nilanjana Som for her help. She was for me, like a musician's accompanist, as I sang the *raga* of CSMVS.

The Sensuous Feminine: Yakshi to Nayika—Speaking with Benoy Behl was as if were together in a cave or atelier discussing the finer points of the piece of art.

The Journey of Our Icons: The Beauty of Sharira—I thank Naman Ahuja for the many conversations I have had with him which made me feel that I was speaking with a *sthapati*. Devangana Desai has been a fellow traveler and when my mind tires and cannot find an answer I always turn to her.

Beautiful is the Word: The Word is Beautiful—It was Sukeshi Kamra and Vandana Prapanna who made the beautiful words speak to me. Mrinalini and Aparna, the *dvarpalas* of the reserve objects were very kind to me and made my entry easy. Saryu Doshi has been a mentor to me in many ways.

Sutras of Beauty: Threads of Life—I have sat beside many a weaver and listened to the whisper of the loom.

The Journey from Kavya to Kalam: From Pothi to Chitravali—The journey from *kavya* to *kalam* of Krishna *shringara* is like going down the Yamuna river and listening to the wind as it brings the dulcet notes of Krishna *kavya*. Even better than that is to listen to Dr. B. N. Goswami's erudite and insightful exposition of miniature paintings.

Gods of Our Shrines: Beauty of Bronzes—I am indebted to Kirit Mankodi and Catherine Mallebrien for their insights into folk bronzes.

Celebrating the Quotidian: Beauty of Everyday Objects—I am particularly grateful to Manisha Nene. In explaining the nuances of the beautiful objects of daily use, it is as if she was conveying to me the voice of Vishwakarman.

The Bombay School: Bridge to Modernity—I am particularly grateful to Prof. Krishan Lal Sharma, the son-in-law of the Late J.M. Ahiwasi. Mr. Dilip Ranade gave willingly of his time and expertise to explain the many nuances of painting in Bombay in the 20th century. Prasanna Mangrulkar as it were opened the doors of the vaults of the storage of modern paintings for me. Manjiri Thakur was always available to help me solve many knotty issues.

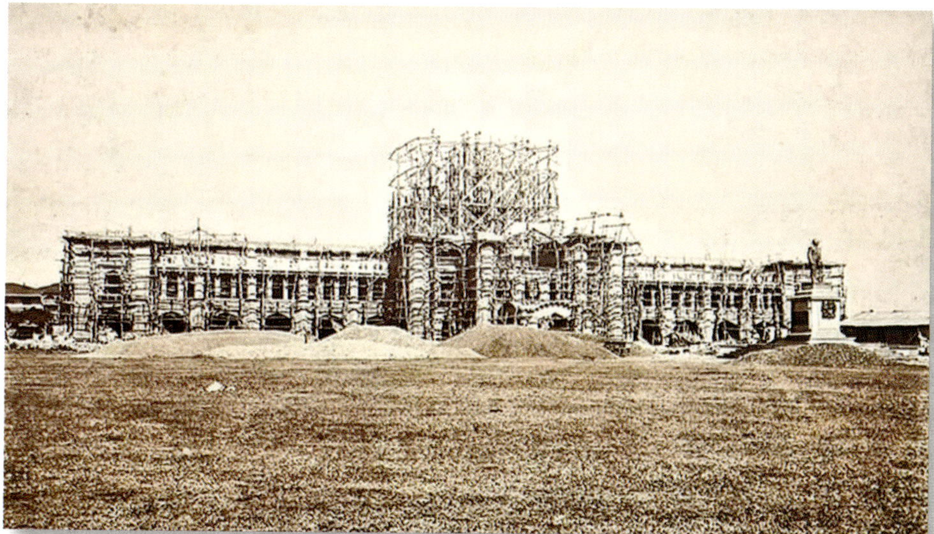

Chhatrapati Shivaji Maharaj Vaastu Sangrahalaya,
formerly Prince of Wales Museum,
under construction at Kala Ghoda junction.

Index

Note: Page numbers in **boldface** indicate images, while *italics* indicate names of manuscripts and selected Indian terms.

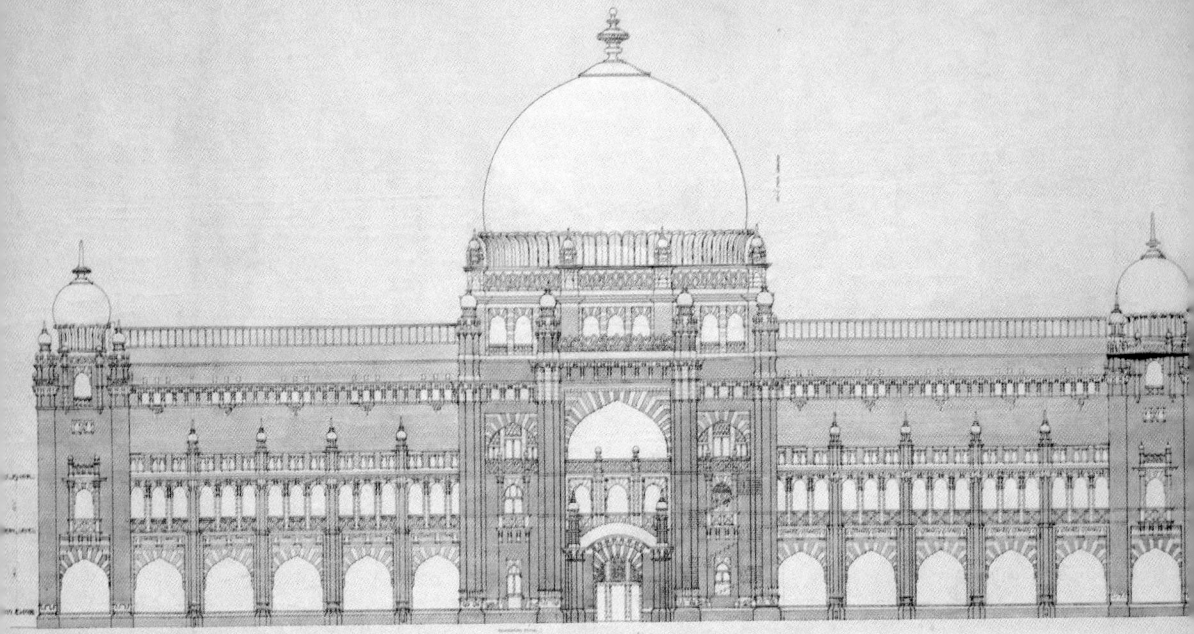

Many a footfall has been heard
in the corridors of this Vastu Sanghralaya,
from the hoary moments of its conception until now,
and many more will be heard in the future.
The many beautiful objects must have revealed
themselves in different ways to them,
some would have whispered of their creator,
others of their patron.
Each had a story to tell, a song to sing,
a mantra to chant, a history to tell .
And all of this the visitor takes home.
But then, when they are touched by the beauty and
creativity of these objects,
they no longer remain visitors,
but return as friends to drink again
from the river of joy
and the fountain of creativity
that flows through this building.

This tribute by Dr. Harsha Dehajia "Musings in the Museum", on CSMVS Museum celebrating its centenary in 2022, is a well-constructed publication. Following academic norms, Dr Dehajia has brought his two loves together—Indian classical music and Indian miniature paintings. He is a well-respected scholar in the world of academia. His *Alap* - The First Notes, and his sensuous feminine *Yakshi* to *Nayika*, are comprehensively studied by this renowned scholar. For those unfamiliar with the classical text, this work goes into detail with its translation. Over and above miniatures and sculpture illustrations, he evokes visual depiction of the written word. The *Alap* creates an ephemeral atmosphere. The *Nayika* in the Indian art form is sensuous and coy, evoking a bygone era and she is always shown in the most imaginative art forms in painting or sculpture. I must state that those who wish to have an initiation to the complexities of understanding Indian Art would treasure this book.

Pheroza J. Godrej, The Museum Society, Mumbai

The Chhatrapati Shivaji Maharaj Vastu Sanghralaya was founded with a a visionary purpose, has evolved and grown through a century of important political and cultural shifts, and today exists as a dynamic cornerstone of India's art world. I send my best wishes and congratulations to those of you who keep the museum so full of life after 100 years.

Laura Weinstein, Museum of Fine Arts, Boston

What a beautiful stringing together of the essence of Indian Aesthetics and concepts of traditional Indian Art. An incredible Ragamala.

Dr Alka Pande, Art Consultant and Curator

Heartfelt congratulations to the CSMVS on the occasion of its centenary, and to the authors for this beautiful volume. Thank you to the museum's curators, staff, and donors for one hundred years of beauty, education, and collegiality. May the museum continue to prosper and enlighten us all for many years in the future.

Joan Cummins, Senior Curator of Asian Art,
Brooklyn Museum, New York, USA

This little gem attests to the author's credentials as a true 'rasika', a connoisseur to whom an object of rouses art moments of ectasy. If Harsh Dehejia's ilk does survive into the 21st century, the CSMVS is surely the place to experience it.

Shilpa Shah, Tapi Collections

The book looks fantastic and my congratulations to you. Over the years, the CSMVS Museum has been an agora of histories, cultures and peoples – to me, it has been all this and more – it is my home.

Usha Balakrishnan